GOD'S UNDERGROUND

CIMADE 1939-1945

GOD'S

With an introduction by
Marc Boegner
and a chapter on CIMADE today

Translated by William and Patricia Nottingham

UNDERGROUND

Collected by
Jeanne Merle d'Aubigné and Violette Mouchon

Edited by
Emile C. Fabre

*Accounts of the activity of the
French Protestant church
during the German occupation of
the country in World War II*

THE BETHANY PRESS • ST. LOUIS, MISSOURI

© *1970 by The Bethany Press*
Library of Congress Catalog Card Number: 75-127850
ISBN: 0-8272-1214-3

Originally published in French as *Les clandestins
de Dieu,* © 1968 Librairie Arthème Fayard.

Scripture quotations, unless otherwise noted,
are from the *Revised Standard Version of the Bible,*
copyrighted 1946 and 1952 by the
Division of Christian Education, National
Council of Churches of Christ in the United
States of America, and used by permission.

Distributed by The G. R. Welch Company, Toronto,
Ontario, Canada. Other foreign distribution
by Feffer and Simons, Inc., New York, New York.

MANUFACTURED IN THE UNITED STATES OF AMERICA

Translators' Preface

The French ecumenical service agency called CIMADE was for thirty years an organization of the Protestant and Orthodox churches in France closely linked to the World Council of Churches. It now includes Roman Catholics on its Board of Directors and is a truly interconfessional agency. CIMADE has some amazing stories to tell. This book contains only a few from the time of World War II, when CIMADE, with its unique style of service and Christian witness, was born.

Although supported in part through the years by nearly all the major Protestant denominations of the English-speaking world, CIMADE is not widely known to the English-speaking public. It has never sought publicity, and it can be safely assumed that there was much soul-searching and reticence before arriving at the decision to publish this book, which appeared in France in late 1968 under the title *Les clandestins de Dieu*. This work of recollection provides a background for some of our own problems today and food for meditation and reflection.

A few historical reminders will help make the following pages more easily understood. Just thirty years ago, in 1940, after a few months of war French officials signed an armistice with Hitler's Germany. France was divided into a Northern Zone, which was occupied by the Germans, and a Southern or "Free" Zone ruled by the Pétain government located in Vichy. It will become apparent in the reading of this book that not only were the laws different in these two zones for most of the occupation years, but very often the same laws were applied differently in the two regions, thereby permitting a degree of hope to persons exerting pressure in favor of the victims of those laws. To the eternal shame of certain Frenchmen, the laws governing persons of Jewish family and religious background were enacted even against those persons who were French or who had sought sanctuary in France before the war. Some documentation is provided on this in the appendix. CIMADE's first form of action was to resist, circumvent, bend, or break these laws by every ingenious way possible.

Mention is made here of Drancy, the railroad center and temporary prison near Paris from which so many left for the concentration camps of Germany. Words like *maquisards* and *milice* need explanation. The former were freedom fighters in the Resistance movement, while the latter were volunteers in the special military police recruited in France to support the Nazis. As in every occupied country, the fellow citizens who joined up with the uniformed oppression units were capable of similar brutality and torture and were hated even more than the foreigners.

It is thought-provoking and disturbing in a democracy to think of the malcontents who welcomed the Nazis in every country and to remember how few among the people actively supported the Resistance. The average citizen just let the gradual elimination of civil liberties and human rights occur, thinking that it did not involve him personally.

Mention is made of a Nansen passport which was delivered to stateless persons for their security and supposedly was recognized in the democracies as a guarantee of protection and freedom. Vichy violated its immunity.

France is divided into states or regions called *départements*. These appear in this account with such names as Bouches-du-Rhône, le Gard, Indres, Haute-Savoie, Haute-Vienne, etc. A mountainous region in eastern France called the Vercors was the scene of a fearful massacre of Resistance fighters. They were expecting supplies and reinforcements from the Allies, but crack German troops parachuted in on them instead. Maquisards died hanging by their feet and breathing the dust of the earth. For years rusted equipment lay in the woods of the Vercors as a reminder of the slaughter. The German soldiers were particularly vicious because they had been filled with stories about the "merciless atrocities" of the freedom fighters.

Also found here are names that have become well known throughout the ecumenical movement in the last twenty-five years: Marc Boegner is a former president of the World Council of Churches and member of the Académie Française. For more than a quarter-century he was president of CIMADE. Suzanne de Dietrich became widely known for her studies of the Bible. She was for many years a director of the Ecumenical Institute at Bossey, near Geneva. Madeleine Barot was head of the "Department of Cooperation of Men and Women in Church, Family, and Society" and is still a senior staff member of the World Council. Others names appearing in the book are those of André Dumas and Georges Casalis, both of the faculty of Protestant theology in Paris; Roland de Pury, pastor and missionary; André Philip and René Courtin, prominent figures in French political life.

Names not recorded here that we would like to mention include Michel Wagner, executive secretary of CIMADE at the present time, and Jacques Beaumont, his predecessor for ten years. We resist the temptation to list fellow team members, including many Americans, because it would be unfair not to list them all. Their stories belong to a later period: the refugee years, the increase of Orthodox participation in CIMADE's life, the wars of independence in Indochina and Algeria, the Angolan story, May 1968 and its aftermath, migrant workers in the new European affluence, world hunger and international economic justice. These friends know that CIMADE is above all a theological discovery of the involvement of Christ and his people in the sufferings and needs of those who suffer most— and an action which points concretely to the rightful liberation of exploited people everywhere.

Although the World Council of Churches was not officially constituted until 1948, the provisional secretariat was already functioning, and its unique importance is seen throughout this book. It is still a necessary voice of justice and compassion in the world. As Dr. Visser 't Hooft said at the Fourth Assembly in Uppsala in 1968: "The unity of mankind is not a fine ideal in the clouds; it is part and parcel of God's own revelation."

Contents

Introduction: The Struggle of the Church at Vichy

PASTOR MARC BOEGNER

I am happy to be able to write an introduction to the little volume prepared by Miss Merle d'Aubigné and a group of former co-workers and friends of CIMADE,[1] faithful reminders of a period of terrible anguish and troubled consciences. I would like to describe the general context of the time of the events related here.

During the last war, from 1940 to 1944, the German "occupation authorities" progressively imposed upon the Vichy government, with the more or less active cooperation of French leaders, anti-Semitic measures designed to isolate the Jews—foreigners first, then French—to "regroup" them, according to the euphemism of the times, in internment or security camps from which they would be deported to Germany for the "final solution" in the gas chambers and cremation ovens.

It was in this way that we in France were confronted with the gigantic and diabolical Nazi enterprise for a people.

Why stir these tragic memories? Not to perpetuate hate and the desire for revenge, but to say again that where horror and distress originate is born the counterpart of service and love. Also so that young people, who have not lived through these

1. *Comité Inter-Mouvements Auprès Des Evacués.* Today: Ecumenical Service in France.

events, might guard against permitting them to happen again and might know to what crimes certain ideologies can lead.

As to the sequence of events, I think I can do no better than to reproduce here, without changing anything, a few passages of the report that I presented to the Protestant General Assembly in Nîmes, 24 October 1945.

. . . I made a first visit to Vichy during the last days of July 1940. . . . From this first visit the essential themes, which would constantly return in my meetings, were very clearly raised . . . among them, the situation of non-Aryans.

. . . That which I would call obsessive anti-Semitism of several officials was given free rein without any German pressure. "Those people have done so much evil to the country that they deserve a collective punishment," a highly placed official declared to me. I foresaw from that time where we were headed and what would be the responsibility of our churches.

. . . I come now to one of the most tragic aspects of the occupation—the persecution directed against the Jews, or more correctly, because it also concerned Christians having three Jewish ancestors, against non-Aryans. . . . I will try to be as objective as possible. What has been written, said, or done in the name of the member churches of the Protestant Federation is what I must report to you today.

I have already told you of the disturbing impression I had of violent anti-Semitic feeling during my first visit to Vichy. Already in October the first law[2] appeared, which had been preceded by many arbitrary measures. The report of Pastor Bertrand on the activity of the Executive Council of the Protestant Federation in the Northern Zone, will tell you of the immediate reaction of the council. For my part, knowing that I was in full accord with the council, I tried to make contacts with the collaborators nearest to Maréchal Pétain and with several ministers and numerous public figures. The grand rabbi of France was still at Vichy, and his painful existence there filled me with the most profound compassion. Beginning with the month of July, I had tried in vain to obtain for him audiences with the *maréchal* and Pierre Laval. I now found him brokenhearted from all the suffering inflicted upon his people.

2. See Appendix I, A, p. 225.

12

One minister, to whom I had presented our protest, declared to me at the beginning of November 1940: "It is a law of 'defense'; it will bring terrible injustices, but it must be 'absolute.'" "The *maréchal* did not want that," M. Dumoulin de Labarthète, director of his cabinet, said to me that same day. I am convinced that it was true, and that is one of the most troublesome elements of the drama of those tragic years.

In March 1941, the creation of a Commission on Jewish Affairs signaled an aggravation of the situation.[3] German pressure became stronger. When I spoke of this to Admiral Darlan, he wanted to calm the anxiety of our churches by telling me that it was in order to save the French Jews. A high official of the police thought to keep me silent by trying to persuade me that this was a governmental question in which the churches had no business becoming involved.

Unfortunately for him our churches did not share this way of looking at things. At Lyons, where the National Council of the Reformed church met before the end of 1940, Pastor Bertrand had told me of the desire of the Council of the Protestant Federation of France that a written protest be prepared immediately. It had been understood, however, that I would continue for a time with my verbal efforts. But when the National Council of the Reformed church met again in March 1941, it was recognized unanimously that the position of the Reformed church must be affirmed in writing without further delay. Therefore it was upon these instructions, and in its name, that on 26 March I wrote two letters, which were received as expressing the thought of the Protestant churches of France. One was to Admiral Darlan, vice-president of the Council of Ministers; the other to the chief rabbi of France. The following is the text of the latter:

"Monsieur le Grand Rabbin, the National Council of the Reformed Church of France has just met for the first time since the law of 3 October 1940 came into effect. The council has asked me to express to you the sorrow that we all feel at seeing racist legislation introduced into our country and to note the countless hardships and injustices that this law brings upon the French Jews.

"Those among us who think that a serious problem has been placed before the State by the mass immigration of a large number of foreigners, Jews or not, and by hasty and unjustified naturaliza-

3. See Appendix I, C, p. 226.

tions, have always expressed the conviction that the solution to the problem must be inspired by respect for the human person, by faithfulness to the State's responsibilities, by the demands of justice of which France has never ceased to be the champion. They are therefore all the more moved by the rigorous application of a law that, attacking exclusively the Jews, strikes indiscriminately Jews who have been French for generations, often for centuries, and those who were naturalized only yesterday.

"Our church, which knew in the past all the sufferings of persecution, feels an ardent sympathy for your communities whose liberty of worship has already been jeopardized, in certain places, and whose members have been so abruptly thrown into misfortune. It has already undertaken and will not cease from pursuing steps aimed at the indispensable rewriting of the law.

Sincerely yours, . . ."

Of these two letters, this one alone has been known until now. Its history is rather unusual. It was published in the Occupied Zone by *Le Pilori* under the title "An Inadmissible Letter by the Head of the French Protestants." It gave the first glimmer of hope to the Jews who learned from it that the Christian churches were concerned about them. In the Southern Zone, distributed in the tens of thousands of copies under conditions that I was never able to clarify,[4] it earned for the National Council of the Reformed church the approval of some, vehement reproaches from others. The Vichy government—it was in the time of Admiral Darlan— was agitated by the letter and by the commotion it aroused. The minister of the interior, Pucheu, made a point of telling me. Of course, the National Synod of the Reformed church had to deliberate on the issue. Instead of the blame hoped for by some, the Executive Council received thanks, which I daresay it has rarely so justly deserved. The letter to the grand rabbi was the first visible sign in France of the indignation of the Christian conscience against the racial laws.

The same day that the National Council wrote to the grand

4. Editor's note: It was reproduced in 1963 in the preface of the play by Rolf Hochhuth, *Le Vicaire* (in English, *The Deputy*).

rabbi of France it addressed a letter to Admiral Darlan, vice-president of the council, the first letter referred to above:

"Admiral, we have just met in Nîmes for the first time since the law of 3 October 1940 on the status of the Jews went into effect. Just before our session, we learned through a note in the press of your intention to appoint a high commissioner for Jewish questions. We consider it our duty in the name of the Reformed Church of France, which includes the immense majority of French Protestants, to inform you of our sentiments on this grievous question.

"We do not underestimate the gravity of the problem posed for the State by the recent massive immigration of a large number of foreigners, many of whom are of Jewish origin, and by the hasty and unjustifiable naturalizations. We are convinced that this problem can and must be resolved with respect for persons and with concern for justice, which France has always wanted to champion.

"Furthermore, we know that in the present circumstances strong pressure is being put upon the government of France to make it promulgate an anti-Jewish law.

"As Frenchmen and as Christians, we are no less aroused by a law that introduces into our legislation the racist principle, the application of which brings for French Jews cruel hardships and poignant injustices. We speak out particularly against the principle in virtue of which the State has broken its formal engagements taken with regard to men and women, the vast majority of whom have served it with loyalty and unselfishness.

"We are told that the law of 3 October 1940 is not a law of religious persecution. If, then, there is freedom of worship for the Jews as well as for Catholics and Protestants, why is it that their worship is in fact already impeded or threatened in certain localities? In fact, one religious minority is harshly stricken. Our church, which has known all the sufferings of persecution, would be defective in its primary mission if it did not raise its voice in favor of this minority.

"We know, Admiral, that you have the firm desire, by the appointment of a high commissioner for Jewish questions, to do all in your power to avoid the most severe hardships for French Jews. We believe that we can assure you that the Christian denominations will commend you without reserve in your effort. They have weighed all the difficulties. Yet, we earnestly beg of you to go even farther and to examine immediately a reform of the statute imposed upon French Jews that will, on the one hand, prevent or repair great injustices and, on the other, attenuate the disastrous impression made in a large part of the civilized world by the law of last October. The defeat, whose painful consequences we are undergoing, is one more reason for France to safeguard that which, in the moral order, has won for her the respect and affection of Christian nations.

Sincerely yours, . . ."

Admiral Darlan did not make a written response to this letter. He expressed to me the desire to talk over this question. During the month of May, I saw him at length. He told me that a draft for a new law was being studied, including certain measures that would seem very harsh to us but also others that would attenuate the effects. His only preoccupation was to save the Jews established in France for several generations. As for the others, immigrants of recent date, he asked only to see them leave.

The law of 2 June[5]—it was of this that he had spoken—provoked an immense disillusionment. Through René Gillouin, I made known to Maréchal Pétain the emotion aroused in our churches. He was surprised that the cardinals had not spoken to him on the question. In the month of August I wrote a long letter to René Gillouin intended for the *maréchal*. Gillouin hurried to communicate it to him, adding a personal letter, which I must say does the greatest honor to its author. Shortly thereafter I saw Cardinal Gerlier, who earnestly promised me to broach the subject of the racial laws to Maréchal Pétain at the first opportunity. He did so a few days after our talk, and upon his return from Lyons, the *maréchal*, more and more moved by joint protests from the Christian confessions, called Xavier Vallat, high commissioner for Jewish affairs whom the Germans denounced for weakness, and ordered moderation in the application of the law.

However, months passed and the situation became worse. I decided to speak directly to the chief of state, counting on the mandate given me by the Executive Council of the Protestant Federation through Pastor Bertrand. Maréchal Pétain received me on 18 January with his habitual courtesy. It is indisputable that all that he learned about the terrible effects of the racist measures caused him real suffering. He saw clearly that great injustices were being

5. See Appendix I, D, p. 226.

committed. But it is no less indisputable that he was painfully aware of his powerlessness to prevent these injustices or to repair them without delay. "Certain things cannot be straightened out until after the war," he told me. Furthermore, he was not at all surprised that our churches made known to him their indignation; their silence would have surprised him.

You know how, at the beginning of the summer of 1942, the persecution in the Northern Zone suddenly took on a character of odious violence, which resulted in the most atrocious scenes in Paris and elsewhere. The Council of the Protestant Federation, meeting under the presidency of Pastor Bertrand, decided to express directly to the chief of state the feeling of the churches in the Northern Zone. I was asked to see that its letter got to Maréchal Pétain. To be more sure, I went to place the letter in his hand on 27 June, reading it to him myself. Here is the text:

"Monsieur le Maréchal, the Council of the Protestant Federation of France, meeting in Paris, takes the liberty of addressing itself with respectful confidence to the chief of the French State in order to express to him the sorrow felt by the churches under his responsibility concerning the new measures taken by the occupation authorities regarding the Jews.

"The regulation of 29 May, requiring our fellow citizens of Jewish race to wear a distinctive emblem, has profoundly grieved Protestants in the Occupied Zone.

"Our president, Pastor Marc Boegner, has had the honor to make known to you some time ago, as well as to the Admiral of the Fleet, Darlan, vice-president of the Council of Ministers, the unanimous desire of French Protestants to find, in a spirit of justice and understanding, the solution to the Jewish problem, the importance of which we all recognize.

"But today we find before us a measure that, far from contributing to a normal solution of the problem, seems to make it more difficult. Socially and economically inoperable, this law inflicts upon Frenchmen, many of whom have shed their blood under our flag, an uncalled-for humiliation, supposedly separating them from the rest of the nation. It exposes six-year-old children to the taunting always possible in the troubled atmosphere in which our population lives. Finally, it forces baptized persons, Catholic and Protestant, to wear ostensibly before men the title of Jew while they themselves are proud to wear before God the title of Christian.

"The churches of Christ cannot remain silent before the undeserved suffering that touches Frenchmen and sometimes Christians in their dignity as men and as believers. The Council of the Protestant Federation therefore has charged me, Monsieur le Maréchal, to explain its deep anxiety to you. It hopes that you will please consider as a witness of its confidence and respect the fact that it confides this pain and emotion to the heart of the great soldier, the chief of the French State.

Sincerely yours, . . ."

The meeting that followed left me with the same impressions as did the preceding one: deep emotion, complete impotence.

. . . In June 1942, several tens of thousands of Jews, arrested during three days of terror and shame, were thrown into the Vélodrome d'Hiver [Indoor Bicycle Racing Stadium], piled pell-mell in sickening promiscuity, with no thought for hygiene or sufficient food. The stench from this human enclosure defies description. . . . Feeling was intense in Paris, where a sinister atmosphere reigned. One remembers how women, in order to escape arrest, threw themselves from windows with their children in their arms. . . .

Pastor Bertrand wrote to M. de Brinon, French governmental delegate with the occupation authorities, the moving letter that follows:

"Mr. Ambassador, at the time that the German authorities made the Jews in the Occupied Zone wear the special emblem, the Council of the Protestant Federation of France gave a letter to the French chief of state, which the *maréchal* graciously accepted, and a copy of which I have the honor to enclose herein.

"It was possible to believe at that moment that the anti-Jewish regulations had reached their culmination with this humiliating measure, which sought to set the Jews apart from the rest of the nation and to signal them out for mistreatment, which has been systematically undertaken since the day of occupation. But the month of July has seen violence multiplied against these persons at a magnitude never before reached. We have observed in the Parisian populace an anxiety of pain and reprobation that generations now living will doubtless never forget.

"The churches of Jesus Christ, to whom God has confided the message of love and peace, as well as mutual respect among men, cannot remain silent in the face of these events, which risk compromising for many long years all possibility of normal relations between two great peoples. Because the French at the present time have no possibility of making known their opinions or sentiments, it would be false to conclude that they remain indifferent to the extermination of a race, to the undeserved martyrdom of its women and its children.

"Cannot the men who profess to work toward a reconciliation between the victor and the conquered populations make the occupying power understand that years of well-meaning explanations will not erase the effect of the cruelty that we have witnessed? A Christian church would be unfaithful to its vocation if it permitted such sowing of the seeds of hate without raising its voice in the name of the One who gave his life in order to break down all separation among men.

"I leave it to Your Excellency, Mr. Ambassador, to judge if the step I have taken today with you will be brought to the attention of the occupation authorities, if a few Christian voices, solely preoccupied in alleviating sufferings and putting out the flames of hate, will be listened to rather than those wholly profane voices who know no other answer to violence than that of hatred.

"Before closing this letter, I must explicitly specify that only the message to M. le Maréchal was deliberated by the Council of the Protestant Federation—now dispersed—and is a collective responsibility. As for this present letter, I bear before the church, as before the French and possibly the German authorities, the full and entire responsibility.

Sincerely yours, . . ."

Events raced on. After the Occupied Zone, it was the turn of the so-called Free Zone. Through camps, villages, and cities, we saw a wave of horror unfurl. In the following months our chaplains, CIMADE, and ministers of parishes accomplished in the midst of terrible distress a labor of Christian love that was a powerful witness to Jesus Christ. I helped their effort as best I could. But new measures were required. I decided that at this tragic hour the Catholic and Protestant churches should try at least to synchronize their interventions. I suggested this to Cardinal Gerlier on 18 August. It was agreed that each of us would write an urgent letter to Maréchal Pétain. Mine was dated 20 August. It was broadcast a few days later by British and American radios. The text follows:

"Monsieur le Maréchal, when you did me the honor last 27 June of meeting with me, I put into your hands a letter wherein the Council of the Protestant Federation of France confided to your heart as a Christian and as a soldier the pain and distress felt by the Protestant churches in the face of new measures taken in the Occupied Zone with regard to Jews and to Christians now considered Jewish by the law. I am compelled, alas, to write to you today in the name of this same council to express the unutterable sadness felt by our churches at the news of decisions made by the French government about foreign Jews (converted or not to Christianity) and the manner in which they have been carried out.

"No Frenchman can remain unmoved by what has happened since 2 August in the security and internment camps. One knows that the answer will be that France is only returning to Germany the Jews that were sent here in the fall of 1940. The truth is that men and women who came as refugees to France for political or religious reasons have just been delivered to Germany, and they know what terrible fate awaits them.

"Until now, Christianity has inspired in the nations, and in France in particular, respect of the right of sanctuary.

"The Christian churches, in spite of the diversity of denominations, would be unfaithful to their primary calling if they did not raise protests of grief at the abandonment of this principle.

"I must add, Monsieur le Maréchal, that the 'delivery' of these unfortunate foreigners was effected in many places under conditions of such inhumanity that the most hardened consciences were sickened and witnesses to these measures were made to weep. Crammed into freight cars with no consideration of hygiene, the foreigners designated to leave were treated like cattle. The Quakers, who do so much for those who suffer in our land, were refused authorization to give them food at Lyons. The Jewish Consistory was not allowed to distribute food. The respect for the human being which you insisted on inserting in the Constitution that you wish to bestow on France has been trampled upon many times. Here again the churches must raise a protest against such grave ignorance by the State of its undeniable responsibilities.

"The Council of the 'Protestant Federation calls upon your high authority to see that entirely different methods be introduced in the treatment of foreigners of Jewish race, Christian or not by religion, where delivery has been consented to. As you yourself have reminded us, no defeat can compel France to let her honor be stained.

"The obstinate fidelity of France, even—and especially—in the tragic days through which it has lived these last two years, to its traditions of human generosity and nobility of spirit, remains one of the essential causes for respect that certain nations continue to show her.

"As vice-president of the World Council of Christian Churches, which groups all the great churches except the Roman Catholic, I cannot fail to inform you of the deep emotion felt by the churches of Switzerland, Sweden, and the United States at the news of what is happening at this moment in France, already known throughout the world.

"I beg of you, Monsieur le Maréchal, to impose the indispensable measures in order that France not inflict upon herself a moral defeat, the weight of which will be incalculable.

Sincerely yours, . . ."

The persecution continued to increase. The nightly scenes at Vénissieux, where Father Chaillet and Mlle Barot, general secretary of CIMADE, exerted ferocious energy to save Jewish children from deportation, and the heroic action led by Pastor Manen in the camp at Milles, both deeply impressed our churches. And the delivery of political refugees seemed to spread with new vigor. On 27 August I wrote the following letter to Pierre Laval:

"Monsieur le Président, qualified to speak in the name of the Protestant churches of the whole world, several of whom have already solicited my intervention, and knowing the facts growing out of these last few days, I have the honor of requesting with the greatest insistence that you give me the assurance that no foreigner who has been condemned in his country for political reasons or who has requested asylum in France for similar reasons be directed to the Occupied Zone.

Sincerely yours, . . ."

Several days later, at the *Assemblée du Désert* [annual meeting of Protestants in the historic Huguenot country above Nîmes], I had occasion to meet with nearly eighty pastors. The hearts of all were heavy with shame and anguish. My colleagues wished for an intervention as vigorous as possible. I retraced the road to

21

Vichy, passing through Lyons, where again I met with Cardinal Gerlier in view of taking common action. As soon as I arrived in Vichy, 9 September, I went to see the head of Pierre Laval's cabinet, whose first words were to tell me that, the night before, taking stock of the total ignorance in which his minister seemed to be concerning the strong reaction of Christian opinion, he had suggested that Laval call Cardinal Gerlier and myself to Vichy. He was sure that his chief, learning I was there, would receive me immediately.

. . . I write these pages of my report a few hours after the execution of Pierre Laval (October 1945). Thus, I have wished to be restrained in the recital of that meeting and of those that followed. . . .

. . . At the time I arrived in Vichy, the archbishop of Toulouse, the bishops of Montauban and Marseilles, and Cardinal Gerlier himself had already sent pastoral letters to their dioceses, several of which showed great courage, about the persecution of non-Aryans.

At the *Assemblée du Musée du Désert,* our colleagues had insisted that the voice of the Protestant churches be heard without delay. But, aside from the fact that it is not as easy for a committee of fourteen members to meet and speak to the church or in the name of the church as it is for a bishop to publish a decree, I have always thought that before protesting to our faithful or to the nation against the faults of a government, we should first go to the persons concerned to say what we think and to show our care not to blame publicly anyone without having first tried to have the unjust measures changed. It was for this reason that I wished to see the head of the government before convoking the National Council of the Protestant Federation, which alone was qualified to express the thought of our churches in the circumstances in which we found ourselves.

Therefore, I saw Pierre Laval, and from the moment I entered, I told him all that I had intended to say to him. His answer was in two short sentences: "I cannot do otherwise." And: "I am taking preventive measures."

He declared that he was unable to do otherwise in face of the German demands, which, in fact, were becoming more and more pressing. To save the French Jews, it was necessary to deliver the foreign Jews (and naturally those Christians considered Jews by the law of June 1941). Certain exceptions were foreseen, which I reminded him were rarely taken into account. Except for them, all foreign Jews had to leave. That would be that much gained for France, which they had invaded under the administrations for whose faults the nation was now paying dearly. And that was his "preventive measure"!

"Will you make it a manhunt?" I asked him.

"We will look for them wherever they are hidden."

"Will you consent to our saving the children?"

"The children must remain with their parents."

"But you know full well that they will be separated."

"No."

"I tell you they will be."

"What do you want to do with the children?"

"French families will adopt them."

"I do not wish it; not one should be left in France!"

Furthermore, Pierre Laval declared to me that he had given orders that all should be done humanely. "There have been 'abominable things,' " I answered.

What could I obtain from a man whom the Germans had made to believe—or who pretended to believe—that the Jews taken from France were going to southern Poland to cultivate the land of the Jewish state that Germany said it wished to establish? I spoke to him of massacre; he responded with gardening.

I cannot reproduce the whole meeting. At the end I said to him: "Mr. President, I am obliged to point out to you the gravity of the situation. The churches cannot keep silent before such facts."

"The churches? They have done other such things! I said the same to the Vatican representative who came to see me. And besides, let them do as they wish; I shall continue to do what I must."

. . . I shall not tell of all my efforts on that day and the next: interview with the American chargé d'affaires, who promised me to cable Washington for authorization to tell Laval that America would accept the children of deported parents; long conversation with the general secretary of the police—in prison at the moment —whom Laval made me promise to visit and who could not give me satisfaction on any point; more than an hour's visit with Admiral Platon, a Protestant, who strongly reproached the churches for betraying the government. I tried to make him understand that he should be proud to see his church speak out against the iniquities we had seen. . . . Unable to meet with the council of the Protestant Federation upon my return to Nîmes, I called an emergency meeting of the National Council of the Reformed church.

Then it was that the council addressed the message to the faithful dated 22 September, which was read from almost all the Reformed pulpits in spite of the efforts made here and there by the departmental authorities to seize the document. Published by the Reformed church, it was, for all the Frenchmen who heard or read it, the message of the Protestant churches of France:

"The National Council of the Reformed Church of France, meeting for the first time since the laws that have struck at the Jewish refugees on our soil, among whom numerous Christians are to be found, has been informed of the measures taken by its president, in the name of the Protestant Federation of France, in writing and by word of mouth before the highest authorities of the State. The council fully associates itself with him and thanks him for his action.

"Without ignoring or misunderstanding the extreme complexity of the situation before which the nation's authorities are placed, resolved more than ever to exercise with loyalty, in the midst of the nation, the spiritual vocation to which God has called it, and faithful to its historic principle of refusing all intrusion in the political domain, the Reformed church cannot keep silent before the sufferings of thousands of human beings who received refuge in our land.

"A Christian church would lose its soul and its reason for being if it did not maintain, for the very safeguard of the nation in which God has placed it, the divine law above all human contingencies. And the divine law does not allow that God-given families be broken, children separated from mothers, the right of asylum and pity denied, respect of the human person transgressed, and defenseless people delivered to a tragic destiny.

"Whatever may be the problems that are not within the province of the church to resolve, but which it is her duty to affirm must not be resolved against the law of God, the gospel orders us to consider all men without exception as brothers for whom the Savior died on the cross. How can the church ever forget that the Savior of the world was, by birth, one of the people whose descendants are the Jews? And the church in which the unity of the body of Christ is affirmed—how can it not be deeply wounded by the measures that also strike the non-Aryan Christians, members of our Protestant parishes?

"Before such grievous facts, the church feels compelled to make heard the cry of Christian conscience in the name of God to entreat all those in authority in the world not to add to the natural horrors of the war, which themselves violate the commandments of Christ, still worse violations whose result will be to hinder in the most fearful manner the necessary reconciliation of the peoples in a world finally repentant, submissive, and in peace before God.

"It demands that the faithful, with the compassion of the Good Samaritan, reach out toward the distress of those who suffer and intercede without ceasing to God, who alone can deliver us all from evil by the grace that he has manifested in Jesus Christ."

CIMADE

CIMADE *(Comité Inter-Mouvements Auprès Des Evacués)*, whose name quickly became known the world over, transformed itself into a work of Christian witness, evangelization, and social work in the camps where thousands of foreigners, largely non-Aryan, lived under frightful conditions. The name of Gurs remains the symbol of intense distress to which CIMADE received the vocation of bringing a spiritual remedy, even more than a material one. Later, with the consent of the authorities, some of the unfortunate ones that CIMADE cared for were able to be received into homes like le Coteau Fleuri, near le Chambon-sur-Lignon, and surrounded with brotherly concern. But once persecution broke loose and the manhunt was organized in the Southern Zone, CIMADE organized the crossing of the Swiss border by non-Aryans who called upon it for help. I must say that the Executive Council of the Federation, without having been able to give its opinion, was committed in a very special kind of work.

I had always upheld CIMADE, in which the churches of other countries saw a manifestation of the Resistance and of the vitality of French 'Protestantism, of the faith and the will to witness of our youth movements and our churches. I upheld it even more energetically in the action undertaken during the persecutions and because of them. In September 1942 I negotiated at Bern for the admission of non-Aryans coming from France, naturally under false names, and for whom the president of the Protestant Federation of France would accord his personal guaranty. And with what joy I gave it to all those brought by the men and women team members of CIMADE in the face of great danger, up to and beyond the barbed wire with which Switzerland had had to encircle itself. One of our young pastors, André Morel, was arrested for having been such a guide. My colleague Eberhard kindly represented me when the affair came before the court at Bonneville, and threw into the balance of justice, with passionate eloquence, the weight of the authority of the Protestant Federation of France. Result: one little month of prison. Moreover, the sentence will soon be reconsidered.

Oh, I assure you that during those years the general secretaries of police, the officials of National Security, and the inspectors general of the camps came to know the Protestant Federation of France. I sometimes made them angry, irritated at its name. I daresay that they came to know it as a federation of churches that will never take the side of iniquity and attacks upon human dignity.

How can I end this introduction without expressing our gratitude to the World Council of Churches, which constantly supported CIMADE morally and financially during those terrible years, and without the help of which those border crossings would probably never have been possible? Pastor Freudenberg himself tells of all the measures accomplished for the reception of the refugees in Swiss territory [see chapter 2]. I must express to the authors of the following pages the gratitude of those in whose name I have had during many years the right and even more—the duty—to speak. Many have not known what was being done in the name of their church, and even more in the name of Jesus Christ, in a hell of anguish, sufferings, and death. Miss Merle d'Aubigné, the team members and friends of CIMADE in the midst of the camps and on the borders, pastors and laymen in the parishes of refuge, brought to this hell a presence of love—generous, disinterested, completely fraternal. May they know that their names are forever in our hearts and that when we think of them we hear the word of the Lord: ". . . as you did it to one of the least of these my brethren, you did it to me."

1.

CIMADE: Presence, Community, Action

MADELEINE BAROT

How is it that CIMADE came to concentrate all its efforts on helping the Jews during the four years of the German occupation of France, to the exclusion of all other activity, in spite of the obvious needs of innumerable refugees and war victims?

Nothing seemed to have prepared CIMADE for that. It had been created by the Protestant youth movements, the Boy Scouts and Girl Scouts, the YWCA and YMCA, and the Federation of Student Christian Movements to help the displaced persons from Alsace and Lorraine, who had been "evacuated" from the Border Zone in September 1939, toward the departments of the Haute-Vienne and the Dordogne.

The secretaries of the movements, the Scout leaders, all women—because their male colleagues had been drafted—had spent the months of *"la drôle de guerre"* [the peculiar war] in the villages where the displaced persons had been installed. They took care of the women and the children, and had created a center for the girls sent to Bergerac to work in the gunpowder factory. They served as a link among the Alsatians, speaking

27

their dialect and helping them as Protestants. The Alsatians were considered foreigners by the population whose prejudices were aroused by the war, and who were narrowly Catholic or completely detached from the church. There were ten women in all, whose principal capital was two cars which permitted them to visit a number of villages regularly.

When, repatriated from Rome where I had continued my studies until 10 May 1940, I was named general secretary of CIMADE, this organization had one clear conviction: the youth movements must unite in a common service to those whom the war had torn from their homes, the "displaced."

I was to do a study of the situation of the displaced Alsatians after the defeat of May-June. They were returning to their homes or spread out looking for work. They no longer needed any special help. On the other hand, the foreigners, especially the refugees who had come from Germany since 1933 to flee the anti-Semitic Nazis, were particularly improverished.

During the beginning of the war many of them had been put under surveillance in camps because they were aliens of enemy nationality. In May 1940 those who were still free fled toward the Southern Zone. They could not possibly remain in the Northern Zone, which had been occupied by the Germans. Those whom France had generously welcomed were particularly exposed because of the ambiguity of the French political situation. They had to be given priority.

They were scattered all over, except those who had been the object of the internment law and were grouped in the camps. It was these camps that we had to try to penetrate, to be with the people, present among them, during this difficult period.

In the Southern Zone the most important camp was Gurs, near Pau, set up in 1938 for the Republicans from the war in Spain. But how to get admitted?

From the pastor of a nearby city who was authorized to enter as a chaplain, but whose role was strictly limited to the holding of religious services, I learned that there had been several births in the camp. I arrived at the gate with a package of layettes and was given permission to distribute them myself. What I saw was enough to convince me that our place was definitely in the camps. The YMCA, although well known for its work with prisoners of war and interned civilians during the First World War, was refused entrance to the camps by Vichy. We thus decided not to make an official request, but for two of us to go to a neighboring village and to work our way in little by little.

The guards became accustomed to our daily visits, without asking too many questions. Besides, who in high places was interested in what happened in Gurs way down at the Spanish border?

Suddenly one day in October, we learned that seven thousand Jews from the Palatinate and Baden had been arrested and transported to France, and were arriving at Gurs, of all places. Everyone was stupefied. The camp was already more than full. The newcomers were crowded eighty to a barracks. Winter was coming.

The camp management was immediately overwhelmed by all the work necessary just to keep alive this population of old people, women, and children. There was no longer any question as to whether or not we had authorization to enter the camp. We were already part of it. The daily trips to the neighboring village of Navarrenx, nearly five miles away, took too much time. When at last the administration discovered our existence, Jeanne Merle d'Aubigné and I had already taken possession of a barracks and decided not only to have an office and a center but to live there behind the barbed wire. It was too late to evict us.

CIMADE had been created to bring help to the "displaced" in general. We found ourselves at the end of the year 1940 behind the barbed wire of the ghetto of Gurs. We saw in this a distinct calling. Anti-Semitism had taken hold at Vichy. Arrests and internment camps multiplied. All racism is inadmissible from the Christian point of view. It was necessary to give tangible signs of this conviction, alert public opinion, protest to responsible authorities, mobilize Protestant forces, and above all help those who suffered most. Already many Protestants had been aware of this issue by the news from Germany, from the Confessing Church and its open fight against anti-Semitism.

Perhaps also was I personally sensitive because of my life in Italy under a Fascist regime, where anti-Semitism and internment camps, both imported from Germany, had rapidly taken incredible proportions? Would it be the same in France?

Our presence at Gurs was partially justified before the police by the relatively high number of baptized internees, registered as Protestants. Even though we never considered for a moment restricting our aid to Protestants, the label *"Assistance Protestante"* that was given us in spite of ourselves was a big help. How could we explain to the internees, having arrived in the "Free Zone" but now held behind barbed wire under unbelievably miserable conditions, that the French disapproved of the Nazi infiltrations and that the Vichy government was not capable of authorizing them to live in freedom? With Protestant internees we could more easily establish relationships of confidence, and perhaps through them these relationships could spread to the rest of the internees.

Little by little a small parish developed. It is not the place here to recount the fervor of this tiny nucleus of Christians for whom the worship, Bible studies, and choral group represented a haven of peace. The most diverse denominations and sects worked together, and a great victory was won when the parish itself was ready to share with the others the material and moral privileges that resulted from the presence of the Protestant workers and the CIMADE center in the camp.

Of course, our presence was not a complete identification with the internees. We could leave from time to time, prepare a good meal, warm ourselves around the stove of the nearby café, make contact again with the outside world. It was indispensable for keeping up the strength necessary for effective work. It was only later that we understood that we were sharing real risks: when a young team member, Jacques Saussine, died of appendicitis because his removal from Camp Récébédou was not authorized in time; when Elisabeth Schmidt contracted typhoid during the epidemic that ravaged Gurs; or when several team members, arrested at the border, spent time in jails.

Slowly, other service organizations succeeded in penetrating the camps and in receiving permission to live in them: the Quakers, Swiss Aid to Children, Jewish welfare agencies.

Under such exceptional living conditions, there could be no question of staying alone, even for Jeanne Merle d'Aubigné— except, of course, when circumstances did not allow otherwise. It was a question of safety, of physical strength for the work to be done, and especially, of spiritual strength. The idea of working and living in teams, which is one of the characteristics of CIMADE still today, comes from this desire to be present in the camps, and from this solidarity of life with the internees.

The rules and demands of team life were discovered only little by little. They are surprisingly similar, whether experienced by the teams set in the camps or, several years later, by the teams living among the refugees of West Berlin, in a village of regrouped persons during the war in Algeria, or during the time of decolonization in the Muslim quarter of Dakar.

After 1941 the number of camps multiplied and other teams were installed at Rivesaltes, Brens, le Récébédou, and Nexon, using the precedent of Gurs, without ever having their situation fully clarified.

In order that this presence be worthwhile, and to bolster the team members, almost all of whom were very young, it was necessary to maintain frequent liaison. I soon gave up specific work at Gurs in order to go from one camp and team to another, to bring news of the outside world and the fruit of other experiences. In this way a very strong spirit of community was created among the teams who could neither meet one another nor even correspond freely.

This need for community and sharing became so great that a meeting of the teams was organized in January 1942 at les Grangettes in the Alps, giving the overworked team members a magnificent occasion for renewal and rest. We continued these annual meetings during the following years in spite of, and even because of, the difficulties.

The second stage of CIMADE's work was the opening, in the spring of 1942, of homes accredited to receive internees who obtained permission to leave the camps on condition that they be taken in charge by an authorized organization and remain under regular surveillance by the police.

This system applied particularly to old people, to the sick, and to women having young children. Thanks to the financial aid of Sweden and the World Council of Churches, we were able to open the homes of le Coteau Fleuri, near le Chambon-sur-Lignon; Mas du Diable, near Tarascon at Vabre in the Tarn; and the Foyer Marie-Durand at Marseilles.

This was a joyous stage in spite of the poverty of means at our disposal. Father Glasberg had also opened homes, and several months later the administration of the camps put a large number of prisoners in assigned residence in the villages, or new-style camps, whose gates were open and in which life was more bearable. The team members followed the internees at Naillat in la Creuse, in the camps of Douadic in l'Inde, Séreilhac and la Meyze in Haute-Vienne, Combronde and Châteauneuf in le Puy-de-Dôme.

Events pushed us constantly faster than we had foreseen, and this stage of service was not destined to last.

A third stage, this one tragic, began in August 1942 with the deportation to Germany of Jews of foreign nationality, residing in the Southern Zone. In just a few days it was necessary to evacuate most of the inhabitants of our home le Coteau Fleuri, hardly opened. The isolated location of the house, near the woods and overlooking the road, a certain complicity of the population and the gendarmerie, and—why not?—the constant prayers of our friends, helped to get everyone to safety. When the gendarmes of Tence received an arrest order, they took the habit of sauntering along the road in plain sight, of stopping at the café before coming up the little hill to le Coteau, announcing loudly that "they were going to arrest some of those dirty Jews." A lookout posted in a woodpile in front of the house gave the alarm. When the gendarmes arrived, those involved had disappeared. A tunnel in the nearby forest served several times to hide the runaways. It was said to be a hiding place that had served the persecuted Huguenots.

At the same time, it was necessary to remove from the deportation convoys leaving Rivesaltes all those who could have a reason for exemption, to help others to escape, and to hide those who were still living in dispersed housing.

We first thought to use the homes of our friends and the parishes ready to take the runaways. The imaginative and courageous responses were magnificent.

It did not last long. The parsonages were soon overcrowded, food supplies exhausted, our friends suspect. We were driven into illegality even farther. We found ourselves looking for crossing points on the Swiss and Spanish borders, organizing escapes from camps, and producing false identity cards. All this was done in the peculiar ethics of secrecy, of extraordinary solidarity, side by side with Catholics, Communists, and all who, for one reason or another, participated in the Resistance.

None of this had been decided, nor even foreseen. There was simply no other solution any longer.

This period of the "manhunt" is related elsewhere in this book. As general secretary of CIMADE, I had to be on all the fronts at the same time. The repeated interventions of M. Boegner at Vichy necessitated a constant liaison between him and us. It was necessary to tell him exactly how the official laws were being applied in the different camps and grouping centers for Jews being sent back to Germany. We also had to inform him on the attitude of the Protestant parishes, for whom he was the spokesman. He had to be able to propose specific measures, corresponding to concrete situations. It was also to him that we turned to plead especially tragic cases.

At the same time, I had to remain in constant liaison with those who assured the escapes into Switzerland, to preach moderation to them, to demand that they act cautiously, to discover what had happened when they did not return from their mission. To all this were added the furnishing of false identity and ration cards, the moving of those hidden persons who were too threatened or who were putting their hosts in danger, and the constant knowledge of the best crossing points on the borders.

Curiously, in this tragic period ecumenical and international solidarity became a tangible reality for the team members,

a solidarity that has remained a permanent dimension of CIMADE.

We well knew that it had taken considerable sums in order to open and support our homes—sums that came from Sweden and Switzerland, through the International Committees of the YMCA, YWCA, and the World Council of Churches, which followed with deep concern the work of CIMADE since 1939. This solidarity took on a concrete and touching form when the border crossings took place. What became of the children and the sick once the barbed wire had been passed? It was necessary to reassure families and friends.

We learned that in Switzerland, too, the refugees were generally regrouped into camps, but above all, we discovered that their admission posed difficult problems to the Swiss Confederation. Was it possible that it would come to the point of sending back the Jews condemned to deportation, to death?

We had to know what was happening. M. Boegner went to Switzerland; then I made a secret visit in order to inform our friends and, through them, the authorities.

It was a great victory when Bern agreed that the lists of refugees in special danger would be received for consideration. We could continue our crossings without the fear of being pushed back at the border, almost inevitably followed with arrest by German patrols.

But what work for our friends at the World Council of Churches! They had to establish lists from the scraps of paper that we succeeded in getting to them, discuss them at Bern, fix the priorities, then run to the border posts: with danger at our heels, we did not admit delay and started our convoys en route without having received an answer to our requests.

To spend a few hours in Geneva between two difficult crossings was quite an event. Sometimes it was at the price of a night spent in prison; one dared not be seen openly in the city for fear of being recognized. One was suddenly seized with a guilty conscience for living in secrecy. Nevertheless, we set out again more convinced than ever of the work to be done, of the place that was ours in France, never tempted to prolong this parenthesis of peace and comfort.

The events that overwhelmed us, and the trivial details of our daily labor, took on meaning when they were discussed with a Dutchman such as Pastor Visser 't Hooft, an anti-Nazi German like Dr. Freudenberg, the Swedes, and the Swiss. That brought us back into the totality of the events of the moment. We were a link in the immense chain of distresses of the Jewish people, but also a link in the chain of Christian forces trying to witness and to serve.

It is from this effective solidarity that my conviction dates— my conviction that CIMADE needs team members of different nationalities and religious traditions in order to understand the complexity of the world today and to provide valid responses. For the duration of the war, it was necessary to be ourselves, Frenchmen, with our limited vision of the world. But it was also necessary to prepare an ecumenical future in which our churches would no longer accept their isolation. Our Geneva friends, feeding that nostalgia for unity and community which is the basis of our international and interconfessional recruitment of team members today, maintained in us this revolt against separations and isolation.

The more the situation deteriorated, the less it was possible to respect legality. Besides, what was the authority to which we were ready to submit? That of Vichy? That of the occupation authorities? That of Free France? It became more and more clear to us that there could be no neutral or apolitical action for a Christian who wanted to be fully involved in the milieu in which he lived. If the structures of the society do not permit all to live, and condemn some to a brutal or slow death, these structures are evil and must be changed or, as a temporary solution, ignored and disobeyed.

Therefore, it was no longer a problem of asking if it was legitimate or not to profit from the means of action offered to us by the network of the Resistance. Nevertheless, knowing that a certain "Pat," who led the convoys of refugees in the area of Bellegarde, was armed, we were unanimous in demanding that he give up this security. Perhaps it was from fear of the consequences if he were captured; more probably it was the conviction that certain methods were incompatible with our desire to witness.

Using false papers, or even making them, did not seem to us to pose such a serious dilemma. Nonetheless, it was instituting the lie as a method of action. As for myself, I had considered it almost amusing to change identity, to go around with a card in the name of "Monette Bertrand." I knew I was sought after. It was part of the war. However, we found it difficult once the German occupation ended and the Liberation government was established to have to request—then to wait perhaps weeks —permits to travel which we had been in the habit of making ourselves.

Life behind barbed wire was one adventure. Clandestineness was another. All adventure brings risks. Those that we ran were in every way less serious than those faced by our Jewish friends. How could we be present among them if we also had not taken spiritual and physical risks?

Nevertheless, political options cannot in any case make one forget that all human beings, whatever their ideology, have the right to be treated as men, respected and served. This is why, at the Liberation, we agreed to go to work in the camps of the "collaborators" at Drancy, Mauzac, Poitiers, Ecrouves, and Noé, at the risk of being misunderstood by our friends of yesterday. For him who wishes to be a part of the reality of this world and at its service, these risks are inevitable.

2.

Across the Border: The Activity of the World Council of Churches

PASTOR ADOLF FREUDENBERG

Editor's note: Pastor Freudenberg had belonged at one time to the diplomatic corps of Germany. The coming of Hitler made him quit. He decided in 1935 to study theology and to enter the service of the Evangelical Confessing Church. It was due especially to Pastor Martin Niemöller that he made this decision. The courage and straightforwardness with which Niemöller preached and made relevant the Word of God had been a great help to him in the middle of the cowardice and opportunism that reigned at the time. After the burning of the synagogues in November 1938, the anti-Semitic violence grew from day to day. Mme Freudenberg was of Jewish origin and the couple had to leave Germany in March 1939 to become refugees in Great Britain, where they were received with open arms in the great ecumenical family and by Dr. Bell, bishop of Chichester and president-founder of the International Committee for Refugees. Dr. Bell had personally sponsored about thirty German pastors fleeing for similar reasons.

At first, Pastor Freudenberg was made responsible in London for directing the service to refugees for the World Council of Churches "in the process of formation." In September 1939 he moved to Geneva, where his department was transferred to the headquarters of the World Council of Churches, and where he worked during the whole war in favor of refugee "victims of Nazi persecution," in constant liaison with CIMADE for those who had sought refuge in France and whose reception he assured in Switzerland.

We asked him to gather together the memories of his activity during this period. Here are some extracts from the documentation he prepared.

1. Free

"For freedom Christ has set us free."
—Galatians 5:1

The actions that we are going to describe here are of very modest importance. Our resistance was very weak against the attacks on liberty and humanity during that tragic epoch.

Nevertheless, we were able to act and we would like to bear witness here to the marvelous liberty and active fraternity that we knew in the ecumenical milieu.

At the time that I was searching through the archives of the World Council of Churches in Geneva to edit these notes, I renewed contact with hundreds of friends with whom I was in direct relation, and I have maintained an abundant correspondence, often touching the ultimate problems of existence. Behind these men and women stand thousands of refugees who were then in France. There were eighty thousand at the beginning of the war. They had fled there because of their Jewish origin and because of their political opposition to the Hitler regime. In 1940 France itself was handed over to the persecutors; and flight into Switzerland, last bastion of freedom, was the final hope of most of the fugitives.

Before recounting the events, one must recall the names of some of those who formed the crew of the little ecumenical vessel. It was an active crew, conscious of its responsibilities, which prevented the newborn ecumenism from rusting in the calm waters of the port and permitted the development of Ecumenical Aid to Refugees (which was later to be called the

Division of Inter-Church Aid, Refugee and World Service [DICARWS]).

There was, first of all, the general secretary, Dr. Visser 't Hooft. He had been kindly invited to settle in the United States. His decision to remain in Geneva contributed much to the development of ecumenical action in Europe. We worked together in the little house at 41, avenue de Champel. He guided my actions and helped me to establish contacts.

Active, indefatigable, he had confidence in me and gave me complete freedom of action. We had the same mentors in theology, Karl Barth and Eduard Thurneysen. In the daily tension between the Christian life and that of the world, we founded our faith upon the experiences and the trials of the resisting churches in Germany, the Netherlands, and Norway. Visser 't Hooft likes to quote Hans Ehrenberg from this period: "The Confessing Church is the secret guide of ecumenism." We had had the same experience of freedom given in Jesus Christ, and it was up to us now to try to return freedom to those who had been deprived of it.

Dr. Visser 't Hooft was in constant relation with the European members of his committee: Pastor Marc Boegner in France, Pastor Alphonse Koechlin in Basel, Bishop George Bell of Chichester, and Archbishop Eidem of Uppsala.

I myself was in touch with my friend Pastor Heinrich Grüber and his office in Berlin, which tried to help the "non-Aryan Protestants" leave Germany. This dauntless Christian, arrested on Christmas 1940, paid for his courage with almost three years of concentration camp. His assistant, Pastor Werner Sylten, paid with his death in the course of internment after atrocious sufferings. Several of his co-workers, neglecting their safety for the sake of others, perished in the gas chambers. For several months in 1942 we were still able to show signs of friendship to a small Protestant parish in the ghetto of Warsaw, whose leader was Max Honig, of Grüber's office. The silence of death ended that.

During the first year of the war, it was necessary to find means to finance the exodus of Jews from Germany. Expenses were considerable because of the often exorbitant cost of travel and the excessive guarantees required. That is why until the summer of 1941 we had been able to help only seventy-one Jews to leave Germany. What was that in comparison to all those who were condemned to death!

The Swiss committees for aid to refugees were submerged with demands from Jews who had left Germany and Austria since 1938 and were not able to earn a living in Switzerland. We found very little help from our American colleagues, in spite of the zeal of Henry Smith Leiper and Conrad Hoffmann, and especially of Swiss professor Adolf Keller, who lived in the United States from 1940 to 1941. He tried to interest numerous ecumenical friends in the refugee cause. The little that we were able to do at that time we owe, above all, to him. Even though we showed that it was a question of certain death to thousands of people, we were up against the incredulity of public opinion, of governments, and even of the Christian churches.

We should remember here the International Conference which met at Evian from 6 July to 15 July 1938, upon the initiative of President Roosevelt, to discuss the problem of refugees. Thirty-two countries participated. The delegates from all the European countries declared that their nations could not take in larger quotas of refugees in the future. The Swiss delegate, Dr. Heinrich Rothmund, chief of the Federal Division of Police, emphasized that his country, overburdened with refugees from Germany and Austria since March 1938, could no longer be more than a country of transit for such persons. The delegate from the Netherlands expressed this same point of view. The only "success" of the conference was the creation of an Inter-governmental Committee for Refugees, with headquarters in London.

How can this lack of reaction to racial crimes be explained? Foreign policy, of course. But is it perhaps possible to say in defense of those responsible that the unimaginable inhumanity of the Nazi extermination plan for Jews, coldly planned and executed, made it impossible to believe? Besides, who would have been ready to admit his powerlessness in the face of such crimes? Who would have been ready to make common cause, without restriction, with the Jews, tortured and put to death, and to take the necessary measures while it was still possible?

If one were realistic, he could hear what was often left unsaid: "Let's admit that these extermination measures are intolerable. It is not necessary, anyway, to get too upset: they are only Jews!" It is not too much of an exaggeration to think that anti-Semitic feelings had already contaminated the Conference of Evian.[1]

All during the war we tried different ways to transmit exact information to the influential circles in Allied and neutral countries, on the development of the plan for extermination of the Jews. The governments themselves were directly informed by their secret agents, who were very numerous in Switzerland.

The secretaries of the World Council of Churches and of the World Jewish Congress established a joint memorandum in March 1943 on the catastrophic situation of the Jews and on the steps that needed to be taken. It remains incomprehensible that this memorandum could have been considered at that date in Great Britain as "Zionist propaganda" in government circles, by some influential Christians, and even within the Intergovernmental Committee for Refugees. And this, at the same time that the House of Lords was echoing the great speech of William Temple, archbishop of Canterbury, on the same theme and on the duties of Great Britain.[2]

We were not alone in this attempt. The international Christian organizations were grouped under the name Emergency Committee of Christian Organizations (ECCO), which formed a subcommittee for refugees. ECCO consisted particularly of the World Student Christian Federation, the World Committees of YMCA and YWCA, etc.

I frequently visited Dr. Gerhard Riegner, general secretary of the World Jewish Congress. All during the war we exchanged

---

1. Cf. *La politique pratiquée par la Suisse au cours des années 1933 à 1955*, pp. 72–73.
   On the imponderables of that conference, see the novel by Hans Habe, *Mission* (Berlin and Weimar: Aufbau-Verlag, 1966).

2. Preface and text of memorandum: see Appendix VII, pp. 234-37.

information. Usually he was better informed than we. Sometimes, however, we ourselves received precious news, particularly from Dr. Hans Schoenfeld, of the Department of Studies of the World Council of Churches, who visited in Germany and in some occupied countries many times, in spite of the enormous danger of these trips.

We met with only a weak response from the International Red Cross, notwithstanding its indisputable humanitarian spirit. It was in a delicate position because of its traditional work in the prisoner of war camps, which it feared would be endangered by working for the Jews.[3] Its Mixed Service Commission had some contacts that were more candid, and we collaborated closely with them in material aid activities.

As I look back, I can only be amazed at the mutual confidence that reigned among all of us—Swiss, Dutch, Swedes, French, British, Americans, Germans, Christians and Jews—in our work relations, which intensified continuously. In the midst of the struggle of ideologies, of the abolition of freedom, we felt, wherever we came from, completely free in a common service to the victims of terror. It was ecumenism in action.

The German armies occupied the Netherlands and Belgium, and crushed the French army in June 1940. At Vichy a French satellite government was constituted. Confused news came to us about the chaotic flight toward southern France of refugees and foreigners coming from countries that were enemies of Germany. At the end of October, the Swiss newspapers told us of the deportation toward the south of France of persons considered Jews from Baden, the Palatinate, and the Saar. By telegram, we received a plea from Dr. Else Liefmann, my wife's cousin, interned at Gurs with her brother and sister. They were in their seventies and fragile in health; the conditions of internment were inhuman. The individual destiny of men and women known to us made us feel the frightful situation of all.[4]

And then the news came to us of the work of CIMADE,

3. On the position of the International Red Cross, see Appendix VI, pp. 233-34.
4. See the tragic letter of Mme Marthe Besag in Appendix V, pp. 232-33, a letter that confirms the descriptions of Gurs given by Jeanne Merle d'Aubigné.

which in a surprising manner was already at work in the Gurs camp.

One thing was sure: our French friends could not, in their own distress, support this additional responsibility alone. Switzerland was the neutral neighbor from whom they had every right to expect the first fraternal assistance. The ecumenical secretariat had to act rapidly, and by all imaginable means. Solidarity with the suffering brother in the crucial moment was demonstrated throughout all Switzerland with comforting simplicity. Three generous Swiss friends in particular gave us their entire help, friends in whom we had total confidence and thanks to whom many doors were opened. Without these Swiss friends, our French friends would not have been able to accomplish so much. Pastor Alphonse Koechlin, of Basel, president of the Protestant Federation of Switzerland, a modest man and "grand monsieur" open to all that is human, rendered eminent services to the young ecumenical movement and to its Refugee Service. Two other indispensable friends were our dear brother Paul Vogt, Swiss pastor to refugees, and the extraordinary "mother of refugees," Gertrud Kurz, of Bern, president of *Service chrétien pour la Paix,* founded shortly after the First World War by the great Frenchman Étienne Bach.

It was decided that all possible aid would be granted. In a few weeks large sums from the Swiss parishes came to us for the aid to be sent to France.

It was also in the course of the year 1940 that the World Council of Churches in process of formation had confided to it the task of keeping watch over the ecumenical communities in the refugee and prisoner of war camps, a responsibility covering not only all the religious needs but also, in the case of the refugees, the battle against unlimited misery. Although it is not possible that the World Council of Churches could ever become a super-church imposing itself upon others, in exceptional circumstances like these, it was necessary to be ready to take its responsibilities alone in the name of the universal church of Jesus Christ. Thus, beginning in 1940, the Ecumenical Commission for Spiritual Aid to Prisoners of War devoted itself energetically to bringing help behind the barbed wire to the Protestant and Orthodox communities. For the first time these communities became conscious of the concrete existence of a universal church. And it was the same for our parishes of refugees at Gurs and in the other camps. There were moments when their spiritual élan and their faithfulness were our joy.

Pastor Boegner in France had given to Pastor Pierre Toureille the post of chaplain to foreigners. This was a pastoral service intended for the very numerous Protestant foreigners who were not in the camps, and who were scattered in the countryside or in groups of migrant workers. They all belonged to the parish of Pastor Toureille, who, during the critical periods, received an average of sixty letters a day and distributed the funds that we sent him for the most needy. A large traveling library was a big success. We sent to the chaplaincy many Bibles and Bible extracts as well as hymnals and brochures in German designed for the major holidays. In France the chaplain to foreigners distributed them through the intermediary of the French pastors in the areas where those people were living.

Other organizations developed during this period, such as Jewish Aid, Swiss Aid to Children, Quaker Service, and American Unitarians, which fought with courage, and not without success, the destitution of the camps.

Much less than our French friends, we had to bear the "conflict of loyalties." However, it was necessary that we accept certain risks. It was in the liberty given us through Jesus Christ that we and our French friends knew the limits of legality and the boldness sometimes to transgress the laws and regulations.

And so it was that one night while sitting tranquilly at home, my wife and I were visited by a stranger, reserved and polite, wearing dark glasses. As an introduction, he presented me with a scrap of torn paper whose message fully satisfied me. We talked a little of his unstable life in Savoy, and he disappeared after having stuffed into his clothing, appropriate for the circumstances, a well-filled envelope. He was to return another time and leave the same way.

We were fortunate that almost all the members of the German Consulate in Geneva were anti-Nazi. After the complete occupation of France by the German troops in November 1942, the consul general of France in Geneva depended even more than before upon the goodwill of his German colleague. Each of them had to avoid calling attention to himself by the Nazi secret service. Nevertheless, this surprising story happened:

With the interest in our work in France growing, we received large gifts in Geneva, as well as numerous packages of clothing. After 1942 we could no longer send them by the normal routes. The consul general of Germany, Dr. Wolfgang Krauel, my colleague and friend of bygone days, told me in passing one day that he could help me to send our packages across the French border, and he gave me the name of an official at the French Consulate. This official authorized me to give my parcels to the building superintendent on certain days before eight o'clock in the morning, the hour when he opened to the public. They would be sent the same day to Annemasse by diplomatic pouch, then sent to the proper address. In this way they reached CIMADE and the chaplaincy during a certain time.

What is so unusual in this story? What is it that made the officials so bold? The desire to remain free and act humanely? The shrewdness that permits one to recognize at a glance a comrade in whom one can have confidence, that look of generous nonconformity in the time of dictatorship?

I think with gratitude of other German friends in the consulate: Albrecht von Kessel, who encouraged us to continue our activities; Gottfried von Nostiz, who served us as courier for the Jura; M. Drescher in the passport service, taciturn and generous; he and the others kept in check a dull little civil servant who was the "Nazi ear" of the consulate.

In a universal Christian organization on quai Wilson, there was a lady from Geneva who was a simple and honest Christian. She was responsible for the rather ticklish French mail that crossed the border at Annemasse and often concerned Pastor Boegner. Because of her sangfroid and her good-heartedness, she was also charged with another more dangerous task. One morning at Annemasse she met a friendly French customs

45

man who asked her jokingly, "Well, Mademoiselle, how much money are you smuggling today?"

"Oh," she said with a sweet smile, "a million French francs. They have been a good bargain in Geneva lately."

The employee burst out laughing and, patting himself on the stomach, said, "Good luck then, Mademoiselle!"

Like a good Christian she had told the truth. The money was hidden in her old torn pocketbook. There are some customs men who are not far from the kingdom of God.

We should also remember here two French friends who kept up the liaison between Geneva and France: Charles Guillon, mayor of le Chambon-sur-Lignon, once the place of refuge for the Huguenots and, at that time, for innumerable refugees. In Geneva he was a member of the World Committee of the YMCA. His double domicile was most useful. And Mme André Philip, of Lyons, who several times fearlessly crossed the border between Annemasse and Geneva, disguised as a fireman on the coal car of the locomotive, blackened with coal dust. *Merci* to the French railroad men!

What can I say about the money without which it was impossible for us to act? The graph of our resources indicates the development of our Service to Refugees, whose beginnings were modest and which became an ecumenical enterprise of great breadth.[5]

The effort of Sweden was considerable, thanks in part to our friends the Cedergrens: Mme Cedergren, related to the royal family of Sweden; and Hugo Cedergren, of the World Committee of the YMCA. He divided his time among Sweden, Switzerland, and sometimes the United States, where he helped to transmit our information about the extermination of Jews. The cruel truth did not really sink in until after the shock of Pearl Harbor (7 December 1941).

One day in 1942 I was very discreetly called to the United States Embassy at Bern, where I was informed without ceremony—I, a German—that a monthly sum of 20,000 Swiss francs would be put at our disposal by the American Christian

5. See Appendix III, pp. 228-31.

Committee for Refugees, coming partly from the government in Washington. This explains the surprising difference between the American subsidies of 1942 (44,000 Swiss francs) and those of 1943 (241,000 Swiss francs). But restrictive conditions were imposed upon our use of these funds: it was forbidden to use them in "enemy territory or in countries under enemy control." Only the contributions from Switzerland and Sweden were thus able to be used in France for CIMADE and the refugee chaplaincy.

The American subsidies were spent mostly in Switzerland, where our responsibilities grew rapidly because of the influx of refugees fleeing France and soldiers deserting from Italy.

In principle, the needs of all the refugees in Switzerland should have been covered by the federal government and the many Swiss organizations of service to refugees. But it was right that we help to take care of those who had already been our protégés. They were friends who counted on our faithfulness. They came quite naturally to our office; it was impossible to send them elsewhere. How many steps, how much time was spent to help them solve their problems, which were born of the separation of couples, of parents and children, and to support them in their desperate efforts of readapting to a more normal life, to their studies, to their professions. After the persecutions undergone in France, the secrecy, the cold, the hunger, the flight to Switzerland in the midst of so many perils, and the inexpressible anxiety of crossing the border, they were received in Switzerland with great reserve. Indeed, Switzerland guaranteed them personal security; their lives were no longer in danger. But still it was with the utmost difficulty that they emerged from their nervousness and exhaustion. Many of them imagined they were arriving in a paradise where the men, particularly the sick, would be accepted and treated as brothers in the sunshine of freedom. One can understand their disappointment, their depression, and their grief when they found themselves once again interned in schools or other establishments, sometimes under very primitive conditions. The Swiss guardians generally showed them kindness, but sometimes they met distrust and pettiness. In the mountain hotels they were very isolated. It was terribly hard for them to bear total inaction. Their liberty of movement and work was tightly controlled by the Swiss authorities.

Here is an example of a day's work at the Ecumenical Secretariat for Refugees:

The Swiss are early to bed and early to rise. Before eight o'clock a telephone call comes to my home from the Pastoral Office for Refugees at Zurich:

"Couldn't you please help little Marie-Claire at last to come to Zurich to live with her grandparents?"

"We have written already several times. Our friends on the other side of the Jura Mountains must struggle with incredible difficulties. She will be arriving soon." In the meantime, she shows up; such joy!

"Walzenhausen?"

"The construction project is going well. Can we count on the ecumenical movement then?"

"Yes, our friends of the Christian Committee for Refugees in New York cabled that they are in agreement. Our young refugees can build with their own hands a nice house for themselves, and for the whole ecumenical family afterward."

Our friend Merz, of the Federal Bureau for Emigrants, calls from Bern: "Have you news of Peter, my apprentice?"

"The poor boy almost succumbed, but his mental troubles have disappeared. His doctor hopes he can work again in three months."

I finally arrive at my office, 41, avenue de Champel:

"Are our proposals for the federal list of 'nonrejectables' ready to leave for Bern?"

"Not yet. Here are fifty new names that CIMADE just sent from Annemasse. Will they give authorization?"

"I think so."

And then the mail: sufferings of the refugees, letters of appreciation, appeals for help, calls from parents in distress, complete lack of money, sickness, scattered families.

"I have been in the camps for five years now. I am middle-aged. Is there any way to recover my freedom and take care of myself?"

Some visitors arrive. When one hears their story firsthand, the human misery grips the heart. A disheveled courier arrives from France: "Message from. . . . They are holding on courageously, but they need a lot of help without delay." Where to get it? We have our dollars, but it is as if we did not have them; we cannot use them in France, and in addition, at this moment they are frozen. Our Armenian treasurer has brought a proposal to free them. The question will be brought up tomorrow in Bern. . . . Noon. My wife informs me of packages and letters to be sent to isolated individuals in the receiving homes or work camps. . . . Afternoon starts with a phone call from the "mother of refugees," Mme Gertrud Kurz, of Bern. It is about some "difficult cases." Her remarks sparkle with the lovely humor of the Appenzell.

We are in Geneva, headquarters of numerous international organizations. Scarcely a day passes without meetings. The year 1944 is coming to a close. The outcome of the war is no longer in doubt. It is time to prepare for the future, so as not to be taken by surprise. Our group on the Study of Postwar Refugee Problems, of which I am the president, has already taken up several questions. . . .

The evening mail brings a letter from Max, bubbling with joy. He is an actor. After five years in camp, he can begin to work again in complete freedom. In France he discovered the "young church" and was baptized in Geneva. He writes: "Today, it is no longer a poor refugee who speaks to you; it is someone who has rediscovered his homeland. Everywhere the universal church exists, I feel as if I am in my own country; and everywhere there is theater, I am at home. Two things make my life now: the church of our Lord in whose grace I can live, and the theater where our heavenly Father has placed me. . . ."

In the evening I write several letters, or I prepare a sermon or a talk for a parish. I must devote some time to theological reflection. . . .[6]

I would like to speak again of the problem of board and lodging in the Swiss families, which was my responsibility along with my friend Paul Vogt. The Swiss police were inclined to let the refugees leave the internment camps on condition that they be housed through the care of the voluntary organizations. The director of the Federal Police for Foreigners made an astute proposition to the friends of the refugees: "If the philanthropists who continuously reproach the Federal Police for its

6. Extract from our brochure: *Cinq années d'aide oecuménique aux réfugiés.*

bureaucratic inhumanity can find housing in receptive Swiss families, we are ready to liberate the refugees." Director Rothmund had calculated well. Even in Christian homes there was little willingness to give a warm welcome to strangers. They were foreigners so different from the Swiss, and—alas! I am thinking aloud—they were almost all Jews. Nevertheless, here and there a few doors opened. And as generous hearts are often found in poor homes, we helped financially in certain cases of long duration.

May he who has never refused to do such a thing, himself, throw the first stone at the Swiss! I would not do it myself. Our apartment was open to refugees, and experience showed us how difficult it is to give complete and open hospitality in one's home for an indefinite period.

2. The French-Swiss Border: Hope and Fear

Let us see now what was happening along the border during the tragic summer of 1942. We have slightly abridged the following story of Mme Gertrud Kurz:

It was a very somber summer for many Jewish refugees, who looked in vain for sanctuary in Switzerland. Yes, it must be admitted, they were sent back from our border, and our consciences were burdened terribly.

. . . One morning in August, Dr. Oeri, of the national congress and editor-in-chief of the newspaper *Basler Nachrichten,* telephoned me from Basel: "Something decisive must be done. I was firmly decided to go personally to the federal official von Steiger, on vacation now in Mont Pèlerin-sur-Vevey. But because of another very urgent affair I must leave immediately for Paris. I have advised M. von Steiger that you, *chère* Madame, would go in my place. I beg you to go right away to Mont-Pèlerin accompanied by some well-known Jewish person."

It was not easy to find such a person. The Jews had been hurt too deeply to accept a meeting with M. von Steiger. Finally, at Basel, it was Paul Dreyfus from Günsburg who accepted.

Our meeting at the hotel of Mont-Pèlerin lasted three hours. It was primarily a question of knowing whether or not the people sent back were going to certain death, as I believed. The federal councillor had great difficulty believing that there existed in "Goethe's Germany" people who had fallen so low as to send numberless Jews to their deaths. To lay stress upon what I had said, I spoke to him about Dr. Silberschein, of Geneva, formerly deputy in the Polish parliament, who told me with deep feeling that he had been called to the bedside of a Swiss coming from Poland. This dying man described to him the atrocities committed against the Jews. This story, and many others, seemed to make an impression on Councillor von Steiger. He admitted to us that our words confirmed what numerous Christians had already told him. When we left, we asked him if we could "hope." He said he had to think about it; the decision would be made the next day in Zurich jointly with the cantonal directors of police, who were to meet with Dr. Rothmund. I went immediately to Zurich for that meeting. . . .

En route I was besieged with questions: "What did M. von Steiger say to you? Are there quislings at the federal capitol?" No, there were not. But there were those responsible who could not bring themselves to decide, solicited as they were by members of the "Patriotic Federation" who complained of the influx of foreigners and demanded the closing of the borders for military and economic reasons, and by many Christians who considered that closing a sin, saying they were in solidarity with the persecuted. . . . The former fought for our "well-being"; the others thought only of the life of the persecuted. He who is motivated only by his faith discerns the value of the two positions.

In Zurich the next day, there were very long discussions at the conference of cantonal directors of police with the representatives of refugee service groups. I had had enough, and I asked Dr. Rothmund if M. von Steiger had not telephoned. "Yes, Madame. He has just done so."

"And what did he say?"

"He has just made a statement in favor of the opening of the borders!"

It was an unforgettable moment. Tension subsided. Hope was reborn. The police directors seemed to approve the resolution, with some reservation.

. . . M. Dreyfus, of Günsburg, immediately gave me fifty thousand francs for the bonds of ten Jewish women deported to France, whose husbands were in Switzerland. The joy and gratitude of these ten families were unlimited. The borders were now open!

. . . Who in Switzerland carried the principal responsibility for what was not done for the refugees from 1939 to 1945? M. von Steiger wrote to me once: "I learn with great surprise that you always repeat in your talks that we have committed a great injustice in closing our borders. I have trouble understanding this attitude since I personally asked that you, the only laywoman, be elected to membership on the Legal Committee for Refugees." I answered: "It is true that I have done this and shall continue to do so if it is necessary to awaken the conscience of my audience; but I shall never hold you and your co-workers the only ones responsible for this injustice. I shall always speak of our collective guilt. We have lacked faith, love, and courage to speak out publicly, in a democracy where each individual has the right to express himself according to his conscience."

These pages by Gertrud Kurz help us to understand the politics at the Swiss borders during that critical summer. But her joyous exclamation, "The borders were now open!" unfortunately does not give an exact description of the situation. Though it is true that at the end of August the admissions were much more numerous and those sent back even more rare, the principle of the closed borders was maintained. All the protests and interventions ended only in momentary, though major, relaxations of the law.

In the beginning of the 1950s, this Swiss policy was violently criticized, accused of having denied, through fear of the German danger, the essential principles of the free Swiss Confederation, such as the duty of resistance to violence, inalienable democratic liberty, and the generous practice of the right of asylum for victims of tyranny. At the request of the federal authorities in 1956, Professor Ludwig, of Basel, prepared a rather complete and very impartial documentation, published under the title *The Policy Practiced by Switzerland with Regard to Refugees During the Years 1933 to 1935* or, more familiarly, *The Ludwig Report.*

Professor Ludwig recalls that a report was made by the assistant to the Division of Police, Dr. Jezler, on the border situation at the order of Dr. Rothmund- 30 July, 1942. It is said in this report:

The mass arrests, in view of deportation in the east, begun in July 1942, constituted a very serious aggravation of the situation for the Jewish population in France, first for the foreigners and those without legal residence. The first fugitives who sought asylum in Switzerland were sent back. . . . Recently, however, we have not been able any longer to bring ourselves to order rejection. Many concurring reports on the manner of execution of these deportation orders and the conditions of life in the "Jewish regions" of the east, give such astounding information that one must understand the desperate efforts attempted by the fugitives to escape such an outcome. We can no longer take the responsibility of sending them back.[7]

At the beginning of August, M. von Steiger communicated the Jezler report to the Federal Council. All of those responsible knew from that date on the death road for which the Jews were destined. His evasive and dilatory response to Mme Kurz three weeks later was not honest. . . . It is small consolation to know that so many other men in government, similarly informed—and even those in the churches—in Allied countries did not wish to recognize the hard truth either.

The common man often showed more human understanding, and numerous people condemned to death were saved on the border by the Swiss police, who interpreted humanely the orders they received, as did a number of their French colleagues.[8]

In spite of the more flexible measures taken at the end of August, the situation remained unsatisfactory for the fugitives. Proof is seen in the telephoned instructions given 28 September 1942 by the Division of Police. Here is an extract:

The growing stream of refugees from France . . . brings the division to give, with the consent of the Federal Council, the following instructions to those charged with control at the border:

I. Foreigners entering secretly should be sent back.
II. Not to be sent back:

7. *The Ludwig Report,* pp. 84–85.

8. When that margin of interpretation becomes impossible under a regime of terror and one comes to a mechanical obedience of the laws, he is degraded. Such was the case of the Nazi nation, where rigidity excluded all flexibility of interpretation.

A. Deserters. . . .
B. Political refugees. . . . Those who have fled only because of their race are not political refugees, in conformity with the interpretation up to the present time.[9]
C. Cases in which refusing entrance would be an extremely hard measure:
1. Persons obviously sick and pregnant women
2. Refugees over sixty-five years of age. Their spouses. . . .
3. Unaccompanied children under sixteen years old
4. Parents with their own children of less than sixteen years
5. Refugees who from the beginning spontaneously declare that they have close relatives in Switzerland . . . or special relations with our country (previous residence)
III. French Jews must be sent back because they run no danger in their country.[10]
IV. In case of doubt . . . immediately contact by telephone the Division of 'Police.

These regulations were so ambiguous that it was necessary to complete them by a sort of "border recommendation" for the persons named in the lists. Thus were established the lists of "nonrejectables." Some of the names were given by the federal authorities, but most of them came from the organizations of aid to refugees, which transmitted them to the federal Division of Police. The Swiss organizations were in contact for that with their corresponding organizations in France or with trustworthy persons. Thanks to the personal and pressing steps taken by Pastor Marc Boegner at the Department of Justice and Police of the Confederation, Ecumenical Service to Refugees was able to put on these lists the names given by CIMADE, the refugee chaplaincy, or known persons. The intervention of Pastor Boegner doubtlessly permitted a more generous use of this system of lists.

9. Note the untenable distinction. The Jews were a thousand times more in danger than many of the "politiques." Note also the use of the Nazi term "because of their race."

10. This distinction was no longer exact at that date.

In spite of that, we sometimes had to battle a long time still to avoid the rejection of our protégés. The resolution voted 9 May 1943 by the Synod of the Evangelical Reformed Church of the canton of Basel shows this:

Deeply impressed by the information received concerning the instructions given by the authorities to the border control units, and by the tragic destiny in store for fugitives who try to enter Switzerland, the Synod charges the Synodal Council to invite the Committee of the Federation of Protestant Churches to intervene with the responsible authorities on behalf of the refugees, in conformity with the task of the church.[11]

The Ludwig Report underestimates the participation of the Swiss churches in the efforts made to obtain a more humane policy in regard to refugees. This participation was in close relation to the Swiss resistance to the opportunist alignment with the totalitarian system. Here are a few examples:

Already in June 1941, Karl Barth had made a speech on the occasion of the 650th anniversary of the Swiss Confederation, founded upon the oath of Rütli in 1291. This speech, beginning with the words "In the name of Almighty God," had attracted much attention. Its diffusion was prohibited by censorship on 18 July, certainly in consideration of the German neighbors, at the apex of their power, but probably also because of the harsh criticism made by Barth of the too great flexibility of certain cantonal and federal authorities before the threats made to their ancient liberties. The prohibition of the censorship was annulled shortly afterward. Here is part of the discourse, which touches on the conduct of the Swiss toward their foreign guests:

"In the name of Almighty God!" Because these words are found in the Constitution, we pose the question: What is the importance of the manner in which we treat the foreigners in our territory? These foreigners are divided rather distinctly into two groups. There are the "unaccepted" guests. The "accepted" are those whose papers are "in order," which today in ninety out of a hun-

11. See also Appendix VII, pp. 234-37.

dred cases at least signifies that they are more or less convinced partisans of the political system of the power that surrounds us, that they are, freely or by constraint, propagandists and sometimes something more than propagandists. The "unaccepted" are those who, adversaries or victims of that regime, have had to leave their country and have entered ours as "emigrants" to whatever degree. The "accepted" enjoy the protection of our laws, by virtue of their *permis de séjour,* guaranteed by international contract. They can organize assemblies similar to that held at the Foire d'Échantillons in Basel; they can even occupy themselves with preparations similar to those made by their compatriots in Holland before the invasion. The "unaccepted" are investigated at frequent intervals as if they were gypsies or convicts on parole. They must run from office to office to have permission, with every restriction imaginable, to breathe our air. They are exhorted from time to time to pursue their ultimate goal, which is to continue the journey. At any rate, life for them is bearable only if they have brought into our country a rather tidy sum. Here something is wrong. Of course, the *permis de séjour* must be guaranteed to those who possess them because that is a contractual arrangement. Of course, one must take into account our own economic difficulties. And of course, one must keep an eye on suspicious elements among the emigrants.

But can we remain indifferent to the disappointment and the bitterness of so many worthy guests belonging to this second class, who came to us confident in this free offer of a free Switzerland, and who found themselves more or less purposely punished for being here as adversaries or victims of a system opposed in its very essence to Switzerland? Will we be able to erase the blame that we risk in having solved this problem? Whom are we serving by treating our guests in different ways according to their political position? In the eighteenth and nineteenth centuries, Swiss policy relative to emigrants was generous and farsighted. Even taking into account our present difficulties, one could not call our policy generous or farsighted on this point. What do we really want: to give up or to resist? Is it not clear that every franc, every step taken, every intervention in favor of these "unaccepted" constitutes an element of authentic Swiss resistance? Why is it that there are still those high places in which it seems that the question has not yet been faced?[12]

12. Karl Barth, *Une voix suisse,* 1939–1944 (Labor et Fides).

Meeting Karl Barth in 1966, I spoke to him with gratitude about this speech and asked him of whom he was thinking when he talked about every intervention on behalf of "unaccepted" guests constituting an element of authentic Swiss resistance. He answered: "Gertrud Kurz and Paul Vogt. Also Dr. Arthur Frey." The latter, director of the Swiss Protestant Press Service, attacked passionately the partisans of the "new order of Europe."

I also want to say a word about Pastor Walter Lüthi, of Bern. He preached 30 August 1943 in Zurich on Romans 8:31–39 under the title "Resist!" before the annual assembly of the federation of Christian youth movements called *Junge Kirche.* Federal Councillor von Steiger was in the audience. Here are some of Pastor Lüthi's declarations: "There is something that separates us from the love of God; it is our bad consciences. . . . We have prevented the entry into our country of fleeing foreigners who looked to us for protection. . . . In the persons of these needy to whom we refuse entrance, we are rejecting Jesus Christ at our borders, because he declared himself to be in solidarity with 'the least of these my brethren.' . . . Dear Federal Councillor, do not try to assuage our consciences! You will render a bad service to our country. . . ."

The guns were silenced on 9 May 1945, and the Department of Refugees had to develop rapidly in order to help millions of other fugitives and their destitute churches. May the memory of the atrocious events recalled in this book and the liberty that the Lord has given us in service determine "that such things shall not come to pass again"!

3.

Gurs: Hunger and Waiting

JEANNE MERLE D'AUBIGNÉ

Madeleine Barot had succeeded in getting inside the Gurs camp and was trying to install a resident team there. She proposed to me that I be part of that team. I accepted and arrived in Gurs at the beginning of January 1941.

There was an indescribable impression upon entering. Monotonous hardship. A sea of barracks almost two miles long and a half-mile wide. A swamp with a road running through it.

The group of barracks was divided into twelve areas, each one surrounded with thick barbed wire. At the gate of each block, an armed guard. In each block, the barracks of the chief—an internee—then the infirmary and kitchen. Forty to sixty prisoners to a barracks. Total population: 10,000 to 16,000 persons depending on the time. The camp had been set up for the Spaniards of the Republican army, 19,000 to 20,000 people, among whom were members of the famous International Brigade. After the departure of the Spaniards, except for 2,000 to 3,000 men of the brigade, in the spring of 1940 a convoy of German women arrived at Gurs. Most of them—artists, students, businesswomen—were not Jewish. They were able to leave the camp at the time of the armistice [1940], although some of the political refugees, distrusting the Hitler regime, preferred to remain in the camp under French protection.

In May 1940, a convoy of women of various nationalities arrived in Gurs in cattle cars. Most of them came from Belgium. They had been sorted out at Luçon and relieved of all their money at Toulouse. Trainloads of men came from the east, nearly all intellectuals and political figures, swelling the camp. Many of them had lived at Saint-Cyprien on the Mediterranean. They had slept on the sand, were fed spoiled fruit, and most of them suffered from dysentery. With them came a large group of 7,000 to 8,000 people, Jews from the Palatinate. Among those who arrived 20 October 1940 in twenty trains were the patients of the psychiatric hospitals, maternities, and asylums of Germany. The stationmaster of Oloron-Sainte-Marie related to me how from those sealed cars came voices, desperate cries. With the president of the Red Cross at Oloron, he opened the cars and had the sickest ones put on stretchers. The others were piled helter-skelter into trucks to be taken to Gurs. It rained in torrents; their baggage, all their belongings, was thrown on the station platform and not distributed until many days later—emptied, drenched, unrecognizable.

An old gendarmes barracks at the north of the camp was the home of CIMADE. We had the privilege of having a wooden floor and over our heads a roof that did not leak too much. At the entrance, on either side of a central corridor, were two little rooms for my colleague and me, with narrow beds over which was a shelf for our "gear." In the main room a small kitchen and a library were installed. The room was heated, theoretically at least, by a trench stove, a cylinder open at the bottom and on top, in which one burned whatever one could. Only the Spaniard designated for this duty was capable of lighting it and keeping it going without smothering the fire. The camp director, unable to imagine that two women alone could survive in this place, assigned us this Spaniard.

Our visitation service began little by little. From barracks to barracks, from suffering to suffering, from despair to despair. It was necessary to live in the midst of all of them. But sometimes we reached the very limit of what we were able to stand.

I remember my first entrance into a barracks. It was cold. The shutters were closed because there were no windows. It was dark. Electric light was given only from six to eight o'clock in the evening. It was not yet time. Upon opening the door, I saw shiny points in the darkness. They were the eyes of women, fixed upon me, luminous like those of cats in the night. Someone came forward, took me by the hand, and led me between the beds and boxes toward the person I had come to visit. In consideration of the visitor, a shutter was opened a little. The women had beds (elsewhere, they had to sleep on the floor). There was luggage everywhere: the clothes one wished to save from rats were hung on lines. The women were lying down, except for a few who, around the stove, argued over a corner of the lid to heat a poor cup of tea. The fire was lighted only two hours a day.

Next I noticed that the tin can industry was going strong. What one couldn't make with them! First the women made hot plates. They lighted them with anything that would burn. These hot plates diffused such nauseating odors that they could be used only outside the barracks. I often saw women in rags, crouched in the snow, blowing on the embers.

With certain winds, especially in the warm season, we suffocated because of the odors coming from the "châteaus," the toilets in camp language. More than six feet up in the air was perched a shelter over two vats which rolled on a rail. A narrow ladder, the rungs covered with frost and ice in winter, led to the shelter, where there were two holes cut in the floor. How many times at night unfortunate old people, fallen from the ladder, were frozen dead on the ground! Each day a little train took away the vats. The prisoners poured out the contents in the fields near the camp. From there came the odor that seized you by the throat. At each return to Gurs, I suffocated once again.

Opposite our barracks, an infirmary-maternity was set up. As in all misery, pregnancies and births were numerous in this closed world where races were forcibly thrown together. When male visits were permitted in the barracks, it was a problem to make the visitors leave. One must admit that this relative tolerance was preferable by far to the excessive severity in the beginning; with the arrival of the convoy from Baden, the couples had been separated. Armed guards prevented the men and women from meeting. One poor woman learned only long afterward of the death of her husband, whom she had never been able to visit and who was buried without her knowledge.

The infirmary-maternity saw the birth of triplets in the spring of 1943 to a Jewish mother and a Spanish father. Some interned obstetricians, aided by the famous doctor of the Spanish Brigade, brought the children into the world. Two survived and became true camp children. The mother was overwhelmed with gifts—layettes and even food.

Food—the crucial problem!

The unforeseen arrival of the convoy from Baden had put the camp personnel in confusion. Flour was low. There were no mess kits, no emergency provisions. Old tin cans and old gasoline cans became the plates, jars, and cooking pots. Panic at Oloron when the camp director demanded food! The municipal councillors refused to make requisitions. How, in this time of extreme scarcity in the Southern Zone, could enough food be gathered to feed crowds of foreigners?

Some prisoners had managed to keep a part of their money. They looked desperately for food. The region was rich. But what about the rest of the masses?

One of my first jobs was to supply these unfortunate ones. Madeleine Barot sent me money that she received from the World Council of Churches in Geneva. As for myself, I scoured the countryside on bicycle to buy whatever I could find in the region. The farmers raised their prices outrageously, so that I sometimes returned empty-handed. One day, I met the old priest of Gurs, very poor, in a greenish-black cassock. He said to me, "I would like very much to help these poor people, but you see all that I have: one half-pound of butter, one quarter-pound of lard, and two sausages."

"Monsieur le curé," I said to him, "you have no money,

but you have authority. Tell your parishioners to be more generous when I try to buy supplies for the internees."

The next Sunday, the priest made such a strong appeal from the pulpit that it was much easier to make my purchases. I even returned one day, not without trembling a little, with two dozen eggs in the carryall of my bike. Slowly the supplies were authorized by the director, and some prisoners were able to scout the neighboring villages to bring back whatever they were able to obtain. Mlle A. had bought a donkey and a primitive little cart. She amused us when she sweet-talked her stubborn animal.

Some men came voluntarily to help us repair our barracks. They often looked exhausted. I asked one of them about it. "We are so hungry that every effort brings on a dizzy spell." That day we had only a bit of bread from our rations and an abominable raisin mixture. We gave each worker a slice of bread with this, and they were able to continue working.

It was during this period that I saw a spectacle that became too common. Going down the central road of the camp, a man walked in front of me; he began to stumble and then fell. He was carried away inert, dead from hunger.

The number of people dying from hunger was increasing daily. People were talking about it even as far as Vichy. It was for this reason that I received a letter from an American lady telling me that, having sold all her jewels for a large sum of money, she had bought a great quantity of food in Portugal. It was the Reverend Clayton Williams, then pastor of the American Church in Paris, who had been the middleman for buying the food and giving the American friend the idea of addressing the whole lot to the *Assistance Protestante* in Gurs. Mr. Williams was not sure of the authorities in the camp, but he knew me and gave my name for receiving all these riches.

I had hardly finished reading the letter when I saw a big truck stop in front of our barracks. A young woman dressed in khaki jumped out, helped by the driver, who was none other than the Count of la Rochefoucauld! She told me immediately that she wanted the *Assistance Protestante* to distribute the goods in the camp because she could not trust the camp authorities, who had a very bad reputation, unfortunately not wholly unmerited.

I called some of our men to help unload the truck. The count gave a hand; and to our amazement we saw such things as sugar, chocolate, sardines, and even—such a rarity—soap!

But suddenly the director of the camp arrived. (News travels fast in such a place even without telegraph or telephone.) He was accompanied by the head nurse (well known as a Nazi). The director was furious not to have been notified before and astonished to see all those goods.

I showed him the letter I had only just received. I could not have guessed that we would receive such a load, as the letter just spoke of a gift which I thought would be about the same as those we received daily for distribution.

The head nurse became jealous and wanted her share. She prompted the director to decide that only half of the load would remain with me, and she took the other half.

The American lady was quite indignant, and I did my best to explain the situation to her. So an equal division of the goods was made, and I promised to keep an eye on the distribution.[1]

From the United States some personal packages began to arrive for certain prisoners. But the number of people devoid of all personal means and of all outside relations was large. How could we help them? We decided to strike from our lists those who received packages. This step made us commit involuntarily the following terrible injustice.

Professor T. had taught physics and chemistry in the Rhineland. He was a member of the Protestant community of the camp. He was a charming man, tall, thin, highly cultivated. I was concerned to see him grow gaunt and pale. He was on the list of those who received packages. He did not complain. He always answered, "I am fine." Then he missed the worship service. I sent someone to ask about him. My emissary returned breathlessly. "Quickly, Mamie, come to the infirmary of Group D. The professor is dying." I went as quickly as

1. The preceding seven paragraphs do not appear in the original French edition.

possible. At the infirmary I saw an emaciated body, shaken with spasms of agony. Did he recognize me? I don't think so. Around him, the men of his barracks were sobbing.

I turned around, indignant. "Why didn't you tell me?"

One man replied ashamedly, "The professor would not let us."

"He received packages from America, though?"

"Yes, but he shared them with the forty men in the barracks."

I was so furious that I could only make a useless gesture. I went to find the camp doctor, forcing him to come. "Tell me what this man died from."

The doctor, always drunk, answered, "Oh, yes, his heart stopped."

The lesson was tragic; it taught us something. I learned, for example, that Mme K. distributed to her barrackmates all the packages that she received. I begged her to come each day to take the noon meal with us. I put someone beside her to watch her, because she would put a plate on her lap on which to slide what we gave her and distribute it in her barracks.

The number of persons becoming bloated from hunger grew unceasingly. We were seeing swollen faces and stomachs, while the legs and arms remained emaciated. Deaths multiplied. Soon there were more than thirty a day, and eleven hundred for the winter months of 1940–41.

Thanks to the regular aid of the World Council of Churches, by the intermediary of Pastor Freudenberg, the rations to distribute increased in number; but they had to be watched. It was thus that I learned one day that the cans of sardines given to the most unfortunate were selling for fifty francs apiece in the "Prayer Barracks" of the Orthodox Jews. After that, we opened the cans before giving them.

Among the men who had come from Saint-Cyprien, a violent typhoid epidemic broke out. For lack of medicine, they were isolated in a barracks in Group C. They lay upon the floor, awaiting death. It was then that Pastor Boegner announced his visit. Hoping to have some influence in these tragic times, he had just accepted the nomination of national councillor.

While the director was giving orders in every direction to receive this important visitor, Madeleine Barot led M. Boegner to the barracks of the sick before the director could dissuade her. M. Boegner remained speechless with horror before these men—inert, emaciated, dying on the floor. He scarcely listened to the explanations of the director: "We have no more medicine, no beds or personnel." It was true in fact.

The president of the International Red Cross, Dr. Alec Cramer, came also; and after him, Mme Cedergren, née Princess Bernadotte. These visits were a great comfort to us. Medication arrived and supplementary aid for our ecumenical meals.

Quaker Aid took its place in the camp and was very effective. The Quakers were admitted by the Germans. During the war of 1914–1917, they had helped the unfortunate on both sides. They received authorization to enter all the camps and to order supplies from eastern countries, in particular that pea flour from Hungary on which so many internees lived. Twice a month they sent tons of merchandise to the camp, thus furnishing two thousand rations a day.

Swiss Aid settled into the barracks next to ours. For children and adolescents, there were cheese, milk, and dried fruit. The Swiss nurse directed the distributions competently. Control of all the lists was assured by the doctors interned in the camp, under the direction of Dr. Heinrich Mayer.

Hunger grew in spite of all the help. A part of the supplies received disappeared. I went to Toulouse to talk over the situation with those responsible for Quaker Aid for the southwest. I suggested that they organize a refectory barracks and a field kitchen. The camp director promised to do what was necessary and signed a protocol. Each day, while waiting, I did the rounds of the kitchens supplied by the Quakers. I knew that, as soon as I started out, a messenger hurried to the kitchens. Upon arriving, I saw the macaroni and dried peas being poured into the kettles. But the independent kitchen did not get organized, and the black market always absorbed a part of the supplies. The bursar declared without ceremony that the signed protocol would not be honored.

A "Clandestine Council" was decided upon, bringing together Dr. Heinrich Mayer, the nurse from Swiss Aid, a person representing the Catholic group, and another from the Protestant group. I was the only French person free to come and go. They asked me to return to the Quakers in Toulouse.

There, Miss H., director of Quaker Aid, proposed that we go together to Vichy to see Maréchal Pétain. The next day we left by a small plane, Toulouse-Vichy, which shook terribly in the air pockets. We went immediately to the Hôtel du Parc, residence of the *maréchal*. We entered without introduction as far as the desk of General L.—greetings, *baisemain, politesse*. The *maréchal* was not to be seen. Could we explain our request to the general? As I spoke, his expression became very cold. He could do absolutely nothing under the circumstances. My Quaker friend asked if we could intervene with the management of the camps. "Who is responsible?" I was asked. I did not hesitate to say, "The bursar."

What was happening at the camp during these hours of absence? My colleague André Morel saw the director, very excited, drive up in a car. "Where is Mlle Merle d'Aubigné? Why is she on a trip when I need her? I have orders to install the Quaker kitchen immediately. We must decide where to put it." André Morel, suspecting the business, showed the plans already made, and made the necessary decisions. He was rubbing his hands when I returned. "Well done, Mamie!" The director received me rather coldly, but his mood passed. We understood each other sometimes. The bursar called for me to see him under some pretext or other. I went with beating heart because I had learned that he had been relieved of his functions and transferred to a small camp of 130 persons. What a downfall and what a loss after the "rake-off" on 16,000 rations!

The following scene was described by the prisoners serving in the bursar's barracks:

"Mlle Merle d'Aubigné enters, smiling and at ease. The grumpy bursar scarcely greets her. Without transition, he breaks into reproaches and insults. Vulgar words assail her. Always calm, she looks out the window without seeming to notice what is going on around her." In fact, I had decided not to listen to the insults, continuing to pray in order to preserve my inner peace and calm. From the window I admired the splendid view of the Pyrenees, covered with snow, and I did not hear the bursar. When the noise stopped, I turned around and picked up the thread of conversation. "Then I can have the beds taken. . . ." A new volley of insults broke over me. The phenomenon of deafness began again. I left smiling.

After the bursar was fired, the director became more flexible and we had much better relations in our work.

In good weather André Morel managed to augment our supplies. Sometimes he spent the night in pastures where secret butchering went on, and he brought us some good cuts. The noon meal became one of our principal means of service. We nourished our secretaries, assistants, and storekeepers, whose number was growing. To them were added other people pointed out as particularly in need, materially or morally. It is thus that many worthy men were able to endure this critical period: Reichel, talented painter, who had seen his works burned by the Gestapo in the Marktplatz in Munich; Richard Moering, poet and man of letters; Buch, political figure; etc.

Religious services were authorized in the camp. In the beginning we Protestants had the right only to the "bath barracks." Not that one could still take baths in this particular place, but this plank shelter had kept its name. It was empty, with asphalt flooring, always damp, if not wet and cold. No chairs or benches of any kind. We had to remain standing, rolled up in our poor blankets. The services were celebrated by Pastor Charles Cadier. The table was on sawhorses, and upon this table with M. Cadier's Bible was a large cross of wood sculptured by a Spanish Protestant, a veritable artist who died soon after our arrival there. This cross, saved from pillage, is now in the chapel of CIMADE in Paris.

Once the director had given us authorization, the worship service was held in the large room of our barracks. The Spaniards built some benches. Pastor Jacques Rennes was in charge of services at that time. But what complications for everyone! Pastor Rennes came from Sauveterre-de-Béarn, about six miles from Gurs, on the other side of the line of demarcation. How many times the pastor could not pass when he was expected for Sunday worship or for a funeral service! Left to ourselves, in the absence of André Morel, I did what I could. On Sunday mornings, in order to be understood by the largest number, I had to speak in German.

For burials, Pastor Rennes was not always notified in time. At camp one was buried at the last breath. The sides of the coffin were so thin that the boards bent under the weight of the body. It was hoisted onto a cart. The cemetery was to the north of our barracks. It sometimes happened that without notice I would see the sad cart from my window. Two or three friends of the deceased would signal me. I had only the time to take my New Testament, join them, and read in the context of this situation the pages of victory in the Gospels and the Epistles, associating ourselves with the hopes and appeals of the Psalms of Israel, and uniting ourselves in the prayer of the Crucified—descended into hell . . . and resurrected. Sometimes there were Jewish listeners, and I was gripped by a feeling of responsibility toward them.

Our worship services brought together Lutherans, Reformed, Baptists. The Protestants were such a small number in the midst of an enormous Jewish mass that one did not even think of the differences of denominations.

We also had Bible studies. Texts of the Old Testament, particularly the Prophets and the Psalms, were the most familiar to all. They were a tie between us and the Jews who came to one or another of our services or Bible studies. There were even some rabbis who participated at certain series of Bible studies, sharing with us their understanding of the texts.

At the request of several who sincerely desired baptism, André Morel had begun a catechetical group. At the beginning of the summer of 1942, a delicate question was posed. Great fear reigned in the camp; the requests became much more numerous. The candidates hoped that baptism would keep them from the dreaded deportation. André Morel sought the advice of M. Boegner, who asked him to remain rather severe and demanding. No conversion was acceptable that did not correspond with a deep and profound conviction.

I was very impressed by the visit of the grand rabbi, intervening in the same way. He came almost begging Morel to prepare no one anymore for baptism. He said that it would not be honest to profit in this way from the panic in the camp; that these conversions could not be serious; that they put the Jews in opposition to their Law; and that they would be decidedly compromised in the eyes of their fellow Jews.

Our place of worship was very rustic. I had had a few Psalms painted on cloth. These were unrolled each Sunday. We had a small pulpit for the preacher, a lectern for the Bible. A Spanish sculptor had arranged and ornamented them with the initials *IHS* cut from a tin can. The communion table was of nicely polished wood and held the cross of which we have already spoken.

Beginning with our first services, I was surprised to see that our friends preferred to sit on the benches along the wall. There they could lean, exhausted. The effort to listen without leaning against something was too much for them. Sometimes one of them would become sick. I got into the habit of preparing a cup of milk, gift of Swiss Aid, in my little room in order to revive those who fainted.

One day the charming and cultivated young wife of an interned doctor arose suddenly and cried, "Nein, nein, meine Kinder sind verbrannt!" ("No, no, my children are burned!") Screaming, she crossed the room. I took her in my arms and guided her to my room, where she sobbed on my bed. Since leaving the Rhineland, she had begun to lose her mind. When they came to arrest her and her husband, her children were at school and she had not seen them again. They had been moved into Switzerland, but she had not recovered from this terrible shock. She was interned at Lannemezan and died there the same year. Later, her husband was able to find the children and go to the United States.

Before and after the Sunday services, we tried to become acquainted—non-Christians mixing with the others. The house was open to all.

One day I received a message from Madeleine Barot telling me that I was going to receive a load of very good clothes for distribution among our refugees. These clothes had been sent by the Mennonites. They were in excellent condition, and we had lots to do to satisfy the demands of those women who had been deprived for such a long time of such joys as trying on dresses or coats.

We thought that all had gone well when in the evening I heard a knock at my door. There was a very large woman who had been given an almost new coat, made of excellent material, and with a fur collar. But it was black. She explained that in her country—she was Romanian—black was the color of death and she never wore it. We gave the coat to someone less super-stitious and gave the unsatisfied woman a short silk dress of many colors which did not suit her at all.

Something else that caused much talking was the giving of Mennonite coats, of a style dating about 1850 but cut in such excellent material that they could not wear out . . . and there were some remarkable tailors among the Jews.[2]

Our schedule was full. Weekdays, starting at 9:00 A.M., began the distribution of books entrusted to several librarians. We soon had more than five thousand volumes, and our readers, well protected in a room warmed by a noisy stove, lined up at the window.

That was also the mail hour. One of our men went to get the many packages that were addressed to the *Assistance Protestante* (which had become our official name). All that was rapidly separated to accelerate the distribution. A new arrival, Alfred Seckel, was a great help in setting up simple administrative methods and in keeping good order in our accounting.

Our barracks had been baptized by the prisoners *baraque de la culture*. There we organized conferences and musical programs, thanks to the very good pianists and violinists among the prisoners. A special gift from the YMCA permitted us to rent instruments and to buy music. Wednesday afternoons were given to musical concerts. The celebrated Brunner, former first

2. The preceding three paragraphs do not appear in the original French edition.

70

violinist of the philharmonic concerts of Vienna, came to play for us. He loved the contemplative silence of our barracks. With all his art and all his heart, he interpreted the works of Bach, Beethoven, Schumann, César Franck. The theme of Franck's sonata for piano and violin had become the signal of Brunner's presence. As soon as he would see me, he whistled it. We also had the first tenor of the Berlin Opera, specialist in J. S. Bach. He sang the grand themes of the cantatas. Farther on we shall pick up the trace of dear Peters. Often the faces of those who listened were transfigured a moment, escaping the horrors of camp. Here also, some became sick, and I resorted to my Swiss Aid milk in order to restore a little strength to the weakened listeners.

Among our musicians, I discovered Hans Ebbecke, pianist, former organist of the Cathedral of Strasbourg. Non-Jewish, he had wanted to be interned and to follow his young Jewish wife. Often he accompanied Brunner. He loved to convert all of an orchestral rendition to the piano so that we could better know the great symphonic works. These musical afternoons continued until the end. Brunner was hidden by the director of the camp. Ebbecke and his wife had adventures that will be recounted later.

In the group of the Protestant community, I see again the silhouette of Prof. Herbert Jehle. He was Aryan, but an intransigent pacifist, and his being the son of a German general had not protected him. As a member of the Student Christian Movement, he had participated in the great ecumenical youth meeting in Amsterdam in 1939. Very tall, with an ample golden beard and a sparkle in his eyes, he wore in camp a blanket around his waist and another over his shoulders. In this way he preserved his only suit for the day he hoped to leave for America. In this strange costume he went for a walk with me one evening along the main road. Feeling very discouraged, I told him of my horror for these barracks, the odors, the suffering. He said to me, "Do not look at the camp. Raise your eyes and contemplate the magnificent heaven, and the worlds that follow into infinity. I am an astronomer; I live in the sky. Look at that constellation, you see that planet. . . ." He began to describe to me the starry sky which twinkled above us in that extremely cold evening. Then he began to talk to me of Einstein's theories. That lesson, coming from a man who had lost everything and who found in his faith and in his science the means to carry on, did me incomparable good. Herbert Jehle was one of the last who managed to embark for the United States, thanks to the help of friends in the World Student Christian Federation. He became professor of astronomy and physics at an American university.

How many other men and women passed through our barracks and disappeared in the smoke of Auschwitz and elsewhere! Some, however, were saved.

Walter Speigel, who helped us to organize our distributions. M. Schwartz, editor of an important liberal newspaper, who, liberated thanks to French friends, was hidden in the Midi of France. And dear Mlle Reckendorff, French professor in Baden, chief of Group J, who helped me to translate into German the short meditations that I had to give in the absence of a minister on Sundays. She was saved by CIMADE and died peacefully in her country.

Then again our accountant, Alfred Seckel. Fleeing from the racist laws, he had signed up in the Foreign Legion and had left Germany and Lotte, his fiancée. His time expired and he was demobilized at Mont-de-Marsan. But on leaving the office, a hand was placed on his shoulder. "This way, my friend, you are going to the camp at Gurs." He had one-quarter Jewish blood in his veins. Lotte, Aryan, was interned in the camp at Brens. Alfred fell sick from the shock. We wanted to try anything to help him escape from camp and find Lotte.

One day a mysterious visitor, Monsieur L., of whose game at that time we were ignorant, asked what he could do for us. "Help young Alfred to get out!" Promise made. Days passed. Nothing happened. Alfred remained in camp. Who was the visitor? Anything was possible. At that point I was called to Savoy for a meeting of the CIMADE leaders. I had to go, but I could not without leaving the responsibility to someone: Alfred.

At that moment, he came to me. "Hurray," he said, "I am

free. . . ." He saw my joy and worry about my own departure. Alfred said, "I shall stay until your return." When
one imagines the possibilities of counterorders, police raids, and
secret dealings, one can only recognize the "class" of the ex-
legionnaire. Alfred stayed, with his freedom in his pocket. At
my return, he came to meet me at the station in 'Toulouse.
He handed me the keys to the office and left to rejoin Lotte
and to be married.

One must tell, also, of the Christmas celebration of 1941.
It was a landmark in that dark adventure. My colleague and
I wanted to take every care in preparing this Christmas. The
tree was a must, but above all, a solid meal was necessary.
Rich soup, meat, macaroni, mashed peas, oatmeal, cakes,
oranges, and candy. Small presents were bought at the nearest
shops: razor blades, cigarettes, matches, little mirrors, bows.
And above all, we wanted each one of the three hundred guests
to receive clothing. All the packages were ready. The night
before Christmas, the arrival of thirty-six men was announced
to me, and they were in special need of warm socks. I had just
put a pair in some of the packages. What should I do? I had
used up all my reserves. Dismayed, thinking of the disappointment of those who would feel left out, I undid thirty-six gifts
in order to give the socks to the new arrivals. The next morning
some packages arrived for the *Assistance Protestante*. I quickly
opened the first box at hand: It contained thirty-six pairs of
socks!

The tables were set up in a horseshoe. I read the pages of
the Gospel of Christmas; the choir hummed *"Stille Nacht,
heilige Nacht. . . ."* The guests ate their fill. Several of them
took a large portion of their meal back to their barrackmates.
To end the celebration, we were able to give a fair amount of
money to the rabbi for his people.

Soon I was alone. My colleague had become ill and had to
be cared for out of camp. André Morel had left on another as-
signment. Madeleine Barot was occupied more than ever going
from one camp to another, starting new teams and thinking
of the future, which was darkening each day. Valuable aid
came in the person of Elisabeth Schmidt, woman minister with

a degree in literature and a graduate diploma in philosophy. By her lectures and studies, she attracted a large number of scholars and others who loved good French. Unfortunately, that lasted only two months. Elisabeth caught typhoid and had to be hospitalized. I told the director, who asked me to keep it quiet because there were already numerous cases in certain barracks. Alone with so many condemned ones, so many dying . . . I visited more attentively the interned social workers, working with them to promote a little spirit of solidarity among the camp population.

In the spring of 1942, I was obliged to take some rest for a few days in the home of friends. Upon my return to camp, I found the situation a little better. The spring was one of lessened strain and of hope for the internees. The weather was warm and fair; the ground had dried; supplies came more easily since the departure of the bursar and also thanks to the Quaker meals served in their special barracks. I had the idea of cultivating a little land that surrounded our barracks. Vegetables grew as if by enchantment in this rich, virgin earth. Flowers decorated our quarters. For gardener, we had a political prisoner, M. Nethe—non-Jewish, anti-Hitler. Happy to devote himself to cultivating our vegetables, he was able to forget his political preoccupations.

The borders of flowers and the patches of vegetables multiplied. The internees found there an occupation and a supplement to their diet. Discipline became less strict. The director wished that the prisoners could forget their internment and think of themselves only as being in emergency housing. He gave permission rather easily for visiting the city of Pau. Some women even went to the beauty parlor! Finding outside work became possible. It sufficed to produce a lodging certificate signed by a Frenchman living in the district, or in surrounding areas. These certificates became the object of the black market: they were bought for 25,000 francs cash in the money of the times. Thus they became a privilege of the rich and of those who had been able to keep their funds.

At the initiative of a Polish refugee priest, some prisoners were able to leave Gurs to be installed by small groups in various localities and to find work there. Madeleine Barot grasped at the idea and looked for a place where the local authorities and understanding neighbors would give them real help. She fixed her choice on le Chambon-sur-Lignon, and rented a hotel there, le Coteau Fleuri. The budget was supported by the Protestant churches of Sweden by the mediation of Princess Bernadotte, who had come to see us.

Thus June 1942 arrived. What a time establishing the lists of those whom we would take! And the others?

I headed a small convoy of thirty-five liberated persons. Escorted by three gendarmes, whose principal duty was to carry the older women's bundles, we arrived at le Coteau Fleuri.

4.

Deportations

JEANNE MERLE D'AUBIGNÉ

Warning signs of tragic events pierced our isolation at Gurs. I had scarcely returned from le Coteau Fleuri when the head nurse let slip a few pro-Nazi remarks. I was alerted. On one of those days, I entered a barracks at the back of which the nurse had herded a group of women and was cursing them: "Dirty Jews, you don't deserve to be treated better than your relatives in Germany. You'll see what will happen to you." I was petrified. When the nurse had gone, I stayed with the women. "We haven't done anything . . . We asked for an extra blanket . . . She began to insult us." There was a long sob. The wind of hate that they had known in Germany was blowing again. Several told of their fear of being transported to Poland. I assured them, with an illusory conviction, that such a thing would never happen in France.

I went to question the head nurse. She spoke to me about the internees in a tone that horrified me. She told me what was happening in the camps in Germany: people forced to work, certainly, but dressed in "most becoming" uniforms. Had she really visited the camps?

Propaganda for the free return of Jews to Germany began to circulate. Several of ours were taken in by these deceptions. It was said they would be "installed in lovely châteaus, well treated, and nourished for their work in certain factories." We now know what they were, these châteaus of Buchenwald and Auschwitz. One charming woman, a talented couturiere and former first seamstress chez Molyneux in Paris, received letters from her daughter in Germany telling (under what constraint?) of these châteaus. She was convinced; she left. We never again heard tell of her.

The end of July 1942 came, with its unbearable odors and a more and more oppressing anxiety. There was more and more talk of deportations.

In my little room, which I had arranged as best I could so that those who came there would find some relaxation, a young woman came to see me and said immediately: "They are grouping large numbers of freight cars at Oloron. They are to take us away. Where? Do you know?" I kept my smile, but she had taken my breath away.

This forced smile—should I keep it? The camp director called me in and said, "Mademoiselle, this morning there was the beginning of panic among the prisoners. You were seen coming from your place looking so sad that those who saw you thought: She knows more than she wants to tell. . . . I beg you, whatever you know, whatever you feel, keep a smile when you go among the prisoners."

A short time afterward, the director came to see me himself. He was terribly upset. "I have come to say good-bye. I am leaving the camp in a few days. I do not want to accept certain orders that have been given me."

On 31 July we awakened to see the camp encircled by the "black" police (so called because of their uniforms). A policeman every six feet. Sinister. At four o'clock they began to bring out the prisoners from the groups, calling from lists the names with initials *A* to *M*. Anger overcame my fright. I could do nothing. The fifteen hundred people in the first shipment were all known to me; several were friends of nearly two years of communal life. Among those first chosen were two hundred young Jewish girls, among the most beautiful and healthy. I went from one to another in the big hangar where those leaving were crowded. I met the rabbi. With what pain he said to me, "I dare not think what is going to happen to these girls." We learned much later. Of all this group, there was only one who survived: Julie Katz. After her liberation in 1945, she told us how the convoy where they were packed into sealed cars, heading for Auschwitz, left the young girls at the Goering munitions factory. Almost without food, they died of exhaustion one after another. When the Americans arrived, there were two to climb into the rescue plane. Julie's comrade died during transport. Upon arrival at Auschwitz, the rest of the convoy was directed to the "shower room" and gassed immediately. We did not yet know all that on 5 August after the first departure, but we guessed that the situation was very serious and that we must try the impossible to save a few lives.

The small secret committee begged me to go again immediately to Toulouse to meet with the Quakers. The next morning, en route by the first bus, I met our friends, who were already informed: massive deportations had taken place over the whole French territory; desperate SOS's were coming from all sides. We learned that a new departure would take place the next day, 7 August. Early in the morning Miss H. and I left by car, racing through the villages at over sixty miles an hour in order to reach Gurs as early as possible in case we should be able to attempt something. At four o'clock those called were taken into the big garages at the south gate where they were locked in until four o'clock in the morning. There was nothing we could do. Then they put the deportees into trucks and buses, taking them to Oloron-Sainte-Marie, where they were thrown into sealed cars. We have since learned that these transfers to Auschwitz were organized under the direction of Eichmann.

As soon as we arrived at the barracks, we learned how great the disaster was. They had called all those whose names began with the letters N to Z. More than six hundred persons, all Jews from the Rhineland. What could I do? I asked for authorization to spend the night with them in the garage at the south gate. It was granted me. They were there, dismayed, depressed, motionless, sitting on the floor or on their poor bundles. They seemed to have lost all their strength, all possibility to express themselves. Some looked dead already; others seemed to be in the throes of death. A few reacted and said to me, "Is this how France treats us?" I looked for people I knew. Many had become unrecognizable in a few hours. I scarcely recognized Mlle Gertrude, rolled in a heap on the ground. She was the social worker with whom I had so often spoken of the future and had organized talks in the groups. I leaned over her. "Mlle Gertrude, do you recognize me?" Not a word, not a sign, not a movement. I insisted. "I am Mlle Merle d'Aubigné, whom you call Mamie, remember?" Two sad eyes were raised to me, two eyes with a vague look, without a gleam of recognition; then they closed, and the little pile moved no more.

In the back of the garage, I recognized two straight silhouettes, impeccable in their nurses' uniforms, white collar, white cuffs, Jewish emblem in plain sight—two Jewish nurses. I told them of my admiration to see them thus. They answered me, "The Lord is with us," and they recited Psalm 130: "Out of the depths I cry to thee, O LORD! . . . " Tears filled my eyes. And the new convoy was sent off . . . I spent those tragic days going back and forth to the weary director. Often he answered me: "No, I shall not strike that name. The lists are already typed." I offered to retype the lists myself. Poor man! Shrugging his shoulders, he crossed off one more name, one life.

The director left, alas! The next day I was told that the new director wanted to see me. I myself was very curious to know who he was. No one told me his name. Imagine my astonishment when, on entering the office, I found myself face to face with the fired bursar. Smiling and sarcastic, he said: "Ah, yes, it is I. I wanted to see you to say that we are now going to work together." Feeling confusedly that my time at Gurs was coming to an end, I kept up a good front and returned to our barracks.

The new director soon took his revenge, in this way:

I had as gardener a certain Walther. He was Jewish, but

79

we had good reason to believe that a request addressed to Vichy would receive a favorable response. We expected to arrange that all Jews working in our teams would be crossed off the deportation lists. Walther, young and strong, frank-looking, worked for us with care and energy. His wife and baby lived in a barracks close to ours. A new deportation was being prepared. Someone told me that Walther was on the list. That was 13 September. I was sure that this was the doing of the new director. Walther refused to present himself and hid. I did not want to know where. The director called me to his office and demanded to know where Walther was. I did not know. With a cruel smile he solemnly declared, "If Walther is not here at six o'clock, I shall deport your whole team." By the tone of his voice, I understood that he was capable. Sick at heart, I went back to the barracks. Walther came to me. He had a good hiding place where he could await the departure of the police. But the others! One for twenty. He became solemn, told me good-bye, went to embrace his wife and child, and then went alone to present himself to the authorities. He was deported in the night.

Those departures! I must recall a few of them. They will help us to understand the anonymous crowds. There were other Walthers, as there were other doctors, other Gertrudes, other Jewish nurses, other Peterses. . .

The woman doctor in Group X was in the death convoy. I saw her, carrying her baggage, leave her barracks; and with a radiant look she went toward the line of the day's deportees. Those of her friends who remained hugged her and cried. Why her? She had had the name of one of her friends, a young woman with small children, crossed off the list. Simply, without ostentation, she took her place. Her face was luminous with deep joy. She gave herself.

Going from barracks to barracks, I learned of numerous cases of suicide. People were cutting their veins.

Lucy was on the list for the night of the 13th. She had been arrested at Pau. She came to find me. What could I do? I remembered the cases of exception foreseen by the law. Lucy was Romanian. Citizens of countries allied with Germany could be crossed off the lists. Because I could no longer go to the director myself, I sent Lucy to a camp secretary who agreed to scratch her name. But the next day, the name of her son was on the day's list. We repeated the steps successfully, and without delay we sent Lucy and her son to Eaux-Bonnes, where her elderly parents lived.

At the time of one of the first convoys, we had told the men locked in the last freight car that the floorboards had been sawed through by the railroad men. It was thus that several men threw themselves onto the track while the train was moving and were saved. We learned about it afterward.

The departures continued. We lived on the outside of life, in a pool of death. Every day I went to those who were leaving. I gave them fruit, which was abundant that year, and sometimes some woolens received from our faithful friends. The head nurse disapproved. "Merchandise wasted...," she said.

It was on one of those days that I saw before me a woman following the line of deportees fall to the ground, her eyes rolled back, face congested. I ran to help her up; I lifted her head on my arm and asked for a little water. The new director and the head nurse watched mockingly. The woman's face, bathed in a little cool water, relaxed. She opened her eyes and thanked me with a smile. Again she contracted with spasms. Two men carried her off, inert. They put her corpse in the deportation car.

Until then, the gravely ill in the group infirmaries had been spared, as well as several invalids in the central hospital. The new director gave the order to bring them together in a barracks near the hangar for the deportees. He even asked me to assure the care of the most helpless. Care for them, I could not accept. But I could and would be present. Gathered in that cave, they lost all control of themselves. They fought desperately. Women attempted to resist the police responsible for embarking them. Others began to turn upon themselves, screaming hysterically. The spectacle was so frightful that I saw tears run down the bearded faces of some of the gendarmes around the trucks into which these unfortunates were being hoisted. I tried to intervene so that this or that paralytic could be cared for. The director became impatient.

From day to day I attempted everything to save a few people. Or, going from one to another of the last survivors, I tried to help some friend who had just seen his loved ones sent off. Or sometimes, in that nightmare, I could only shut myself in my little room in the empty barracks.

I see again a couple arriving in my room, throwing themselves at my knees, begging. On the table the man had put jewelry and gold ingots, offering them in exchange for their safety. What could I tell them? That I could do nothing more, that we never accepted anything in return for our services. The woman sobbed at my feet. I was heartsick. I repeated in French, in German, "Je ne puis rien faire, rien, rien. . . ." They left.

The partially empty camp at Gurs began to fill up again. The police raids in the region had produced results. I was literally swamped with demands for false papers because people had learned that CIMADE had saved several persons.

It was thus that the months of August and September passed in heat, terror, and despair.

Toward the end of September a delegation from International Quaker Aid [Friends Service Committee] arrived. The "Friends" had obtained authorization from Vichy to collect the valuables that the prisoners carried with them and which were taken from them upon arrival in Germany. The Quakers undertook to keep all that was entrusted to them and to send it to those indicated. The announcement had been made all over camp, and I went to help my Quaker friends in this service.

Again, it was a sort of vision in the manner of Breughel or another inventor of infernal scenes. The heat was suffocating. Before our little tables the people passed, almost naked, holding in their hands a precious little purse or detaching from around their necks a little pouch containing jewels, pearls, diamonds, small gold or platinum ingots. We had to ask the name of the heir, almost always emigrated to the United States. We had to explain to them that, if they kept these valuables, they would be taken from them by the Germans at the end of their trip. We sealed the envelopes, wrote the names . . . and they left. We passed to the next in line. Often these unfortunates looked at us with a bewildered air. They hesitated. We had to hurry them. The line was long. We were afraid to see a counterorder arrive. The German police had not been advised of the operation. We repeated: "You can have confidence in the Quakers. Everything that you give them will arrive at the address that you give." In fact, the counterorder arrived before the end of the day. We had not yet finished. Then I saw men, hesitant until then at what was in fact the announcement of their death sentence, throw themselves at our tables. "Quickly, take these things. Send them to. . . ." They were all deported. They all passed through the gas chambers.

The Quakers fulfilled their mission. In 1950 we learned that all that had been collected at Gurs and in other camps had arrived at its destination. Often one could hardly read the names and addresses written by us in the horror of that day.

Now the days passed without new deportations. I felt easy about our team, which seemed to me protected by order of Vichy. I dreamed of taking two or three days' rest in Ariège to gather my strength and get a little sleep. Scarcely had I arrived when a telephone message announced that another deportation had taken place and that Charlotte Wolff, one of my teamworkers, had been embarked in a convoy leaving from Rivesaltes, the sorting point.

At Rivesaltes we had a very good team directed by André Dumas and Élisabeth Perdrizet. They worked in close liaison with the camp director and the prefecture. Charlotte's departure had to be stopped. I telephoned and took the train for Rivesaltes. I arrived late in the afternoon.

In fact, Charlotte was in the convoy that was to leave that night. I immediately found the director. He gave me a *laisser-passer* to go find Charlotte. Armed with this paper, I arrived, not without difficulty, at the deportation hangar, after crossing barbed wire, barricades, checkpoints and soldiers with fixed bayonets, all surprised at having to let me through. The night was very dark. The deportation barracks stood out in the middle of a flat area surrounded by barbed wire. A few scattered silhouettes strayed in the vicinity. I entered the assembly center, recognized Charlotte, and called her. She turned around and threw herself at me. Her hands grasped my arm. I told her simply: "You are free. I am taking you." People looked at me. They looked at her. Such looks! The guards had to raise their bayonets. It was too late to finish the procedures for liberation and to leave the camp. We passed the night in the CIMADE barracks. Charlotte pushed her bed against mine. She tied a rope to her arm and mine for fear that someone would come to take her during the night without my knowing it. The next day I took her to some friends at Sète. From there she left for Grenoble, where she remained hidden until the end of the war.

At Rivesaltes a new and very difficult task was awaiting me. Convoys from Gurs arrived and I was alone in trying to render some service to the deportees. André Dumas had found a way to gain the confidence of the prefecture and of the person in charge of deportations. They had instituted a sort of court of justice where one tried to save a few of these defenseless beings, with the imagination of some men and women who possessed only their goodwill and a profound sense of the value of a human life. I felt cruelly my incapacity before this task: defend these people with complete competence, where might makes right. I had to explain in a few words the situation of each internee from Gurs. I knew them more or less, and I had to question them beforehand. What hope could I give them? We could count on only those famous *cas d'exception,* and these were taken into consideration less and less. We were each in a small cell where our "clients" filed by one after the other. Those forty-eight hours spent listening and debating each case with these unfortunates were sheer hell. During the night we had to prepare the defense for each one and be ready the next morning at ten o'clock. The "court" met at that hour. I felt criminal to be so inexperienced and to have to try to defend these dozens of persons condemned to death. Whom did I save during these two days except Charlotte? Only a very old woman whom I managed to place in an old people's home where she disappeared in the crowd.

Another means of salvation was marriage. Some men from the area loaned themselves out for this game—for a good price. The marriage was held at the town hall and was duly registered. It goes without saying that that took some conniving. After the ceremony, each went his own way, the internee sent to a safe place.

Upon my return to Gurs, I found the camp almost empty. The deportations had not ended.

At the end of October 1942, I received notice of my expulsion. It was signed by Darlan. I had to leave the camp within a week. The director had prepared his last revenge. I telegraphed Madeleine Barot, who arrived quickly even though she was in danger herself. She advised me to leave without protest: CIMADE was endangered. André Morel was in prison, numerous friends were menaced and had more or less gone underground. "We must not attract attention to ourselves." We decided that I should go to Eaux-Bonnes, a small resort city lost in the Pyrenees where those Jews had been sent who had been able to leave the camps before or after the massive deportations.

I ordered, therefore, a taxi at Pau. It was to come for me at ten o'clock in the morning. It didn't come. It could not enter because the camp was under a state of arrest. The remaining internees came sneaking into my barracks to say good-bye. The taxi arrived at 8:00 P.M. It was dark. A gendarme accompanied it, and two men from our team mounted on the running board came to help me. The taxi went down the main road between the guards who blocked the gates of the areas with fixed bayonets: unusual display of force. What was happening? I learned later. The prisoners had been so outraged at my expulsion that a revolt had begun to spread. The director had closed the camp and forbidden the entrance of the taxi until nightfall. This is how I left Gurs in a heavy, menacing silence.

5.

Les Eaux-Bonnes,
Naillat, Douadic—The Maquis

JEANNE MERLE D'AUBIGNÉ

Dismal arrival in Eaux-Bonnes: little resort town at the bottom of a deep valley surrounded by steep cliffs. One hour of sun per day in winter. Unheated hotels.

The first problem was to overcome the cold. The casino gave us the first floor. We began by painting. Stoves soon permitted us to live there.

I had with me a team from Gurs determined to help me in this new adventure: a pianist, Gunther Freundlich; a non-Jewish political prisoner, Moering; and another pianist, Hans Cahen-Brach. The office soon resounded with strains of Bach.

All seemed relatively peaceful when 9 November 1942 arrived. The Free Zone was invaded. Returning from Laruns one day, I had a surprise: the road was blocked, and men in green uniforms demanded my papers. I pretended to have left them at the house. The less one showed them, the better it was.

That evening, while we were trying to warm ourselves before the fire, there was a knock at the door. A small German officer entered and gave us a lecture on the marvels of Hitlerism.

In Eaux-Bonnes, there soon remained only women, children, and old people. The young men had disappeared in the direction of Spain. Moering had donned the clothing of the son of the proprietor of a sawmill and Freundlich soon followed him.

Our internees were under the surveillance of a police chief, M. Michel. I was soon clued in. As an active member of the Resistance, he had decided to keep the Jews away from the Germans. The latter began saying that they did not want all those Jews so close to the border. They talked of deporting them, so we were very worried. Christmas was coming. We did not have much heart for the traditional festivities. In the salon, however, we decorated a Christmas tree for this festival of light. Christmas took on a larger, more real significance.

It was urgent that the expected convoy leave as quickly as possible. The *commissaire* refused my request to accompany our people, but promised to give me all the instructions for finding them later. He ordered me to continue to care for them. We waited in the midst of the most terrible dangers.

On 17 January 1943, the *commissaire* contacted me. The convoy would leave the 20th. It was to be directed toward Naillat, a lost village in the Creuse, twenty miles from Guéret, eleven miles from all trains, five miles from the nearest bus. This village had been chosen by the prefect, who was known to be a *résistant*. It was a sure refuge. All those who arrived there would be found unharmed at the time of liberation. But some of them, believing that the Italian army, well disposed toward the Jews, would protect them, gave in to the urge to leave and try to get to the Italian border, Nice or Grenoble. They were all captured by the German police and deported.

Let us talk of our arrival and of our life in Naillat.

Madeleine Barot had rejoined me at Guéret. We debarked the next day in the picturesque little village, high on the hillside, where no one was expecting us. At the inn where we ate, they were sorry to serve us *only* three kinds of meat!

The mayor was nowhere to be found. Finally tracked down, he declared that he did not know anything, had not prepared anything, and that his administrators wanted no part of these Jews. We simply told him: "Three thousand people are arriving tomorrow. Where are you going to put them?"

"I do not want to have anything to do with it. Take care of it yourselves."

We wound up obtaining a list of vacant places and the hand stamp from the mayor's office. There were few empty places. Farmers demanded exorbitant prices for their rooms. It was necessary to make lodgings out of barns and the school play-shed piled with straw.

The trucks arrived at the main square, opposite the *mairie* [town hall]. The strongest of our people could be directed to neighboring villages, but we had to house fifteen hundred persons at Naillat itself. It was laborious. The lure of money began to open doors. A canteen was organized in an old store. A cook was found in the person of Jules, a "kosher" meat-cutter by trade. (At the right moment, Jules managed to hide himself and then to find his little shop in Paris on rue des Rosiers.) The rooms beside and below the canteen became the Foyer. Soon a piano and a library found their places.

I had to find supplies myself. The peasants held too much of a grudge against our internees. Such a job! Precious help was found in Tina, formerly of the Moscow Opera. She still had a lovely voice. She had beautiful long blond hair, and wore only red because of the beneficial power of that color, she said. She loved going to the farms to look for provisions for our canteen. One day I had to step in. A farmer had dared to demand an excessive price for 150 kilograms of potatoes. Tina told him forcefully that he would go straight to hell. The startled farmer had chased her away. I went to try to smooth things over. Terrorized by Tina, he accepted the moderate price that I offered him. I had brought two men to carry the sacks and begged Tina to say nothing more, but her eyes shot fire at the trembling farmer. While I was paying for the potatoes, his wife arrived—hard, authoritarian. "I told you to sell for. . . ," she shouted. I kindly remarked that the bargain was made, and that they could not raise the price like that. I left, barely stopping Tina from beginning her maledictions again.

After a certain time, people living with the peasants began to feel at home. They no longer needed the canteen. Jules Levy cooked for me and three or four lone persons.

I had found a room on the ground floor in the home of the former village schoolmistress. A Jewish family lived in the same house. The old grandmother observed the sabbath and the Jewish holidays. She called me "a daughter of God" because I showed her the greatest respect, and I loved to join her on Friday evenings when she read the Psalms, lighted by a large candlestick, before an impeccable white cloth.

These strangers, obliged to live in rather hostile surroundings, sought things to do. They took books from the Foyer and consulted me about the Bible. I had the idea of telling them the history of their people. Most of them seemed to know nothing about it. The Orthodox Jews celebrated the sabbath and ate kosher food, but they were mostly rather narrow and ignorant. Others, whose old parents could recite by heart the Torah in Hebrew, were more open, and they were the ones who invited me to begin the Bible studies. The people seemed captivated. I still hear the deep voice of M. Loebel reciting in Hebrew the chapters of Genesis and Exodus that we were meditating.

Lucy S. was worried about her fourteen-year-old son, a brilliant pupil who had had to discontinue his studies. I decided to see what I could do for the boy. I knew of the existence at Guéret of a Monsieur X., professor of physics and lay leader of the Protestant worship service. Very perplexed, he mentioned the matter to the principal of the high school, who declared that Jews were excluded from the lycées, and that I must present my request myself. I was received coldly. "It is difficult. . . . There is no room. . . ." He did not say a clear no, and I concluded that it was yes and spoke about admission of the boy for boarding. Whereupon, he became angry and flatly refused. But I did not think that John had been refused for studies. Professor X. was delighted when I told him. The question of room and board remained. "Go see Monsieur T. He is a schoolteacher, fired for his anti-Nazi ideas." With some difficulty I found the low, tiny house on the street indicated. Led into a small provincial parlor, I heard men's voices conversing passionately in the next room. I distinguished some dangerous words: "fighting, resistance. . . ." I coughed to indicate my presence. Nothing happened! My presence and my actions among the Jews automatically included me in the clandestine movement. Monsieur T. came to receive me and agreed to house John, who would "share the room with my son, who is also a student at the lycée." And the boy was quickly at the head of his class.

About this time four boys, one of whom was the son of the general secretary of the prefecture, went camping in the woods around Guéret. The maquisards [resistance fighters] were beginning to steal away and form guerrilla forces. What happened? Had the boys been denounced? The Germans massacred them frightfully. One of them was only wounded and managed to drag himself home to break the news. I arrived at Guéret the day of the funeral service for these poor kids. The German authorities would permit no one except members of the immediate families to enter the cathedral. The entire town, formally in mourning, was in the streets and held off one hundred yards from the church. People fell to their knees at the moment of absolution. Still kept at a good distance, not knowing how to show their sympathy and their indignation, the crowd then surrounded the cemetery. This spontaneous demonstration was cruelly punished shortly after. Planes came on market day and swept the main square with machine-gun fire, killing several people and setting fire to houses.

The birth of a Jewish baby evoked so strongly the texts of the Nativity that I must tell of it. In a family of Orthodox Jews composed of the father, the mother, a twelve-year-old daughter, two little ones three and five years old, and a grandfather, the mother was pregnant. I had made all arrangements for her admission to the hospital at the time of her delivery. The maquisards had agreed to help. I had only to let them know; they would take the mother in their car. But this woman was afraid of not being able to eat kosher food at the hospital, so she had given me a false date for the birth. One night around eleven o'clock, someone knocked on my door with such insistence that I went and opened it. The twelve-year-old girl was standing there. "Come quickly. The baby is coming."

"Have you called the doctor?"

"No. They told me to come to you first."

"I am going. You run to the post office and ask the operator to call the doctor for you." My landlady arrived with some old cloths and clean scissors. We went out into the night.

When I arrived, I thought I was seeing the cave of Mary and Joseph. The room had every aspect of a cave: low walls, cracked and blackened. In a corner, a fireplace with a kettle where the grandfather was boiling water. The woman was lying on the ground on straw covered with cloth. The father, leaning over her with his long beard, made me think of Joseph. The baby was already there, held by a neighbor. There was nothing left to do but to separate the baby—a boy—from its mother, and then to bathe him. The father and grandfather rubbed him with oil and salt. Then I held him wrapped in the cloths that we had brought until the arrival of the doctor and his wife, who finished the delivery and settled the woman in her bed. Returning the next day to care for her as prescribed by the doctor, I found the young father facing the east wall, one arm bare, a band across the forehead, a shawl over his shoulders, beating his chest and reciting prayers in Hebrew. He did not move. The grandfather was still at the fire boiling water, and the daughter helped me to care for the mother.

This was her eighth child. She was up and around very soon.

Often I had wondered why our people had been so little bothered in the Creuse. At the Liberation, I was given the key to the enigma. I was told, "Do not leave here without seeing the girl whose quiet courage saved so many people." She was secretary at the prefecture of Guéret and from time to time received lists of people to include in the convoys. She copied these lists, made out cards for each one, put it all in the fire at night, and began again the next day. The representative of the *Feld-*

gendarmerie at Guéret was an Austrian who was disgusted by these raids and did not care to know what happened to the lists. I warmly thanked the young girl in the name of all those she had saved. "But," I added, "how is it that one day the gendarmes came to take our men for deportation?"

"That day I had joined a group of maquisards on operation to Limoges in order to free some of our men from prison, including my brother. We were successful, but I was awfully sorry to return and see that the list had arrived that day and had followed regular channels, resulting in the arrest of your two men."

As a matter of fact, that raid had upset us very much. Someone came to tell me at five o'clock in the morning that the gendarmes were there. They did not seem to be in much of a hurry. Nevertheless, they found Hans Cahen-Brach at his house, as well as another refugee in a neighboring hamlet. The others hid. The passivity of the two men exasperated me. Each of them could have profited from a few moments of the gendarmes' inattention and escaped. Hans Cahen-Brach, however, had no illusions. He told me good-bye. Climbing into the truck, he called, "Mamie, you didn't give me my New Testament." He wrote to me once from Drancy. Then it was all over.

The gendarmes themselves were surprised. They got in the habit of telling me when they received an order to seize someone. One day they went to look for a Polish man who worked on a farm. The man had been forewarned but insisted on remaining. The gendarmes met him on the road. They stepped aside to let him pass. At the farm they asked the usual questions: "Where is X., who works for you?"

The farmer's wife, nervous and blushing, said, "He left a long time ago."

"Don't worry, *ma bonne dame;* we just saw him go by."

Taking again an official air and getting out his notebook, the brigadier wrote, "Monsieur X. disappeared the. . . ." He closed his notebook and saluted. They left as they had come.

When my presence at Naillat was no longer necessary, Madeleine Barot notified me that I should go to the Douadic camp, near Le Blanc, about twenty miles from Châteauroux in the

Indre. On a hot afternoon in August, we both arrived on bicycle.

Our presence was not at all desired by the administration. But the orders from Vichy were clear, and the director, a French policeman under German orders, had to assign me a barracks for the center and give me a room in the same place as the other personnel. It was in a dilapidated state. The room allotted to me was such that I had to stretch oil cloth over the bed and place a bucket to catch rainwater and winter snow that came through the cardboard roof, and through the walls, which were lacking siding: it had been used as firewood. The wind blew and whistled through the room. Fortunately the refugees made me a very soft straw mattress that I curled up in, letting the wind swirl through the strands of my hair. At the end of winter, the YMCA procured for me large pieces of cardboard with which I reinforced the walls. The roof was repaired. An internee was assigned to light the fire. Life became bearable.

The time came to be initiated into the life of the camp. I took my meals at the table of the top staff of personnel. The director, threatened by the maquisards, lived in his office at the other end of the camp, and drank a lot. The assistant director, M. Lherminet, former workman from the north, returned from Syria, was the chief of the local Resistance!

During the course of that winter, I became acquainted with the nocturnal activities. Toward midnight, I was often awakened by the noise of heavy boots. I would hear whisperings, the droning of an airplane. I would see two fires lighted in the field just opposite my room. Heavy steps would return toward the barracks. Everything would become silent again. I concluded rather quickly that it had to do with parachuting arms. I learned that the containers filled with arms that landed here were quickly submerged in the little lake at the edge of the forest. A group of maquisards, mostly students from Strasbourg evacuated to Clermont-Ferrand, came to pick up the weapons and carry them to the Plateau de Millevaches in Corrèze. There was a parachuting each time the British radio, listened to with fervor at the Foyer, played the song "Il pleut, bergère."

New prisoners arrived, women coming from the camp at Brens in the Tarn. From a CIMADE team member of that camp, I received some information about the newcomers. She particularly recommended Mme Werfel as an aide in whom I could have confidence. Happy to be able to count on her, I could now leave to visit other camps in the region and the CIMADE teams. Her help was especially useful in bad weather. The men from the maquis stayed at night in our barracks. There was always some bandaging to do or some mending. M. Lherminet made them some soup, and the next morning before dawn all trace of their stay had to be wiped out.

The coming of spring simplified my visits to neighboring camps or to Châteauroux or Limoges (for the many things I always had to do). Generally I made use of the supply trucks for these trips.

One day the young driver of the truck carrying me said brusquely, "Do you see that farm? The farmer's wife did me a great service. Yesterday I had gone to get vegetables in the station at Limoges. While I was loading, I saw a German armored train enter. From the cars came screams, children crying, yells: 'Papa, Mamma! . . .' Mademoiselle, I could not stand to hear that. I backed my truck up to the door of the last car. All the guards were up front. I opened the locks and made a sign to about twenty kids from five to fourteen years old to jump into the truck. In less time than it takes to tell it, they were hidden under the vegetables. I carefully put back the locks and drove around to leave the station. But, what to do with that merchandise? Passing in front of this farm, I asked the advice of that woman. She told me: 'Unload them here. I'll take charge then.' This morning I stopped and asked how it was going. She answered: 'It's OK. They are all stowed away in the vicinity.' "

At Limoges I met a student who, with an innocent air, gave me the address of a very hospitable and comfortable house where a free room was regularly available to those in the Resistance. It was strange to enter this beautiful home by the back door, to be guided by the discreet maid, and to receive breakfast in the morning without ever having seen the lady of the house. What joy also to leave a bouquet of flowers for that unspoken hospitality!

I was then received by Pastor Chaudier, head of the Resistance in that sector. He had a room with two exits where very recently the famous Jean Moulin had passed the night. Pastor Chaudier received money from America. The Gestapo had searched for his files without results. "They are well hidden in my attic," he told me. I served as intermediary for the distribution of money at Naillat and Douadic.

At camp, arrivals continued to come with little resemblance to one another. Here were two British girls, prostitutes from the Côte d'Azur, in very bad shape. One of them, in the last stages of alcoholism, was a complete wreck without reflexes. The other, of Irish origin and more refined, had a little girl, whom we placed immediately on a farm near the camp. How could we do otherwise when the mother left each evening for Le Blanc to ply her trade with the Germans? Soon we became suspicious of her. It seemed that she told the Germans all that she could learn about the Resistance. This could not continue. They asked me to speak to her, to bring her around to other ideas. I told her what the British were doing to deliver us. She got up—the scene took place in her room at camp—lifted up a picture over her bed, and uncovered a portrait of Hitler. I did not need to know anything more. "Think of your little girl," I told her as I left. Several days passed. Two men came one evening to the women's barracks and asked for the Irish girl. She understood. She gave her handbag to the other English woman, saying, "It's for my little girl!" She left. They led her to the edge of the woods and shot her there. They came to tell me: "We had to do it. We had proof that she was betraying us to the Gestapo." Someone added: "You can go see her foot. It is still sticking out of the hole where we buried her beside the road." I felt that the situation was becoming more and more serious. Positions were taken and were clear for all.

Returning from the rounds of nearby camps, I was greeted by cries: "It's happened! The deportation lists have left the

office of the Gestapo at Châteauroux. You are on the list."
M. Lherminet confirmed the news and added, "When you see
the camp emptied of all the men, you take care of the women
and children, and wait until we act."

Sure enough, the camp was soon empty. That day a young
rabbi arrived. We told him immediately that he had fallen into
a hornets' nest. He cried, "If my people are in danger, I shall
not leave." He prepared a big service for that afternoon, since
it was a Jewish holiday. He told me that all his fellow Jews
wished that I would join them for prayers. Mme Werfel and I
used up all our resources to prepare a snack for the women
and children who were gathering in our barracks, as Lherminet
had asked me to do before disappearing. After the religious
service, the women and children were grouped around the tables
with their packages (in case of deportation), as in the days of
the Exodus.

Suddenly a terrible uproar glued us to our places. Bursts of
machine-gun and rifle fire rang back and forth. The snack was
stopped; there was a heavy silence filled by our prayer for
those who were fighting for us. The battle raged. Lherminet
and his men were posted, with those of our men who could
fight, at the angle of the road, five hundred yards from the
camp. Our anxiety was at its height. Whom were we going
to see appear? It was our side, bringing two buses and three
German soldiers! Lying in wait, our defenders had seen the
buses arrive for the deportation. They had opened fire, killed
one of the drivers and one of the soldiers, and jumped the second vehicle, while the third, opening fire in turn, tried to get
away fast. Our men ate something and returned quickly to the
forest, taking the buses and prisoners.

We expected a terrible revenge. I slept little the following
night. About five o'clock in the morning, I heard the sound of
a horse galloping under my windows. I was ready for any
eventuality. I had a small bag containing what I wanted to
take in case of deportation. I ran to find Mme Werfel, who
was in much greater danger than I. To hide her, I had had
dug under my bed a rectangular hole, lined with oil cloth.
I could not convince her to climb into this tomblike thing.

At the gate of the camp, Lherminet was talking with the chief of the French squadron preceding the German detachment coming to search the barracks. Lherminet wanted to give us time to hide the damaging objects, such as the cords and parachute material with which the women made underwear and other things. Lherminet sent word for me to come to the Foyer in nurse's uniform. On the door someone had put a red cross. I had to quickly group around me some women working. It was necessary also to quickly hide the large packages of bandage material marked in big letters Manchester, Birmingham, and stored in the CIMADE barracks. Wearing a complete uniform, I placed myself in the middle of the women pretending to work on the tables covered with white sheets. I suddenly understood that it would be better to occupy the doorway, barring it with my white uniform. At that moment the German soldiers arrived, after having gone through the camp sowing terror. A small helmeted man stopped before me and stood on tiptoe to see over my shoulder.

"Ah! Rote Kreuz?"

"Ja," I said, "Rote Kreuz."

"Gut," said the soldier and disappeared.

We knew that we could expect the worst. But we also learned that the Germans were lacking men, that they had left very few troops in that part of the country, and that the Douadic camp had a reputation as a stronghold of the maquis. They did not dare come back.

However, the incidents multiplied. We lived in a perpetual state of alert. Emotional crises succeeded one after another.

Two Englishmen were parachuted into our area in full uniform, because without uniforms they would be shot mercilessly. The two men were in secret conference with those of the maquis in our CIMADE barracks. The Germans, informed, arrived like a whirlwind at the other end of camp. Just time enough to jump into the car stopped beside the barracks and for the English to disappear. The Germans began to shoot; the English also, to cover their retreat. No one was hit, and the Germans stopped at the edge of the woods.

There was more and more talk of a possible invasion. The British radio was scarcely audible because of jamming. Nevertheless, we managed to discern strange messages loaded with meaning for some.

One fine morning in June—the 6th—a boy who was messenger between us and the maquis came to say, "Mademoiselle, Robert has arrived!"

"Who is Robert?" I called, and suddenly understood. "They have come?"

"*Oui,* Mademoiselle, they are landing in Normandy. The chief is in direct radio contact with them. *C'est formidable!*"

All day we were glued to the radio. We heard: "They are disembarking. . . . The sea is black with ships . . . the sky with planes. They are fighting on the beaches. . . ." That evening, at the highest pitch of hope, I shouted, *"Vive la France!"* and the *Marseillaise* was sung by those foreigners who hardly knew it. But that day, it was the song of all, the song of liberty.

We were not at the end of our troubles. While the battle of Normandy raged, the Germans brought in that direction all their dispersed forces in France. The armored division *Das Reich* circulated on the roads of Indre and the Creuse, looking for passage toward the west, harassed by the maquisards who endeavored to slow them down.

During those days, I had to accompany my young assistant to Limoges. It would have been safer to keep her with me, but her parents were frantic, and I received the order to take the girl home. The train from Châteauroux to Limoges was blown up every night. We had only our bicycles. The gendarmes warned us very quickly that we would meet the biggest German tanks and that they shot at anything they saw. Had not the gendarmes already this morning picked up the corpses of a man and the wife of the town crier? We were obliged to stop along the way and spend the night in a small hotel. While we were filling in our papers, the hotel owner cried: "You are not going to Limoges? The Germans have just burned a little village on the outskirts and shot the whole population. My brother has just returned from there. He is horrified. Do not go to

Limoges!" With the calm of unawareness I replied, "Madame, so many frightful things are happening that it is senseless to add more." It was thus that I heard for the first time of Oradour-sur-Glane.

That did not keep us from going to Limoges. We arrived only an hour before the curfew. The city was in such a state! The population had built barricades across the boulevards. Spiked stockades everywhere, piles of arms, machine guns here and there. French *milice* [guardsmen] wandered about disorganized. Under their astounded eyes, we climbed over the piles of weapons on the ground. I put the girl in the hands of her parents and arrived at the home of the pastor. The door opened cautiously. "How were you able to get through? The city is transformed into a citadel. We have a German guard in the concierge's room." He told me rapidly that he had just returned from Oradour-sur-Glane, where he had gone with the bishop of Limoges to pray over the smoking ruins of the church. Upon returning, he had led the bishop to the German general commanding the sector. After hearing the pastor's description, the general spread his arms on the table, burst out sobbing, and cried: "It was not the Wehrmacht that did that. It was the SS!"

"Wehrmacht or not, your nation will be marked by this degrading act," said the pastor as he left. The general immediately gave the order to take off the guard who watched the door of the parsonage.

The country was boiling. In a few hours everything was stirred up. Pastor Chaudier had thought to give me a *laisser-passer* to cross the zones held by the maquis, without which I would never have been able to get back to Naillat. As I was pedaling tranquilly enough along the little road in the direction of Souterraine, two forms came out of the ditches on both sides. "Halt!" I jumped from my bicycle. A machine gun, held by a young peasant with a very resolute air, touched my ribs, and a young man, probably a student, serving as the officer, questioned me. After half an hour, with the young peasant still pressing the barrel of his machine gun harder and harder in my back, the student said: "Because you know E., who signed your *laisser-passer*, hurry to get home. Where are you going through?"

"To Naillat by the road to Souterraine."

"You will not be able to pass. We have placed plastic charges under all the cow dung. The armored division *Das Reich* is all around here."

"Well, I'll take the road that goes by the lake. It is a detour, but I'll arrive before night."

"You will not pass that way either. We have dug enormous trenches across the road. It is impassable on bicycle. Take the little trail through the woods. You will find barricades of trees, but you can get over them."

I took the trail. In some places it was steep. With difficulty I passed through the branches with my bicycle. On the other side, worn out, sitting on a mound, I tried to get some strength back. A peasant passed by with his cart. He picked me up with my bike. I knew the man. He said that at Naillat the maquis were going around in broad daylight.

The next morning someone came to find me, saying: "We have found a German wandering in the woods. It can only be a soldier escaping or a spy. We are going to judge him. Come and serve as interpreter. None of us knows German." In the courtyard of the inn there was a tall blond boy. On the other side, the "officers" of the maquis had their heads together. To the rather concise interrogation, the prisoner responded that he had fled the battle of Normandy, that he had walked constantly toward the south, and that to remain alive he had sold his equipment. During the interrogation the peasants came close to the little wall of the courtyard, and soon they were yelling at him, charging him with all the misfortunes that they had suffered because of the war. The tension grew. The officers of the maquis became taut. Hatred blew around us like a windstorm. This lonely man with trembling lip stirred pity. He could not be assassinated in cold blood. A silent prayer rose in my heart that the spirits of these men be opened to justice. An impressive silence settled over us. It seemed as if the wave of hate met another wave, that of clemency. What would happen? A voice in the crowd called out, "Mercy!" Again the silence; a strange calm. Everyone relaxed, and the men of the maquis saw their officer come forward and repeat, "Mercy." The prisoner had not understood the words, but he had felt them. Exhausted, he fell on a bench.

I returned to Douadic without difficulty. It was the last act of the drama. A few weeks later I returned to Paris with the faithful Mme Werfel, on a truckload of wood whose logs bruised us during the whole twelve-hour trip.

6.

Rivesaltes: Sorting Station

PROF. ANDRÉ DUMAS

The Rivesaltes camp, situated between Narbonne and Perpignan in the heart of a desertlike region of old abandoned vineyards near the village of Jalses, constituted a place apart from the very beginning. It had been constructed as an acclimation center for troops enlisted from the colonies overseas. But the administration had had to play it backward. Rivesaltes, continually battered by north winds, without a tree on the horizon, spread out like immeasurable worn-out laundry on the rocks and brambles between the stripped hills and the distant sea, seemed better suited to acclimate French recruits to the plateaus of the North African Atlas than to familiarize foreigners with French nature and climate. Only the Canigou, standing like a Japanese volcano above the plain, gave the place a rugged beauty.

The camp was vast. It consisted of several clusters of buildings separated by patches of brush. Until the beginning of August 1942, there was no barbed wire or watchtowers. At the entrance of each cluster, a gate lowered like a customs or rail-road crossing reminded one that he had to present himself at the guard post, occupied by officials dressed in dark blue uniforms like administrative personnel in a penitentiary.

By euphemism the camp was called a "Housing Center." It was supposed to give refuge to all those anywhere who were deprived of a home and work because of the war. But in fact, it was very clearly a security center, where you found various groups divided approximately by the clusters: a large number of Spanish republicans, especially women and children of the men who were then working on the construction of the Atlantic Wall and the submarine shelters at Lorient and Brest; refugees from Central Europe—Czechs, Poles, Russians, Yugoslavs, whose successive stages had most often been Holland and Belgium, then Paris, the Southern Zone, and finally Rivesaltes; a considerable number of gypsies systematically arrested by the Vichy government; some Dutch, Belgians, and Anglo-Saxons sent back from the Spanish border which they had tried in vain to cross; finally, a category already very special because of the history that had pursued them even before the terrible Nazi menace stood at the gates of this very meridional camp— I mean the Jews. They were there either because they had been arrested individually in the Southern Zone or because they had been expelled en masse from the Rhineland and Baden toward the camps in the south of France, following the armistice of 1940. Thus the Jews had been thrown into conquered France by a unilateral decision of triumphant Germany. Now like the Spaniards or the gypsies, they were part of the refugees which the regime of the Southern Zone was housing under its own responsibility.

Suddenly, during the summer of 1942, Nazi Germany committed itself, and France followed orders a second time without trying protests other than organizing the deportations. It placed in the service of Hitler, up to the line of demarcation, its police, its regional offices, its trains, its camouflage; but due to a certain bias, it permitted private groups that lived in the camps to participate in the work with individuals to limit the number of deportees.

At Rivesaltes the camp changed its appearance after 4 August 1942. One cluster was isolated. It was surrounded by barbed wire, and the guard was doubled with armed police. In the midst of forced housing, the concentration camp phenomenon showed its real face. From the point of view of the Vichy government, it was a case of reaching the figure of ten thousand Jews required by the occupation authorities.

The Jews were to be chosen from among those who, entering France after 1 January 1936, were originally from Poland, Germany, Austria, Danzig, the Saar, Czechslovakia, Estonia, Lithuania, Latvia, and Russia, even if they held a "Nansen" passport. Eleven conditions for exemption were foreseen.[1] The enumeration of these official categories shows that the delivery operation tried to be camouflaged as humanitarian. Also, the motives advanced showed the utmost confusion and hypocrisy. They spoke sometimes of a German political decision to create a Jewish autonomous state in Central Europe; at other times, of the military desire to remove those who opposed the regime from a foreseeable Second Western Front soon to come; or of an economic precaution which consisted of diminishing the number of mouths to feed in the poor southern region; or of the Vichy manipulation to slow down the threats to the French Jews by returning to Germany "its" national Jews; or even of a test imposed upon the Pétain government to verify its loyalty in collaboration.

It was 1942. Rivesaltes seemed far from Drancy, of which one heard little, and from Auschwitz, of which one heard nothing at all. Nevertheless, without being aware of exactly what would follow, there was total anxiety. To fall again into German hands was to head toward hell. At Gurs the news had spread; the camp director had quit. At Rivesaltes it was not the same. Rather, we tried to fight on two levels: to multiply the dossiers for exemption and to argue them with the maximum of stubbornness, and to facilitate escapes toward nearby Spain or, of course, toward Swiss channels, which were more difficult because of the multiple controls.

1. Cf. Appendix II, pp. 227-28.

I do not know the exact number of those who left in the trains that waited at night on the camp embarkation track. It seems that the Ministry of Interior had demanded that the prefects prepare a list of persons who might be hit by the measures, and that these lists in the beginning of the operation contained fourteen thousand names, of which ten thousand were to leave. But I do know that several different times in the evening, when the number had not yet been reached, raids were held in the clusters to find "complementary numbers" at the last minute. Generally they were isolated men or women without family, who were not protected by any file since it had remained in the hands of the police inspector who had left at the end of his day's work. What I do know is that the number required had to be reached, as Vichy confirmed imperatively by telephone, and that each escapee was replaced, man for man. The exemption conditions were only a guide to the good use of the theoretical difference between fourteen thousand and ten thousand, but in no way were they a legal guarantee by which the administration would have exercised what little remained of its honor.

From the time of the enclosure of the special cluster, Rivesaltes—between 4 August and the end of October 1942—became thereby one of the centers of the Southern Zone from which the Jews promised to Germany by Vichy were taken. It was a question either of the older residents of the camp who, in spite of the continual steps taken between October 1940 and August 1942, had not obtained the possibility to emigrate from France and thus remained in the half-opened trap; or of foreign Jews arrested by the police and taken to camp individually or in small groups. Naturally there was no connection between the number of people required for the formation of a train whose departure was generally known five or six days in advance and the changing population of the camp. Sometimes there were many exemptions; sometimes there were almost none at all, either because too much was demanded and was impossible to gather or because the delay granted to furnish proof was too short. Everything depended upon the day when one passed before the police commissioner charged with verifying the certificates, the documents in hand, and the number of conditions of exemption that were currently annulled. The cases were pleaded by comparing afflictions. The legal quality was relatively less important than the family situation. The reprieve, that is to say, survival, was conditioned by the legalized papers. If one was exempted, he rejoined the others in the camp without barbed wire, but naturally he was not freed. Further, it was necessary to be taken in charge by an outside service organization or family—measures which were always a long time in bringing about and which the prefecture did not simplify, since the administrators were always wondering if the number to furnish would not require that they return one day to the categories already exempted. If one was taken in the camp, he could no longer see anyone from the outside. He awaited the trucks that took him to the train around eight o'clock at night. The railroad cars, guarded but not yet locked, started rolling around three o'clock in the morning.

The volunteer agencies had been charged with preparing the "counterlists," containing the names of persons to exempt. Each page had to be marked with the first and last name, nationality, domicile, profession, family situation, the number corresponding to the category of exemption requested, and the special observations that permitted the registering and appealing for a meeting longer than that provided normally with the functionary of the Ministry of the Interior. Knowing that the day of the departure of the convoy was never put off, we had to fight up to the last moment in order that the "legal" exemptions be respected. In acting this way, we risked at any moment becoming objective accomplices of selection. Moreover, everyone knew that this struggle foot by foot and page by page was fought in the one fear that, neglecting by laziness or haste the formal conditions indicated in the circular from the Ministry of the Interior, those responsible for the special stockade might add to the convoy those persons who theoretically had sufficient documents to escape it. Those who directed the operation did not wish to think about its consequences. They obeyed the government in selling to Germany foreign emigrants, who happened to be little-known Jews. It was in this perspective of governmental order that they accomplished a "dirty job," reduced in their eyes to a methodical and rapid transfer from a local housing center to other faraway camps, which some went so far as to insist were more comfortable.

But the Jews were not mistaken about the heart of the matter. On leaving, they left letters of farewell with their valued objects and, for their relatives far away, some personal souvenirs that they might find later on. They were hopeless, but generally very calm and courageous. Those who had been brought by the police thought they could escape en route, more than did those who had lived in the confines of the center for months and years. Several rabbis were in their midst, faithful companions of the Torah, which became again in those terrible days the constant presence of the Eternal. There were more Psalms murmured than exterior revolt, more learning again of the end of hope than cries, more mysterious acceptance of evil than indignation. One of them said, "In France, when a prisoner breaks into hysterics, you are embarrassed. You take him to the infirmary to keep him quiet, to hide him, and maybe to care for him. In Germany, they put him on a manure pile and tell him to play the rooster. Well, we are returning to Germany and we must learn to cry no more."

Naturally, escapes were numerous. A good number of long-time residents of the camp were hidden far from the clusters from the first days of the operation, when it appeared that no category of exemption could work in their favor. The essential thing was not to await the transfer to the special enclosure, but, profiting from the initial disorder, to leave the desertlike plateau where the camp was located. For the escape to succeed, you had to have a nearby place to hide because the trains were gone through with continual identity controls, as were all the neighboring roads. For weeks, some stayed hidden in the vicinity; some even until November 1942, which with the entrance of the Germans into the Southern Zone brought with it paradoxically the end of the administration's collaboration in the work of sorting at the internment center, and consequently greater facility for leaving the grim place. Guards cooperated indirectly in the escapes by offering their homes as rather sure places of refuge. It was often easier to come to that kind of understanding with certain guards than with the neighboring peasants, for whom Rivesaltes remained a foreign enclave. However, concerning escapes as well as exemptions, it was always a case of a small number when one thinks of the great crowd that waited in the special cluster for its transfer to the railroad cars.

Such were the frightful weeks, desertlike and overcrowded, dreary and organized, when by the expedient of a circular on the repatriation of Jews from Germany and Central Europe, the French administration of that time delivered ten thousand foreign Jews. Rivesaltes, in August and September 1942, was one of the first supply centers for Auschwitz. In November 1942 the German occupation spread everywhere. But before that the task had been done without it. The spiritual surrender agreed to at the armistice had continued. Locally, the Resistance had taken no other form than the continual fight over the dossiers, the organization of near or distant escape routes, and a presence until the hour of departure near the nightly convoys of four or five cars, which would soon be attached to an ordinary train rolling toward the demarcation line, where cattle cars significantly replaced the third-class cars of the Vichy administration.

The CIMADE team that spent the summer of 1942 at Rivesaltes had been installed there a little more than a year. So they knew rather well the inhabitants of the camp, in whose midst they lived, as well as the guards recruited from the area, the members of the administration, and the city of Perpignan, which was not far off. But at Rivesaltes there were up to twenty thousand residents of every description. The system of successive selections—free and interned, Jew and non-Jew, exempted and taken—was such that the chance of ending up in these solitary night trains engendered immense anxiety, but it did not start in motion collective measures capable of breaking locally the execution of orders from Vichy in the service of the Germans. Many lives were saved which could not have been if CIMADE and the other groups had not hung onto the exemptions and organized the escapes. However, the question will always be open: Why were some taken in "the night and the fog," while others were left out of the slowly exterminating process?

Also, why did we sort out, in order of the greater and lesser distress, the files that we had to defend to the end, like children adding some shovels of sand to a crumbling castle being submerged by the rising tide? When the storm is there, one struggles to keep a few treasures dry. This rescue task was the only just and possible one, but the storm is a natural phenomenon. The circulation of an anonymous document is a human act that men can refuse if they wish, especially when a border is geographically near. Begin by speaking of "housing" and not of internment, and by extension you will soon be saying that a deportation is a "transfer." You will become anti-Nazi from November 1942, after having kept order at Rivesaltes in August and September. It is *in the beginning* that you must refuse to adapt in order that your *yes* be truly *yes* and your *no* truly *no*.

7.

Diary Notes from the Milles Camp

PASTOR HENRI MANEN

The Milles camp had been opened at the time of the influx of foreigners fleeing the eastern countries in order to try to embark for the United States.

In 1940 the Ministry of the Interior channeled men arriving in Marseilles to this camp. There they were supposed to be able to continue taking steps toward embarkation. The women were placed in hotels at Marseilles. These hotels were controlled by armed guards; sometimes even barbed wire surrounded the buildings. The women received rations as in a camp; their food cards were confiscated. Soon starving, several of them tried to buy false bread cards. One day the police surrounded the bakery where several of these women had come to make their purchases. They were searched. Several of them found carrying false cards were interned. Among them was Hanna Werfel, whom this detention saved from deportation and who later became Jeanne Merle d'Aubigné's assistant at Douadic.

Among all the internees in the hotels and camp, although the "politicals" were numerous, the Jews formed the majority.

Friday, 7 August. They are saying in town that the Jews are being deported.

Saturday, 8 August. I have been in camp since 8:00 A.M. I call together the Protestant community. From the first contacts I have a strong impression: if there is terror before this specter of deportation, there is also the courage with which each one looks his destiny in the face and the love that they will not stop showing one for the other, each one trying to soften the trials of his brother and to save what he can. . . .

Sunday, 9 August. Speaking for Mr. Lowrie of the YMCA, I make known to parents obliged to leave that they can entrust their children under eighteen years old to the care of the YMCA. They will be sent to America. There is great relief for a few families.

Monday, 10 August. The unforgettable sight of the separation of children from parents. Atrocious! A tall handsome boy seventeen or eighteen years old is between his father and mother, arms around their necks. He does not cry. He leans alternately toward one, then the other, his face against theirs, slowly, gently, with all the tenderness in the world. His father and mother cry silently. The time drags on and on. . . . The bus starts. Not a cry, not a gesture. Tears run down the strained faces—faces that in one moment want to see for eternity. . . .

The police around me are pale. One of them says to me: "I was in the colonial army in China. I saw massacres, famine, war. I never saw anything as horrible as this."

No one can move. The bus has disappeared. A mother falls and rolls on the ground in hysterics.

A man and a woman slash their wrists. In a hopeless condition they are taken to the hospital.

Tuesday, 11 August. The internees are gathered in the courtyard. Sorting out of those who leave and those who stay. This lasts from morning until evening. The convoy full, the train begins to roll at 8:00 P.M. The Quakers were able to go through the trains to give food.

Wednesday, 12 August. It is unbelievable. I timed it: in thirty seconds the fate of a man is decided.

Distress, humiliation, disgust, indignation, infinite sadness,

111

repulsion. The Nazis trample and ruin lives. Unerasable stains. There is a witness of the church under the cross in the Milles camp. The Lord made it faithful and worthy to be preserved. There is also a witness of Israel in the Milles camp. The Lord made it great. These people have suffered with dignity, with truth, with humility, with greatness.

Night of 25–26 August. Raids on a large scale. Gigantic dragnet. All who were caught along the coast, in the regions of les Bouches-du-Rhone and the Gard, are brought to the camp. Among them are parents who saw their daughter throw herself from the window of her bedroom to escape the worst. . . .

Night of 1–2 September. Men, women, and children are in the courtyard. All day under a torrid sun. All night. The food service is not working. There are strict orders that all children older than two must go. The smallest stumble, cry, and cling to their parents. Poor little men five or six years old try to carry bundles their size. They are overcome with sleep and roll on the ground with their packages. Young fathers and mothers cry silently while watching this shipment. The little ones have their departure numbers in their hands. They march in step as best they can with their unsteady legs. . . . And the train is ready to leave.

8.

Le Coteau Fleuri
at le Chambon-sur-Lignon

PASTOR MARC DONADILLE

This house played a decisive role in saving several persons.

I arrived in the summer of 1942, sent by Madeleine Barot to help the director, Hubert Meyer. Alarming news came to us from everywhere concerning the deportation of the Jews. We did not believe the official version, affirming that the Jews claimed by Germany were being sent to small villages in Poland. Therefore, we had to make those of our boarders who were threatened disappear. With Mme André Philip, Pastor André Trocmé, and a school principal, we established a plan with the help of part of the population of le Chambon.

The plan had hardly been settled upon when a message from Madeleine Barot told us that danger was imminent. André Trocmé learned that the same night the gendarmerie would come to take all our boarders of Jewish origin. Our plan went into operation. We warned those involved. Many of them had believed in their complete security at le Coteau Fleuri; they were appalled. Three women, paralyzed with fear, refused to leave the house.

Of the non-Aryan group, about eighty persons, a few figures emerge, who were impressive in their self-control during the turmoil: Dr. Mayer; Sister Berthe Lenel, a nurse still dressed in her habit; and a few others.

At the end of the afternoon, by teams, we led our protégés to shelters nearby. I had charge of one group which included, among others, Dr. Mayer, Sister Lenel, and Schmidt, a German physicist completely in the clouds who did not understand anything that was happening. He repeated to anyone who would listen: "I was baptized as a child. I am not circumcised!"

At nightfall all of us leaders were back at le Coteau Fleuri, awaiting events with pounding hearts. We had hidden the three women who had not wanted to leave the house in the gables under the roof. They had passed through an opening cut into an attic room. We camouflaged the opening with a dresser.

We were awakened in the night by police cars and a bus. Someone knocked. I opened a window and asked in the most natural manner possible who these visitors were. A gendarme stepped into the light. I went down to open the door. An adjutant of the gendarmerie explained with a very embarrassed look that he had come to fetch the non-Aryans in order to transfer them elsewhere. I expressed surprise that there was not an officer of a higher rank for such an important operation. A commander and a lieutenant approached who tried to explain that the Jews were to be relocated in some regions of Poland where they would be able to live in peace. I talked as long as possible before letting them in.

A list of names in hand, we made the rounds of the rooms. First room, no one. Second room, no one. Third room, no one. "Then where are they?" asked the lieutenant. I pretended surprise. They were there last night, but we were not a concentration camp, so undoubtedly the rumor of arrests at Gurs and Rivesaltes having come this far, they had fled. The gendarmes seemed rather relieved. While looking at the list they had given me, I was shocked to see Mme Bormann's name. Convinced that she was not considered Jewish (she was a distant cousin—

she said—of one of the big Nazi leaders), she had remained in her room, where the gendarmes found her. They asked her please to dress and to follow them. Scarcely were we out in the hall when we heard hoarse, deathlike shrieks. We opened the door and found Mme Bormann rolled in her blankets on the floor, eyes rolled up, limbs stiff, apparently out of her mind. The gendarmes telephoned a doctor in le Chambon who arrived quickly. When we were alone together for a moment in her room, I saw her wink at me, and she stopped her yells. She explained that she had used this method before in a pinch. The doctor examined the patient and declared that she could not be moved.

We continued the visit of the house, room by room. They were all empty. On the upper floor there was great excitement. In one room Monsieur X., Aryan, jack-of-all-trades of the house, had put empty tin cans on a well-made bed, and I heard a clinking sound, characteristic of drops falling on a metal surface. In a lowered voice I questioned him. Monsieur X. whispered, raising his hand to the ceiling: "The women . . . up there . . . It's the excitement!"

"Take away these cans. Too bad for the sheets." And to the gendarmes who entered the room, I suggested I go see Mme Bormann and find a way to get the necessary medicine.

The gendarmes stayed in front of the house until morning; then they left. Their cars had hardly gone when I saw the old scientist to whom I have referred arrive, looking as though he was out taking a quiet walk. "What are you doing here? Why didn't you stay with the others? You know very well that you are in danger!"

"Please excuse me," he replied. "I wanted to take a walk in the woods this morning. I got lost. Finally I found a road and met a gendarme who very kindly indicated the direction to take. He also said, 'You walk too much.' "

We remained on alert several days. A discreet but rather close surveillance was organized around le Coteau. Each time I had to visit our protégés, I had to play hide-and-seek with the policeman sent to follow me.

André Trocmé had announced that a vast manhunt was to

be organized. We decided to place our fugitives on farms farther from le Chambon, while waiting to send them to Switzerland. This new trip was made at night without any trouble.

All our boarders were saved. Only one young girl among them perished in a cremation oven. Placed in a parsonage, she opened the door to a gendarme coming to look for Mlle X. She answered, "It is I." The gendarme gave her a chance, saying: "I'll wait for you. Go pack your things." IIe thought she would take advantage of another door of the house opening toward the fields, which everyone knew about. She did nothing of the sort but came out with her suitcase.

9.

Border Crossings

GENEVIÈVE PRIACEL-PITTET
("TATCHOU")

I arrived at CIMADE in Nîmes in June 1942, to be part of the secretariat and handle relations with the Récébédou and Gurs camps.

End of August 1942. The first raids took place. We were forewarned and without delay sent a first contingent of those whom we could hide to the Musée du Désert (Le Mas Soubeyran near Mialet, Gard, high point of the Huguenot resistance). We took advantage of buses leaving for the big annual gathering the first Sunday in September, and then we hid those who traveled this way in the region of Pont-de-Montvert and Florac.

I was in charge of organizing a way to pass people into Switzerland via Chamonix and Argentière. This was prepared in close collaboration with Pastor Paul Chapal, of Annecy, and Father Folliet, chaplain of the Catholic Young Workers movement (JOC).

It was necessary to work fast. We had to hide, then move out, those people in danger. Thanks to Father Folliet, the convents of Savoy opened their doors. Pastor Chapal turned over his living room as headquarters and his cellar for storing the baggage of the fugitives. This would be sent later, as soon as possible, by the Véron and Grauer Company of Annemasse. In the Haute-Loire and in the Drôme, all sorts of people hid fugitives entrusted to them by CIMADE. A moving company transported them in its big trucks.

The first crossings of the Swiss border were made above Argentière. I gathered the groups at the youth hostel at Chamonix and turned them over to a registered mountain guide, to whom we paid five hundred francs per person. This system was stopped rather quickly. We soon learned that the guide cheated the unfortunate clients, even abandoning them in the mountains if they did not give him enough money. There were those who, sent back at the border, were caught and thrown into jail without our knowing it soon enough.

At the same time, a team of students, pastors, an engineer and his twelve-year-old son followed another trail, more difficult but more sure, leaving from Chedde. This network was stopped in October 1942 with the snow and the arrest of Pastor Morel.

As one can well imagine, all this illegal travel could not be done without making false papers. Our little factory was the office of CIMADE at Nîmes, where my colleague Clairette and I spent a part of our nights at this job. We had to make the false handstamps with potatoes, corks, and india ink. We had many failures and needed lots of patience. We had to try to find some real stamps, if necessary steal them. I was almost caught in the act at the town hall in Nîmes. Our counterfeit identity cards were not so bad. All had to have the signature of the mayor, two witnesses, etc. The telephone directory gave us good ideas of names to invent. We signed one time with the right hand, then with the left. Our record was making fifty identity cards in one night. The first step was getting authentic blank cards. As sly as Apaches, without being noticed we did the rounds of the tobacco stores where the cards were available. Or we told stories—some plausible, some stupid, some romantic, etc.—in order to have a sufficient number. I bought cards in all the towns where I stopped.

There was also the problem of food cards. We recovered the

cards of those who left. To put them back into shape, we began by washing them in peroxide, then we ironed them out, and they were soon filled in for the following client. The exchange of tickets was more or less assured by sympathetic friends who tried to get them at the same time as theirs. Or else we received some from obliging mayors.

In October 1942, we put into use other passages into Switzerland besides those of Argentière, the Balme Pass, or le Buet and Barberine. There was no problem about climbing the mountains; it was a matter of being clever. We now prepared routes between Annecy, Annemasse, Évian, and Thonon. The pastor of Thonon and the priest of Douvaine were with us and helped us by their knowledge of people and places. On the whole, it was a matter of passing over or under two rows of barbed wire a few yards apart and over six feet high. I made up the teams of *passeurs,* boys about eighteen years old who did not risk being picked up by the S.T.O. (Service du Travail Obligatoire, or Forced Labor Service)—Boy Scouts or former Scouts for the most part. We worked in teams of two—either two boys or one boy and me. The work varied a great deal. Sometimes we passed two people at a time, sometimes six. There were old people who had to be helped to walk, climb, or slide. There were babies to be put to sleep and to pass in a sack. There were children who had to be kept from crying. Above all, there were the scared who had to be reassured. Among the boys who helped us, there were some related to the maquis of Savoy. Due to this fact, they led very disturbed lives and used their wiry endurance to the limit.

Thanks to a Resistance authority in Lyons, we also received some help. Certain places that we would normally not have access to were opened to us for hiding. For example, isolated monasteries in the mountains. A pharmacist was a godsend. Two of his cousins opened their apartment as a hotel for hiding clandestine travelers. We sometimes crossed over ourselves when going after money in Switzerland.

It happened, unfortunately, that the Swiss began to turn people back. It was then that Pastor Marc Boegner obtained permission from the federal government at Bern for those whom

119

he guaranteed and who were in CIMADE's care to cross the border.

December 1942. Sprain and slight fracture of my foot. Here I was, handicapped by a plaster cast. I was no longer agile enough. The people I was leading turned on me and had me captured by the gendarmes. Arrested with the others, twelve of us spent the night in a cell in Annemasse. There the gendarmes forgot to feed us. At last on 24 December they took us—frozen, hungry, and handcuffed—to the prison at Annecy.

A month and a half of prison at Annecy! My feet were frozen, especially the one in the cast. During this time I made contact with some prostitutes, some thieves, and some black marketers. One prisoner gave me lessons in picking pockets. (It seems that I have no talent.) We were completely idle. Everyone told her little story fifty times a day. We worried about what would happen after leaving prison, if we ever left. Boredom at thirty-five and uneasiness in a group are terrible. After the trial at Saint-Julien-en-Genevois, I was freed sometime during the first days of February 1943.

After leaving prison, I took up the border crossings again. We used the cemetery near Annemasse. The French side of the border was the cemetery wall. The people arrived in great mourning: black veils, wreaths . . . The same ones were used each time. The people were left trembling and crying from fear, kneeling near a tomb. During this time we checked to see if the way was clear. Then we passed them over the wall; the grave digger's ladder made that easier. Then we wrapped up the veils and wreaths and left. One time, one of the boys jumped from the wall onto a German customs man that he had not seen. We had to knock the man out gently in order to cross over without any more trouble.

How could we shelter all those who arrived from all directions? At Annecy, to the few monasteries that were open were added individual offers by sympathetic persons. Someone proposed the rectory at le Bout-du-Lac, at the far end of Lake Annecy. To avoid police controls, the trip was made by rowboat. The priest was a bit senile and very deaf—to say the least. He was ninety-two years old. He would never know that he had housed dozens of people. It all took place between his house-keeper and us. She was a grumbling old dragon, but devoted. In case of extreme urgency and total lack of housing, we used the bedroom set up in the storefront of Rev. Folliet's father (a strong collaborator). However, it was not very practical. We had to wait until the iron grille on the store was lowered, and get up very early in the morning to put everything back in place to make sure that the proprietor would not be suspicious.

CIMADE moved its offices to Valence. It was handier for communications between the Haute-Loire and Savoy. But the region of Aix-en-Provence became a center of hiding places. In order to pass people, we had to go after them. The trains arrived and left at night. In Aix all that I was familiar with was what I could see at night between the station and Pastor Manen's house, the meeting place. Along the way, I knew all the doors and porches where one could hide in case a patrol came along. Our false identity cards were improving. Now we made "real false cards," signed by the prefect and registered. We had the connivance of certain offices. Our material situation was better. At Valence we had a canteen with the Youth Movements. There we exchanged information, polished plans, found food tickets, addresses, resources. In brief, it was a "den of gangsters." The minister's house was another; you could go in day and night; you asked questions of no one. When you woke up, you found the most unexpected people.

The problem of hiding while waiting, of hiding immediately, was always there. At Valence there was a hotel of the Croix-d'Or requisitioned by the Gestapo. Therefore, it was one of the rare hiding places we could be sure of. No identity check there! Our "clients" were terrified and could not understand why we put them there, of all places, to wait.

End of summer 1943. Near Annemasse, the roads were being watched too closely; we could no longer cross over. We scouted the Jura on the other side of Geneva. Means of access were difficult. The region was not suspect, but it was over fifteen miles from Saint-Claude to Les Rousses. Our headquarters at Saint-Claude was set up in the home of an old Communist, a friend of friends of ours, a pipe cutter by trade. When one spent the night at his place, it was in the same bed with Monsieur, Madame, and their two daughters. On days when there were many of us, they found a folding bed. With these routes, we could pass only people able to walk twenty miles. As time went by, we reduced the distance by taking the bus to Les Rousses. The risks of identity checks were greater, the German police dogs ferocious.

As well as I can determine, our little traffic from August 1942 to December 1943 permitted the evacuation of about four hundred persons, either sent to CIMADE or gotten out of camps, or sent to me directly.

All of this lasted for me until December 1943, when I had to decide for personal reasons (and because strange people had come several times to my sister's home, where I could be ambushed) to leave for North Africa to join the Free French forces by way of Spain. Two other team members of CIMADE took my place.

10.

Brens: From the Empty Cell
to Children's Cries

SUZANNE LOISEAU-CHEVALLEY

Spring 1942. It all began with great uneasiness in the camp. Two German political internees condemned to death in their country had been arrested, placed in cells, and guarded by the police in such a way that no one could approach the barracks.

The first of the two women was Protestant. On several occasions I arranged to go near the barred window at ground level. I found her with serene heart and face. She awaited the moment, the instant. One morning the cell was empty.

This departure, then the following, caused a stupor in the camp. The occupants of the German, Russian, and Polish barracks felt threatened. Several days passed, and then I received from Drancy an astonishing message in a beat-up, used envelope, which said thank you for "everything." It urged that I not be sad for her because she had been happy in her solitary cell, where she had felt surrounded with love. She wrote, "In the night a candle burned." She was surrounded by the politically condemned and numerous foreign Jews. "Each one must prepare himself . . . it is not necessary to take anything along."

So, everyone knew for sure that "it was coming." Consternation spread over the camp. Soon I received a message from Madeleine Barot: massive deportations would take place for Jews and political prisoners. A list of eleven exceptions had been fought for and established; however, we could count on no one to respect these exceptions.

With this list, I went to the head of the camp. He did not want to do anything, having received no orders. "The more Jews delivered to the Germans," he said, "the less chance that one of us will be claimed by them." And our zone was still said to be free! The zeal of so many people to satisfy the Germans astonished me. I insisted. I threatened: perhaps one day the situation would be reversed, and with our many ways to inform certain organizations, he would regret his attitude. He was afraid.

It was my advantage to have been told before him what was in preparation and to have had that list. To be a lawyer, also! I had permission to use the internees' files. The lists had to be established taking into account the aforementioned exceptions. Therefore, we had to come to an understanding with one another. There was a constant coming and going to and from my barracks. What could I give to most of them? I could give without reserve that profound compassion which filled my heart, and I could listen to what remained to be said by the traveler who was leaving forever. . . After getting the information, I went to the prefecture of Albi. In the case of the elderly, it was rather easy to decide. Not one of them left the camp of Brens in convoys during the summer and fall of 1942.

Delicate problems were involved in cases concerning nationalities. Recent border changes complicated things. Some birth certificates permitted me to obtain from the prefecture the exemption of some Jewish women. For the sick and infirm, the collaboration of the camp doctor would have been necessary. He refused, then made a few promises.

Two women, political internees Wanda and Erika, both Jewish doctors of Polish nationality, were looking for outside help to escape, ready for any risk. They did not ask my help because they did not want to make it necessary for me to lie and endanger the work of CIMADE.

To gain time, they soaked their feet in water in a basin heating on the barracks stove. Their feet were horrible, like boiled meat. I took care of them. These two young women had known the ghettos of Poland. Condemned to death, they had escaped the first time. They fought again now to escape death. Several of their barracks companions, all Communists, blacklisted them because they wanted to save themselves. Wanda and Erika were therefore very much alone. The betrayal of the doctor took away my last scruples. I offered to help them by taking a message to the outside. It was my first step in illegality, the one that cost me the most! I did not know then that the time would come when it would no longer be necessary to ask questions, but to act to save lives, make false cards, steal seals, help a team to hide the corpse of a German in the snow.

The internees were in the habit, one might say, of thinking each morning that it could be the last. An unknown death was accepted. In spite of the desperation, they continued to live with a courage that left me amazed. We were constantly on the alert. The slightest unexpected noise made us jump. We were afraid of being brutally surprised.

Nighttime was the hardest for those who could not sleep. One had to "live his own death." The rounds of the guards each time awakened the anguish in the depths of their hearts. Numerous internees, kept awake by the ever-burning lamps, preferred not to sleep. Often, sitting in small groups on one of the bunks, we had long whispered conversations. The internees were in the habit of seeing me go softly from one barracks to another, passing a bit of the night with those whom I found open-eyed.

One night, I knew for certain from several signs that the hour had come. Someone from the administration warned me that I should stay in my barracks because the newly arrived guards would not be able to recognize me. There were some unusual furtive comings and goings. I had promised to warn those who waited. It is less intolerable to be awakened to hard reality by a friendly presence than by the brutality of the guards.

Quietly, against orders, I went from one barracks to another. Each one understood without a word, no cries or lamentings—there was a conspiracy of silence so that I could continue to the end. When I had gone, the unfortunate ones would get dressed without leaving their mattresses. One moment I thought that I could not go any farther. I shall never forget the infinite compassion with which several women looked at me. "She is not yet in the habit. . . ." Not yet in the habit of seeing around me these defenseless beings, caught in a trap, condemned to death, delivered like animals. Habit! It seemed to me that too many people had this habit in our sweet France.

At two o'clock in the morning motorized troops roared into the camp and like a well-rehearsed ballet, with brief orders, the clicking of arms, went into the barracks of the foreign political prisoners. There were several men to seize each woman lying on her bed. Soon the whole barracks, the whole camp, rose up and showed its anger. Not all the women were taken, but we knew that those who were went to their deaths. The future did not belie it. There was something great, in spite of the useless violence, in that protest of all the camp internees, as vain as it might be. The condemned were silent. With blows of nightsticks they were pushed out of the crowd. The others were thrown back violently into the barracks or cells. Soon there was only a small group of terribly pitiful women with torn clothing and strained faces, who tried to cover themselves under the eyes of the armed guards. The Red Cross nurse, whom one saw only on rare occasions, offered packages prepared for the trip. Not one woman went forward. No one would take anything given by the "Administration." I had some fruit, six cans of sardines, and some cookies. The women understood that it came from CIMADE, and hands reached out.

There was such an appeal for help in the eyes of those women that my decision was made, without words, and each one understood. Where they went, I would go. Because I was free and they were not, I gave them a little of my freedom as a last sacrament for hope and courage.

Clara Neubauer, who had cared for me like a mother hen since I had come to camp, and who was there for reasons I never knew, had understood. She disappeared and came back bringing my knapsack, and she forcefully put on me her own boots, a special rarity in camp. I had not noticed that it was raining. Everything happened fast, very fast. One last time I shouted in vain for the doctor to remove a paralyzed woman from the convoy. Her seventy-five-year-old mother joined us. The daughter could not get along without her. The doctor answered, "Where the girl is going, she will no longer need her mother." However, he did make out a temporary certificate for Wanda and Erika. For one, it would be salvation; for the other, a short reprieve.

The women were pushed out of camp and loaded into a truck. Having remained in their group, I found myself there also. A clamor arose in the camp. Undoubtedly starting from the barracks of the French politicals, the singing of *La Marseillaise* broke out in all the barracks. A rough bump, and then we left with this last adieu ringing in our ears.

We rode for a long time. When the truck stopped, dawn was breaking on the radiant countryside washed with rain. All alone on the sidetrack of a little station, there was a freight car, a common cattle car. Someone pushed us. The doors closed on us and on six armed guards. Inside was an acetylene lamp. We waited a long time. Our car was finally attached just behind a locomotive, and then the long grinding of old metal pounded in our heads. It seemed at times that we could not endure it another instant.

Each woman seemed to have reached the limit of suffering: one had left her child at camp, another the hope of ever seeing again her crippled husband at Camp Djelfa. Others had left only their solitude and their misery, everything having been snatched from them; but even that misery was a precious possession and they were full of nostalgia because they had lost it.

There was hunger and thirst. Food was to have been provided, but the insulting little packages had been refused. There was the terrible constraint and shame of being treated like animals, to have only a little pile of straw in a corner to satisfy the need of each one under the eyes of the guards, obliged to remain in the closed car. And of course there was the terrible odor that

127

was not long in taking over. At the stop the guards were let out, the door shut again. To be fair, I must say that they were human within the limits possible. They attempted to explain that they did this work reluctantly and in fear of reprisals on their families in Paris. They gave a little of their food.

Night came. The lighted lamp, swinging with the rhythm of the train, projected deceptive shadows on the walls. It was a relief when it went out a little before dawn of the first morning, leaving us in a half-light by day and complete darkness by night.

In this night, in the noise, with the hunger and cold and half-dried clothes, the interior silence of each one was more profound. I stretched out near one or the other of these women, and we spoke in low voices. Each one told a little about what was most dear to her. And in spite of the essential solitude in the heart of each, a kind of peace was born from the shared suffering.

"I am content," said the friend who had left her child in camp. "I am going to know what it is to suffer with those of my race." She thought she was going for a time into the ghettos of Poland with the Polish Jews.

I remember the good-looking face of a Russian Communist. We were talking about hope. I told her that I could not live without Christian hope. "I am not without hope," she said to me. "I believe in human progress." Did that moment come to her when, in complete hopelessness, death would appear to her as a hope of resurrection in Jesus Christ? Did death bring to that other young Jewess the answer to her anguished question: "If it were true?" These exchanges with several Jews had followed a rabbi's visit in camp shortly before the departure of our convoy. He had affirmed with the help of scripture passages that the Jews suffered and would suffer again because they had the truth. After that visit, while talking with some of them we had compared passages of the Old and New Testaments.

Toward the end of the fourth day, the train stopped. The car was opened. A guard asked if there was a nurse among the internees, because in the next car most of the men suffered from dysentery. Our doctor friend refused, afraid of being separated from the others. They all advised me to go, perhaps to bring back some information.

In the neighboring freight car, the situation was worse. No medication. And since there were more men than women in the convoy, the crowding in this car had made the trip even more terrible for them, if possible. The politically condemned came from prisons, others from the camp of Saint-Sulpice-la-Pointe. Still others were brutally snatched from their hiding places. A few days had sufficed to give these unshaven, hungry men the appearance of living corpses. Haggard, dull-eyed or bright with fever, they were like drunks, staggering or piled on the floor.

I learned then that our convoy was made up little by little as it went toward the south: Toulouse, Tarbes, Pau, the area of Bayonne. Almost all the arrests had taken place at dawn, which explained the interminable stops of the convoy. A young Jew was there, his ardor contrasting with the apathy of the others. All his loved ones were dead. He had only life left; he did not want to die.

The train changed direction. Night came. We could not be far from Châteauroux. Two guards were leaning against the door. Without difficulty I persuaded them that to avoid the contagion of dysentery the portable toilet had to be emptied as often as possible and not postponed until the station stops. The plan worked. The car door was not entirely closed. A brief stop. The young man holding the bucket threw himself from the moving train. Two shots. The guards leaned gloomily against the car door.

A last stop near Vierzon. The line of demarcation was near; the guards went no farther. The convoy would be taken in charge by the Germans, delivered to the Germans. The guards begged me to leave because I was not on the list and because there was nothing more to do. They refused to open the women's car for me, so I lay down on the tracks. I could do nothing else. Would they understand that there is a limit to the sufferings one can let fall upon others? They gave in. They opened the car and I saw my friends again. The elderly mother and her invalid daughter had not left their corner since the departure. Suffering seemed to be nearly over for them.

My friends begged me to leave them, to return to camp where, they said, there was much to do. Then, in that freight car, that straw, that horror, we sang the song learned at Brens, harmonized by Liselotte, our orchestra leader:

Let us join our voices before we separate;
I am going to travel other places.
Life is beautiful and the world so lovely;
Sing out this last good-bye.

And if I meet death along the way,
Reaping among us the row of beggars,
Yes, I shall be ready for my last good-bye;
I leave for a very long journey.

It was the fifth night; another station siding. Through the cracks in the car I distinguished some German uniforms on the platform. The soldiers formed a double line. They had dogs with them.

Someone opened the door, and brief orders rang out. The sorting was going to begin. I embraced my friends. Some would go through Paris, the politicals, I thought. The others would leave directly for Germany. No one ever came back.

The guards hid me behind them, helping me to catch a freight train. I lay down on a platform loaded with big tree trunks. As "merchandise," I would make the return trip much quicker. In the middle of the night, the train started off.

Now I was alone. I was seized with anxiety. I must go back to life. I understood better our friend who said, "I am going to be happy suffering with those of my race." Solidarity in trouble, sympathy in the real sense of the word—they alone make it possible to endure certain things without revolting and to find peace.

During my absence from the car, my friends had put papers, birth certificates, diplomas, letters, two wedding bands—all that they had not yet had to give up—into my knapsack. A can of sardines, a few cookies, a little scarf for a present . . . Often I was gripped with anguish and sorrow in thinking about the fate of my deported friends and the little I could do for them. But one day I received a note from a Communist deportee whom I had not known very well at all. She spoke of the "Protestant barracks" and said: "When I went into your barracks, which had nothing more than ours, it was as if I were received by a very dear host, with all the best spread upon the tablecloth." May she not have forgotten, at the end of all the sufferings that must have preceded her death, the "tablecloth" symbolic of her who, having nothing to offer, received her in the name of Jesus Christ.

In the night the train stopped: Châteauroux. I climbed down from my platform. Soon I found myself surrounded by Romanian and Hungarian Jews escaped from the Occupied Zone. They were hiding here and waiting for a chance to try something. With their help, I found the young man who had thrown himself from the train. He had been given false papers. Later, he was able to reach the Spanish border and send me a message.

At Châteauroux I met a secret correspondent from London, an Austrian. He forwarded all the information I gave him about the convoys, the identity of the deportees. In a few days all of that was repeated by London radio and heard in France.

I was exhausted. I could no longer eat, and fell asleep when talking. I had to return to the Brens camp.

And even the children . . .

It was a summer day with flowers, birds singing, sunshine. A day for vacation, a day when it would have been good to hear the laughing of children. I had to leave at dawn with two policemen in a covered truck. The camp director sent me like this—was it because of sympathy or to get rid of me by giving me an occasion to put him definitely in danger? I said to him, "You know why I am going."

It was hard to be almost officially with the police, determined to "fulfill their duty to the end." I had no choice. All that I could do now was to inform quickly those whom I could speak to when we stopped. "The half-Jewish children they are looking for will not be put in children's homes, as the police are supposed

131

to say." I tried to slow down the comings and goings of the truck in order to give time to hide the children. This was possible a few times, but not always.

Thus we covered the Tarn and a part of the Haute-Garonne —a nightmare of a trip. How was it possible that they spotted this tiny hamlet of La Montagne Noire, where, in an isolated house, three girls from six to thirteen years old were hidden? Informers, probably. The gendarmes inquired in the hamlet. When the truck arrived at the house indicated, the oldest of the girls fled across the fields, but the younger ones, wearing summer dresses and without baggage, understanding nothing of what was happening, were thrown into the truck. The youngest said in a clear voice: "Tomorrow traveling is not permitted. It is Saturday." Each stop brought more suffering.

At the hospital at Castres, they wanted to take the child of a sick man lying in bed, despairing, whose wife had already been arrested. He refused to tell where she was hidden. When a nun entered, I begged in a low voice, "Sister, do not say anything." But she serenely gave an address and some directions. When I was leaving, I heard the dreadful cry of the father, who had grabbed a knife to kill himself. I tossed at the sister, "Aren't you ashamed to turn in a child?" She didn't flinch. The address in the small village she had indicated was false. Much time was lost. Furious, the police could not return to the hospital; they did not have time. I suppose that the nun has forgiven me, as I myself have forgiven a man who said to me, "You could be a mother and you do this kind of work?"

At Dourgne in the Tarn, nighttime, lightning all over the sky. We stopped at the village square. The doctor was pointed out as hiding a little girl two years old, whose parents later were arrested. The doctor refused to say where the child was. The police called for the mayor. He was spiteful, saying that the doctor should be arrested as well as the pharmacist, a French Jew. The police answered that they had not yet received orders to arrest French Jews. The doctor explained that the child was crippled from polio and that she would never be able to walk if she was not cared for. Then, there on that village square, I explained loudly what the life of that crippled child would be like in the transports and the camps. The police were ashamed. The obstinate mayor talked about a search. I realized that the doctor risked internment. I believed that I could save the child. It seemed to be impossible that there was nothing to be done to avoid deportation. The police themselves assured me that we were returning to Brens with the children. I told all that to the doctor. The mayor and a policeman went to find the child. It seems that the whole family, with happy faces, was at the table for the evening meal. A beautiful blond baby was tapping its dish with a spoon. Someone put the child in my arms. The doctor promised to send me the X-rays and medical certificates. The police were disgusted with their task. "If we had not taken the child, the mayor would have sent word that we did not want to do our job." I understood then how one learns to hate.

The truck continued its journey in the night. The storm broke out with violence. Lightning illuminated the woods. The truck covering had been adjusted because water was coming into the truck full of children. They did not talk. When a "grown-up" twelve years old reassured the others, his voice trembled. They did not ask questions; what would I have been able to answer? The interrogation of those eyes—anxious or confident—was already intolerable. It was enough to make me feel guilty for living in a world that persecutes children. " . . . as you did it to one of these little ones, you did it to me." Why? Confident, the smallest had put her arms around my neck. In order not to hear the thunder, we sang children's songs and rounds. Crouched against one another, several finally fell asleep. They could take no more. Some of them had been in the truck since morning.

Those little faces on that terrible trip haunted me. I tried in vain to think of the others, of those who were able to escape. But it was no consolation.

In the middle of the night the truck arrived at camp—not at Brens but at Saint-Sulpice-la-Pointe. They had lied to me from beginning to end. This camp was for political men prisoners. Other trucks were there, waiting to be unloaded in the morning. The children were cold. And I saw again the trembling hands of a woman who had tied a scarf around her child's neck at the moment of departure, and the hands that were held out, held out for a long time . . .

Day came; columns were formed. Children, women, men. Another heartbreaking occasion. Stumbling from sleepiness, the children were taken from the truck. The little one was torn from me. They turned back with pathetic looks before following their group. Tears, cries. After getting out of the trucks, parents were separated from their children. Heartrending screams.

Here was Saint-Sulpice, the sorting camp. Internees from Brens were brought here a few days ago. Were they still here?

Some time earlier, at Brens, knowing that a deportation was to take place, the little group of Protestants had gathered in the chapel. I led the service and we prayed for all those who would leave and especially that Carla Neubauer and Erma Maier be saved. The service had been interrupted abruptly. They had come to take the latter by force. I was terribly sad and discouraged. But when she was leaving, Erma said to me, "I have trust," and her look radiated her faith. A few days later a word from her told me that she was in the camp at Saint-Sulpice and awaiting her departure. (This camp was for punishment of male political prisoners at first; then it became a detention center for foreign Jews. At this time it was a relocation center prior to deportation.) After Erma left Brens, I reexamined her file very closely and found after the name of her father, written in very fine German handwriting: "Belongs to the Protestant church." Thinking that mentioning her father's faith could keep her from deportation, I went to the prefecture of Albi. I learned later that this was no help at all.

Now, here I was at the gate of the camp so strictly forbidden that Madeleine Barot had not succeeded in having a CIMADE team admitted. Since the children had been taken away, I wanted to go in. I mingled with the Jews being pushed into the camp. At the window I received a blanket and a bowl like the others. Inside: barbed wire and more barbed wire. Isolated by still more wire was a barracks, that of the "politicals." That was it! Through the grilles I saw friends from Brens, and we had a joyful reunion. In this world saturated with anguish, it was good to feel that God permits trust and friendship to fill hearts and to shine in eyes. Someone told me that they were waiting for a sorting commission from the Swedish Red Cross with a Princess Lieven. All the cases would be examined and they would keep everyone possible.

My friends helped me to find the mother of the sick child from Dourgne. Poor woman. She became almost crazy upon learning that her daughter was in the camp. May I say right away, the mother and child were to be admitted to the camp infirmary. From there, with considerable effort, they would be sent to the hospital at Albi. The mother, guarded by a policeman, refused to sign adoption papers prepared for the child. It is thus that suffering and anguish can take away all ability to listen and to believe a word of hope.

My friends' joy attracted the attention of the guards. Immediately and rather brutally, I was led out of the camp. It was necessary to find a way to enter again. When the sorting commission arrived, I would have my say!

However, it was the camp doctor who helped me involuntarily. I had gone to him to plead the case of the child from Dourgne and her mother. He confirmed that there was nothing to be done and took me to his office in the camp to show me that they were on the departure list, and in fact already gone. When, unsuspecting, he brought me back toward the exit, I returned, presumably to leave the child's X-rays. I found my internees rather easily in spite of the confusion that reigned because of all the arrivals awaiting deportation.

Thus I lived two unforgettable days in secret with my friends, blending myself with them in the eyes of the guards. Together we ate from the one large kettle because there were not enough bowls for the "politicals," and the soup did not seem to us to be so bad.

After two days a guard entered the barracks with a representative of the sorting commission and said, "If anyone has absolutely valid reasons for not being shipped away, she may follow us." I stood up and the internees exclaimed, "Here is the social worker who has come to defend us!" In the commission room, it was difficult to distinguish the representatives of the camp administration from those of the commission. I said bold-

135

ly that I had been sent to validate an exception in favor of Erma Maier, since her father belonged to the Protestant church. Then I spoke of the crippled child. I remember that I was very angry and that two guards took me by the arms and led me out of camp.

In what turmoil I returned to Brens! A few days later I saw Erma Maier arrive. Deliverance! We all remembered our prayers for her. Later at le Coteau Fleuri I saw her again, as well as some others. With what joy she told of her deliverance!

But because of these activities I was put out of the Brens camp. I left it with a heavy heart. CIMADE sent me to other tasks.

11.

An Escape from Camp Nexon

LAURETTE ALEXIS-MONET

April 1943. The camp of Nexon (Haute-Vienne) was gradually emptied of those who survived the rigorous winter. It had been observed that the camp was not suitable as a hospital camp. Until then, it had sheltered cripples, children, and old people. On the other hand, to competent authorities it seemed very suitable for internment of people needing serious and strict surveillance. So the barracks were filling up again, but this time with future deportees for the so-called work camps and with French political internees.

Rather small, surrounded by a double row of fences, then barbed wire staked out with spiked wooden barriers, and guarded by many watchtowers where the guards changed constantly, the camp seemed at first to dispel all hope of escape. Nevertheless, at the time this story begins, these precautions were still insufficient. One noticed a gang of workmen around the "special cluster," made up of two sets of barracks isolated even in the interior of the camp by another enclosure. This enclosure was being reinforced. A few days after the work ended, about forty prisoners arrived who had the disquieting privilege of being called by name at the time of their transfer from the police vans to the barracks. Such precautions were not taken for the poor troop of anonymous emigrants destined to die anonymously. Like a state within a state, the special cluster benefited from a special guard also. My activities stopped at the entrance of the enclosure, watched over by two guards.

Even the most generous of the personnel did not let the tiniest bit of information filter through. However, camp discipline relaxed a little. Forty prisoners, even the "hardest," are not many to occupy a full corps of personnel who had guarded six hundred lame and dying all one winter. People were bored; they chatted and exchanged cigarettes. First I obtained permission to distribute packages through the fence. Then, I talked a little, and gradually I convinced each guard to let me do what perhaps his predecessor had permitted me to do.

Conversations were begun; friendships were formed. Then the camp director went to Vichy to learn what to do with his nearly idle employees.

The Allies were secure in North Africa. They occupied several Mediterranean islands, in preparation for landing in Italy. We believed in the Allied victory and hoped it would be soon. The guards were told by their prisoners that perhaps tomorrow the roles would be reversed, which gave the guards reason not to be too mean. And so I became acquainted with the "specials." One, after having fought in Spain in the international brigades, had attempted to organize an anti-Nazi resistance in Austria. Another had been part of the court that condemned Hitler after his *putsch*. From yet another I became acquainted with drawings of pacifist inspiration (Christ on a cross with a gas mask) before knowing the artist: a hunchback with weak eyes, whose use of a pencil was dangerous for the Führer. And there was also that ex-sailor, tattooed up to and including his scalp, who still became excited at the memory of Scapa Flow. Each one had done something personally. That was why their names appeared on the list for which the camp director was directly responsible to the German police.

The camp was well guarded; no one had escaped in years.

Twice already a patrol wagon had stopped before the gate of the stockade. Each time a prisoner had been made to climb in. Each time it was a deserter from the German army, caught in the region.

Five miles from there, they said, was an "execution wall." About half an hour after each of these departures, the straining ears of the prisoners picked up the crackling of a volley. Suppers went uneaten; but no other more serious reaction would be forthcoming from these men, who had been imprisoned several times and, in addition, were spied on by one another. Rumor had it, in fact, that there were police spies among them, trying to earn their confidence.

Upon his return from Vichy, the camp director did not announce any increase in prisoners assigned to the locale. But to console his underworked personnel, he promoted everybody. The brigadiers became chief brigadiers, the inspectors became chief inspectors, and all these chiefs toasted one another at a lively banquet. Two "special" prisoners were given the right to leave the enclosure to work in the kitchens, where I arranged to be fairly often. At nightfall many of the new chiefs finished celebrating their success by snoring on the table or throwing up in the washrooms. Some others got weepy and looked for a kind soul to whom to pour out their confidences. One of them, with tears in his eyes, put his arm around my neck. I was disentangling myself when he announced, " . . . something awful, it's secret, but it's terrible. . . ." I accepted a few moments of this annoying intimacy, listening carefully. "All those in the stockade . . . adieu. In two weeks, three at the most, they all will be taken by the Gestapo. But first, next week, they are going to shoot six, the worst ones . . . but I can't tell you which, shh, state secret."

It was Easter. I was able to obtain permission to share a holiday meal with the prisoners. I bought some rabbits on the black market. They got into the enclosure secretly one after the other, enclosed in a violin case which was carried back and forth for this reason. The women of the stockade would cook the feast in the evening on the pot-bellied stove. They washed the sleeping bags, which on Easter would serve as tablecloths because this banquet to which I—free in these prisons—was invited was a solemn occasion. They gathered bouquets of dandelions by stretching their fingers through the barricade to grasp the flowers in the barbed wire.

Later, I would lead the Easter service of the Reformed church. I had received pastoral authorization giving me the right and the mission to give Communion: the bread of life and the cup of the covenant. To those who awaited death, I would announce the victory of Easter.

We shared dinner among the dandelions, which were drooping on the old sheets. The camp director, wearing white gloves, returned from mass. He passed in front of the stockade without telling me to get out as he should have done. After drinking the contraband coffee and scrutinizing all the faces, for once smiling and relaxed, I would choose him in whom I would confide: six among you will be shot during the week. I don't know which ones. I cannot—but I must, I must absolutely—prevent it. Choose among yourselves. I shall try, God alone knows how, to organize an escape.

Fritz called me. He gave me a German Bible on the first page of which was written the name of a woman: Josephine. "It is for Josephine. She is in the camp at Gurs. Give it to her when 'they' come to get me. I think that will be soon. Adieu. We shall meet again. . . ." His finger pointed to the sky. He said "up there." Thus Fritz helped me to reveal this difficult secret. I left it to him to guess who the candidates might be. I wanted to help them to escape, but how? Fritz was far less emotional than I; he knew how to envisage death. Even in recognizing the weakness of my possibilities, he found there the only hope left to him. But he was a realist. We should not prepare more than four people for the escape. Two would be caught, and if all went well two would get through. Most likely, no one would make it. It would be uselessly foolish to try to have everyone escape.

I had heard talk of the Resistance. I did not know a single face. I was nineteen years old. For nearly a year I had been shut up in the camps with hardly any contact with the world. The week before Easter, I had camped in the Alps for a few days with students of the *Fédé* (French Student Christian Movement). There I had heard about the Resistance from people who seemed to know. Pastor Georges Casalis had told me: "If one day you are in trouble, you can come to my house in Lyons, day or night, even without sending word. And if you have someone to hide. . . ."

But that was at Lyons. In the area of Haute-Vienne I knew no one except the pastor at Limoges, who I knew had been bothered by the police because of several sermons that were a bit too courageous. He would listen to me; but could he help me?

I had outlined a plan, with many important pieces missing. Two pairs of wire cutters stolen from the camp workshop would be put in the soup by the two prisoners working in the kitchens. I saw them often, but as discreetly as possible. The wire cutters, after being removed from the soup, would end up in Fritz's straw mattress. The tattooed man, the sailor from Scapa Flow, suggested insulating the handles with tape in case there was an electric alarm system functioning in the fence. In the evening I made the rounds of the barracks, looking for a part of the enclosure that was not reached by the floodlights. The shadow from the nearest watchtower seemed to be the only possible point. It would be necessary to work at the very feet of the guards. The first fence had to be cut from a window; then the escapees had to section a roll of barbed wire, cut another fence, and cross a ditch full of barbed wire. Then they would find themselves at the foot of a wooden fence about thirteen feet high, behind which was the road. It would be necessary to find a weak place in the fence, a rotting board whose nails would give without noise. Finally they would be outside. And then, once they were outside?

Those who were going to escape spoke only a few words of poor French. They had arrived in a police van and were totally ignorant of the topography of the area. The railroad tracks were guarded at night by teams. The roads would be barricaded as soon as the escape was announced. I would be the number-one suspect of the camp, and my every move would be watched. There was little time. I had to set up a system that

141

could function without me, that could be utilized by people knowing nothing of conditions outside the camp and in constant danger. I decided to tell the pastor at Limoges of my plans. He could perhaps come to the rescue later if I myself were deprived of liberty. He proved to be as gracious and willing as he was uninformed of clandestine activities. I unknowingly gave him his baptism into the Resistance, because I learned later that this initiation would take him along the road that led to the presidency of the Liberation Committee of Limoges. Leaving Pastor Chaudier, I bought a map of the region. Through the camp kitchen, Karl and Franz passed it toward the enclosure.

The map! Here is the road, the roads. Here are the traps. The dirt roads are hazardous. A person can easily get lost in unknown country and be spotted quickly. Fortunately, a few hundred yards from the road alongside the camp is a railroad track of little importance where a local shuttle train passes only rarely. The track is not guarded at night. It goes toward Saint-Yrieix, the neighboring town across the hills. The track passes over several bridges under which flow little streams from the forests. There are no houses too close, no roads. Listen well, Karl and Fritz. You will find two big sacks of supplies at the fourth bridge along the railroad track, in a bush behind a rock. You will take them and climb back up the hill after having walked in the water. You will remain hidden there until you find a message in one of the sacks of provisions, which will give you a rendezvous. These sacks will be brought there several days after your flight by one of the pastor's parishioners. I do not want to know her. She has never seen me. She lives in Saint-Yrieix and can easily get supplies from the surrounding farms. Afterward, we shall see. Now, time is pressing. Each day there is the risk that the camp gate will open and let in the patrol wagon coming to get the victims.

Franz, the tattooed man, Karl, and Fritz were the team. It was a maximum. No one counted on a totally favorable result. We would be happy indeed if one of the four was able to make it to freedom.

Finally! The two cooks told me that they would make the attempt that night. I spent a sleepless night, straining my ears, waiting to hear a whistle, yells. The next morning, apparently with their usual composure, Karl and Franz took up their work in the kitchen. We tried, they said. We had sectioned a few of the big wires that hold the fence. Then the tattooed one had taken an irrepressible coughing fit that was heard before we could get back into the barracks. When the guard called, he had answered that he had gone outside to cough so as not to awaken everyone. A minor incident; but if the cut wires were noticed, all hope of escape would be lost forever. Karl and Franz were depressed. They confided to me that the operation was almost impossible; they seemed to have lost all hope of success.

In the afternoon Fritz, who already had a stiff leg as the result of a wound received in Spain, sprained his ankle, making any attempt impossible for him and dangerous for the others. He courageously withdrew from the team and even offered to create a diversion at the proper moment if it was necessary to distract the attention of the guards. I shall never be able to forget the serenity with which Fritz saw this hope disappear. (I learned ten years later that by an almost miraculous series of circumstances Fritz nevertheless had escaped death.)

Night fell again. We were all anxious. The blue skies of recent weeks had clouded during the day, as had our hearts. I did not sleep. I listened. Soon I no longer needed to strain my ears; a rumbling was becoming louder and louder. The storm broke. A torrential rain started; flashes streaked the sky, thunder cracked, and hail fell. Electricity went out in the whole camp. What a blessing! I have never welcomed a storm with such fervor. The guards huddled in the back of their sentry boxes, each one searching for shelter from the downpour of such unheard-of violence. Dear God, if only it lasts . . .

It did last, so long even that Chief Brigadier Miramont, who should have proceeded with a check of the barracks in the middle of the night, preferred to remain sheltered from the rain, quite comfortable. Quite comfortable, poor Miramont. But the next morning, what bedlam in camp! Three prisoners missing at roll call; holes in the fences showed their trail. The director and the commissioner of the camp, panicked, frightened, and anxious, telephoned in every direction. The camp was explored also, but the hole eliminated all hope for the searchers. Each one affirmed that the escapees would not go far. But I thought that the rain would erase all the traces and that my supply sack was well sheltered under the arch of the bridge.

This was the last time Miramont would guard anyone. He was sent to Camp Saint-Sulpice as an internee, with the black marketers and the counterfeiters of false papers. He was a good man, and after a brief moment of compassion I told myself that on liberation day he would be happier to be part of the liberated than to be among the guards.

For myself, of course, troubles began: searches, interrogations. The judiciary police of Limoges did not leave the camp for several days. Neither did I. I acted as if I had nothing to do elsewhere. I expected no visit, no mail. I also pretended to be terrified by the interrogations. I wanted to go home to my mother. What had I come to do in this terrible place—I, so young, so ignorant . . . ? Consequently, they left me alone. But suddenly the cell of the "punished" had an inhabitant! A hand appeared at the window and waved a greeting. Yes, one of the prisoners had been caught; no way to find out which one. The inspectors of the judiciary police called me back and, furious, told me that they now knew that I was an accomplice. The captured escapee had confessed. I had sworn to myself never to confess at any price. That saved me. Demoralized by the sight of that hand waving at the window, exhausted emotionally, I doubted my friends and suspected the unlucky one of having given in. But I continued to deny that I had any part in the escape until the inspectors opened the door to let me free, thus giving me proof that they had been bluffing.

Poor tattooed one. The truth was that he had given himself up, having lost his way, driven by hunger and sickness after several days of wandering. I never knew anything more of him, except his departure in the van.

A week had passed since the escape. Pastor Chaudier telephoned directly to the camp director, arguing that he had friends at Vichy and that it was scandalous to consign to camp a child of my age, who had come there freely on her personal initiative, and for whom there was nothing to reproach. He explained that I knew no one in the region and that I must be very discouraged by the solitude and abuse I had undergone. As pastor, he wished to see me; and because he could not enter the camp, he requested that I come to the parsonage at Limoges to be comforted. I was surprised to have the director suggest a visit to the pastor. But a greater surprise awaited me: Franz and Karl threw their arms around my neck upon my arrival and wept without shame. I thought them in the woods, supplied by my unknown helper. They explained that they had found only the first packages placed by me. The others must have been placed elsewhere by mistake. After a week of waiting and hunger, they decided to walk to Limoges at night, hoping to find the church without betraying themselves by asking their way. All went well, and they were now in the shelter of a friendly home. But that house was also the meeting place of the Scouts and the ladies' aid. Things could not continue this way. I decided that we should wait the minimum of days sufficient for me to leave the camp without arousing suspicion. For some time now a CIMADE team member had worked with me and would be able to replace me. Returning to Nexon, I spoke of my fatigue, my low morale, and the necessity to return to my family.

The day of departure, I had a meeting with my friends at the station at Limoges. I bought their tickets for Lyons. We went out onto the platform separately, and were to go separately into the cars. I was to circulate in the corridors, once the train was moving, in order to spot my protégés. Alas! My inspection was in vain. Neither Karl nor Franz was in the cars for Lyons. When we arrived at the station at Châteauroux, I had no time to lose. Half the cars left from there for Lyons; the other half for the Occupied Zone. I heard the cars being unhooked. I had time only to leave the train for Lyons and to jump into the moving train going toward the other zone. Interzonal controls were going to come along. It would be a catastrophe. Here was Issoudun, last station in the so-called Free Zone. And the train got under way once again when I finally recovered my escapees! The three of us jumped in the opposite direction from the moving train to land, frightened, in a wheat field in the early dawn. It was necessary to await the train for Lyons by prowling along the roads.

At Lyons, where I had not judged it wise to announce my arrival, many difficulties awaited us. First, we arrived after the curfew. In exchange for the ticket returned at the station exit, we were given a piece of paper verifying our arrival by night train. We were to meet at the top of the stairs of the Perrache station. I had never been in Lyons. I intended to ask the way from some policeman. Franz and Karl would follow me, ready to hide in a doorway at the least sign of danger. Ten minutes passed. Karl was there and questioned me with a look. Where was Franz? A quarter of an hour, twenty minutes. What had happened? Would it not be wiser for us to get out if Franz had had the misfortune to betray himself? We decided to wait another ten minutes, and we were about to give up all hope when at last Franz arrived, pale but smiling anyhow. Terrible coincidence: he had recognized an official collecting tickets at the exit as a former guard at Gurs! He preferred to run the risk of leaving by the baggage room, waiting for the right moment.

So then, our trio was on its way. I turned around from time to time to be sure that my protégés were following. It was during the blackout and their silhouettes were hard to see, but so much the better. I called to the windows from which a little light showed to ask the way to the Montée des Lilas. I even went first to a policeman, who was ready to ask for my authorization to move about, and while he was giving me explanations that I took the longest time possible to understand, my companions quietly passed by.

No one answered when we arrived at Pastor Casalis' house. But he had foreseen everything and had explained how to enter in case of his absence (at the time, I had been surprised and perplexed). I shinnied up a cement electricity pole to the top of a little wall, at which point the roof of a shed touched it. Going down the other side was easy. Entering the house itself, also. With what joy and pride I welcomed my friends to a house that I had just entered myself for the first time! Dear friends, we tasted well the sweetness of your home, the beds that felt so good after the boards in the camp dormitories. And there were even a few supplies—cans of sardines, which were a heavenly feast! I think there were also a few bottles. Karl the Communist began to understand the usefulness of pastors when they were "like this one."

I do not remember the date of that day which stands out among the others. The radio, turned on very softly, announced the capture of the island of Pantellaria by the Allies, and we made a point of celebrating the fact with a couple of drinks. It was like a held note in the uneven and hurried rhythm of our lives as runaways.

The next day I went to see another pastor at Lyons, Roland de Pury, who I knew was not afraid to become involved. I found Mme de Pury. Her husband had just been arrested and was imprisoned in the fortress of Montluc. All of this was told to me with a surprising calm, and if Madame de Pury showed any anxiety, it was because we three, so deprived and uninformed, were in a house so exposed. It was not by chance that Georges Casalis was away from his home after Roland de Pury's arrest. "He runs a strong chance of being harassed," Mme de Pury told us. "Your refuge is a trap. You must get out of there as quickly as possible." But where could we go?

The next day I went to look for the address of a possible protector who could lead the two men to the maquis. Karl and Franz, during this time, were reading the works of Karl Barth in German. They admitted that Christians of this kind would not bother them in the least in constructing a new world.

Evening had come. Someone rang the doorbell. The doors were locked, the lights turned off or invisible. Whoever it was rang again, called, and shouted. I listened. "Hey, you bum, if you don't open the door, I'll break it down." Karl asked me if there was a fireplace through which to escape; if not, would a pastor have a revolver in his home? Our hearts were beating so hard that it seemed to me they could be heard in the street. And then, heavenly voice, a woman's voice coming down from I know not which neighboring apartment: "There is no one there. They left eight or ten days ago. You can keep on knocking if you wish." Discussion. Steps going away. The remains of the bottle with which we had celebrated the fall of Pantellaria were used on the spot to calm our nerves.

The very next morning I led my men to a rehabilitation center for juvenile delinquents, directed by Gaston Riby, who was later deported. He received young delinquents whom the war, illegality, and privation had led astray. He tried to have them cooperate in social service projects. With these youths, he sometimes mixed a few illegal ones temporarily, who joined the maquis afterward. At *La Chaîne* the past, the origin, of the boarders was questioned by no one. The police were not liked there. Helping one another was the lifesaver for all. While Franz and Karl were at *La Chaîne,* I received from my co-worker at Nexon the news that the special stockade had no more inhabitants. Franz and Karl were the only ones to survive, and as I was to learn later, Fritz, I know not how.

There was an office of *La Chaîne* at Grenoble, that is to say very close to the Vercors maquis. From one *Chaîne* to the other, then from Grenoble to the maquis, Karl and Franz followed the road to liberty. Jean Weber, who directed *La Chaîne* at Grenoble, had to involve me a bit in his network. He also was jailed in Montluc at Lyons, then became president of the Liberation Committee of Grenoble.

I saw Karl and Franz again a few times during their training at Saint-Laurent-du-Pont, which was in a peat bog. They were waiting for their integration into the maquis. Their courage earned them the croix de guerre. At the time of the armistice I received a postcard from them, mailed at the border as they were returning to Germany. I do not know what has become of them. I hope that they remember that there are pastors who "understand life" and to whom they owe theirs.

12.

Along the Border

SUZANNE LOISEAU-CHEVALLEY

January 1943. I found Mme André Philip at Annecy. She described to me the routes to use. I admired her courage; she did not let fear stop her.

We were to leave together the next morning to begin the work. She was told during the night that she would no longer continue to work in that region. She left me to shift for myself, as she herself had had to do.[1]

First day. Annecy train station. I was waiting for the "packages" that I was to receive. In my blouse I had a packet of

1. Concerning this episode, Mireille Philip has sent us the following details:
"In January 1943 I had to choose, because I worked for a network connected with the maquis of the Vercors, passing the parachuted coordinators from France to Switzerland; and I was no longer in contact with CIMADE. My work with CIMADE had consisted principally of hiding Jews in the Haute-Savoie. Before passing them into Switzerland, it was necessary to wait for the agreement of the Swiss authorities. Those with whom I had cooperated a great deal were Father Folliet, chaplain of the Young Catholic Workers at Annecy, and Father Rosay, priest of Douvaine. I had a meeting with Father Folliet at six o'clock in the morning in a church where he celebrated mass. That permitted us to make our plans and guaranteed a certain security. He put me in contact with the convent at Chavanod so that I could request shelter for the women. The mother superior proved to be very understanding and kind. For the men, still by the intermediary of Father Folliet, I worked with the Trappist monastery at Tamié. After an animated discussion with the reverend prior, I was able

documents given to me by Madeleine Barot. These documents had to reach Switzerland for the security of the refugees. There was a long wait. Heavy surveillance: Germans and policemen were all over the place. I had to be careful.

A train arrived. Two women, then a third, attracted my attention. They were carrying poorly tied bundles; panic was on their faces. They saw me and their expressions brightened; they had the impression of being taken in hand. They were armed with false Alsatian papers. One of them was the sister of the writer Stefan Zweig. We took the train as far as Annemasse after I had given a ticket to each one so that we could sit in adjacent compartments. Suddenly, one of them ran into my compartment. *"Fräulein,* I lost the ticket that you gave me!"* There was amazement among the other travelers. The women were nervous wrecks, incapable of controlling their panic. I explained to the conductor that I could pay for the lost ticket, and I rearranged some of the scattered packages. All the travelers were upset. The trip was going to be difficult. At Annemasse I had to go back and forth to "pass" each of the three women separately. They were afraid to show their cards. My presence reassured them.

We had to go eleven miles to get to Douvaine. It was necessary to take the bus pretty far to avoid inspection. We decided to obtain permission to hide the boys there. They were admitted under the pretext of being on a religious retreat. In their company I often covered the many kilometers that led to the Trappists. I conducted some and brought back others whose turn had come to cross the border.

"As for Father Rosay, his hospitable parsonage sheltered me many times, even at night, with boys in great danger. Members of the Young Catholic Workers lent their support in looking for and showing the best routes. These two priests—alas!—are dead: one shot, the other deported, victims of their unpretentious devotion, which had its roots in a living faith that left a great impression on me. Two brothers in the Young Catholic Workers, one nineteen and the other twenty years old, suffered the same fate for the same reasons.

"I am overwhelmed by a feeling of humility and gratitude to many of these refugees who became friends. Whether it was at Rivesaltes, or le Chambon, or in the Haute-Savoie, they often gave me the example of a dignity and courage that the circumstances made particularly impressive. It would have been so easy for them to founder in discouragement, fear, and egotism. For some their faith, for others their simple human quality, was at the base of that attitude. Finally, it was we who, in helping them, received most from them. It was so much easier to be in our place than in theirs—a place that we had chosen ourselves, and which in my opinion was privileged and normal."

for the same reason to leave the bus before Douvaine. We were loaded with packages. The walk was nerve-racking.

The priest received us graciously, but he was worried. He was being watched more and more, and when I told him of the sudden departure of Mme Philip, he was hardly reassured. The simple folk who helped him in his work could no longer continue to show the crossing points without very great danger. It would be less dangerous for us to leave right away and without help. The priest drew me a little map on a scrap of paper. Outside, a freezing fog blurred the shapes of things. We could not see much ahead. Perhaps that would help. In spite of my hesitation about taking all the parcels, we took them anyway. In order to carry them, I was to make two trips beyond the police post on the priest's bicycle, then we would meet and walk together. Twice, customs men on bicycles passed us. They were curious to know if I was going to cross the border with the women. Of course we said no, but we had the strong impression that we were awaited farther on.

We could not go back. Where would we go? We still had about four miles to go. The fog became thicker and thicker, the cold more and more biting. Here was a road to the left. Was it the one indicated to me? But I did not see the cross drawn on the map. I went on alone to try to reconnoiter the place while my friends waited for me. I was not alone long before two gendarmes called me, demanding my papers. Seeing that I had double nationality (French and Swiss), they accused me of trying to make a fortune helping Jews cross the border. I could not give a valid explanation for my presence. At the end of the road there was only one farm, whose inhabitants were already endangered. So I had to follow the gendarmes to the border post. I was afraid for the women and for the papers that I was hiding. It did not take long. A gendarme told me harshly to leave and not to roam around there anymore. Did they want to catch me in the act? I hoped that my companions had waited for me. While I was still within sight of the post, I was stupefied to see them approaching. The gendarmes on bicycles quickly caught up with them. What should I do? Continue on my way with the priest's bike and let the inevitable happen, without running the risk of being arrested myself and not being able to continue my work any longer? My choice was quickly made. I was convinced that there was always a chance to save what seemed lost. I joined the little group. "Are you with these women?" asked the gendarme. "No, but I must help them." The only solution left to me was to convince the gendarmes. They encircled us, and we found ourselves on the way to the border post. I had to get rid of my documents. It was not easy, but it was night and the fog was even denser, which helped to counteract the gendarmes' flashlights. I stumbled and fell and threw my packet as far as possible into the ditch. I was to find it by crawling in the wet grass when I came back.

Here we were at the post. Examination of identity cards. A gendarme declared them false, that the women were probably Jewish. He telephoned; an inspector was going to come and they would be arrested. With the energy of desperation, I defended their cause. I had to win the gendarmes over at once. "No, these women are not Jewish. But even if they were, if they were threatened by the Germans, do the French have to hinder their flight to freedom?" I spoke of the camps, of deportations. My refugees also spoke. A great fear came over me of what they might unwittingly say that would endanger CIMADE. They wanted to explain that I was not a "passer" and that CIMADE had taken them in charge for nothing. I had paid for the tickets, and they would not be sent back at the border. They said all this in spite of my desperate gestures. One of the gendarmes even said, "We are not asking you for all that!" Outside there was the marching of soldiers, orders in German. Terrible anxiety. Then it seemed that the patrol was going away. The relief man left for his rounds. The one left with us brusquely let us go. "Get out, and don't stay near the border." I could scarcely believe my ears. Were they afraid to show themselves human when they were together? Did they want to save us from being caught by the German patrol?

We found ourselves again in the night, free but still having much to fear. I abandoned the cumbersome bicycle at the crossroads. We took the little path, finally identified, that went along the border. Suddenly I heard a man's voice. "Can you help me? I heard everything. I was near the post." It was a navy officer in danger. He had succeeded in crossing the border the first time but had been sent back by Swiss customs. He had crawled here. Yes, later, if he would stay there, I would try to come back. Continuing on the path in the night, we saw a tiny light in the distance. The farm was there. In total darkness it was not easy to find a path to cross the border stream. Each tree and each bush seemed to threaten us. When my friends were on the other side, we were too emotional, too unstrung, to have a feeling of deliverance.

They were safe. The navy officer was waiting in a shack. Tomorrow there would be daylight and he could get the necessary papers to take the route for Spain. Curled up in a barn, I looked for a little warmth; I thought of our work, sustained by the prayers of others, of the whole team in Brens. When all seemed to me to be lost, I thought of those who prayed, and I felt supported as if by wings.

Again the station at Annecy. A young woman showed me my "packages" and disappeared in the crowd. On a bench were three children, poor, darling little things, two little girls three and four years old and a baby about one year old. The tired baby was leaning against one sister; the other held a small bundle. These children were Polish Jews whose parents had been deported. The paper work had been done for them in order for them to be received in Switzerland. Now to pass them. They seemed exhausted. We remained on the bench a few moments in order for the little ones to gain a bit of confidence in the new person caring for them. The baby cried. She was thirsty. The station lunchroom was not far.

We had to go past the police inspection stand. I pushed the oldest ahead. "Go quickly with that lady. We are coming right behind you." Then I told the other, "Go join your sister." They passed unnoticed, and I followed with the baby in my arms.

Once more we were at the priest's home in Douvaine. He was moved to see the little ones. With a diaper found in their bundle, I changed the baby. She was burning with fever. The oldest one told me with a worried tone that we should put her to bed because she had the measles. Already the little arms clung to my neck. The children did not want to see me go away. In their eyes there was such anxiety, such a need to be reassured.

The comings and goings at the rectory were never-ending. I was brought a handsome eight-year-old boy, with a sensible and determined look. He was Hungarian. His parents had been deported. He showed me what he possessed in his little suitcase and the papers that he had hidden in the lining of the lid. It would not be possible to take this suitcase. He had this heart-breaking remark: "I have lost my parents. Without my papers, I shall be nothing at all. Even my name will be lost." I very neatly sewed his papers inside his jacket, and he was content. He helped me to write the names of the little girls on their clothing, and we left.

I bundled up the baby, holding her in my arms. Very soon the other little one did not want to walk, and I had to sit her on my shoulders while the big one held onto my skirt. The boy walked bravely in front of us and felt that we went very slowly because of the whimpering girls. Would we arrive before night? The burden was too heavy for me. A French customs official joined us and took one of the little girls on his bicycle. He showed me a place to cross secretly: I should go as far as Veigy (the other location on the border was guarded by a German patrol), and there wait for him behind the church until dark. We took the road for Veigy; the customs man continued on his way. A woman passed us and said, "Beware of that customs man!" Thus I learned that a bounty was offered by the Germans for catching the "passers" in the act. Worry gripped me, but I continued along my way; the baby cried— she was sick.

We waited a long time behind the church. It was completely dark. I pressed the baby against me to keep her warm and quiet. The others leaned against the wall. They kept asking if we were leaving soon. A gendarme roamed past and asked me harshly: "What are you waiting to cross for? You are known: the girl with the turban."

How did he recognize me in the dark? We started out again, but I did not know the place to cross. At each step we stumbled. The boy, who had walked as a man before, could not any longer. I heard steps in the night. It was a boy from the area who showed me the road, the stream, and beyond, Switzerland. I found footing on the stones, and once on the other side of the stream, I quickly placed the baby on the lap of the oldest beside a rock. Her sister pressed against her, and all of them, the boy included, burst into tears. Cry loudly so that some guard will come pick you up, poor kids! I hid behind the trees, and in the night, in the light of the lanterns, I saw the customs men and knew they were saved.

January 1944. With a refugee sent from le Chambon-sur-Lignon, whom I was leading to Switzerland, I fell and hurt my leg while going over barbed wire along the Annemasse road. Lost in the fog and night, we went in circles between the lines. A man's voice called in German, "Who's there?" We thought all was lost and followed the soldier. When the light struck his belt, we saw that we were with a German-Swiss! The police at the Swiss post were very angry. They explained to me that the Swiss police were better informed than I could imagine. They read several notations to me dating from January 1943. Without admitting it, of course, I recognized them, and in every one I was "the girl with the turban."

13.

The Bridge of Manne-en-Royans

PASTOR E. C. FABRE

What a setting for the drama!

How transparent the water of the Bourne! One of the clearest rivers in France, they say; one of the coldest. It gushes out upstream at the Goule Noire bridge. They say that the temperature in summer is not over forty-two degrees where it comes out of the ground. Where is this Pont-de-Manne? Take the road on the left bank at Romans-sur-Isère. There is Saint-Nazaire-en-Royans, where in a red burst the waters of the Isère meet those of the Bourne. They take a moment to mix, and for a very good reason: nature and industry. On going up the Bourne toward Pont-en-Royans as far as the bridge where two roads appear, you are at the Pont-de-Manne.

Today you no longer see the little house built against the

bridge, behind which was the long building that is the hotel. The house, constructed for the toll officials, has been torn down recently. It obstructed the view of the river from the hotel. But that house, with one large room downstairs open on all four sides, was the perfect place for those who had to be "sheltered" in that unfortunate time.

Thanks to Abbé Glasberg and his friends, this hotel had been rented to serve as a refuge for a few liberated people from Gurs and other camps. The abbé's committee had placed an Egyptian director as head of the house, and the owner of the refuge had agreed to live with his family in the outbuildings, very simply furnished. How were these people chosen to be here? We have never been able to pierce the mystery. No one talked about it.

It was in the beginning of summer 1942 that CIMADE told me of the presence at Pont-de-Manne of several refugees from Gurs whom they held dear. Among them were Jews and resisters to the Nazis. There were about fifty boarders in all. The shelter seemed safe. The German police, acting through the French *milice,* did not at first grasp the role that this wide-open refuge could play. They accepted its existence, which was the thing that mattered.

In those first warm days of 1942, the buzzing of life came up from the meadows, the brushwood, and the forests, suddenly delivered from the grip of cold. The news came to me that I was to go to Pont-de-Manne to meet the guests at the refuge. There was the house, the one room. Almost all the refugees were there. Missing were those terrified by despair. Among the latter were those who stayed in their room, others who distracted themselves by any means. One must not think, look, understand, or listen. The others were there, those who dared, between the open windows of the building. There were the Ebbeckes, the Peterses (he was first tenor at the Berlin Opera), the Gaucks, the "politicals," M. Blumenfeld, Mme Marx and her daughter, who were part of the group coming from Gurs and especially watched over by CIMADE. What is there to say, to do, when one is "in life" while the others are "in death"? Be still, watch and look, listen and listen again.

And to the house by the Bourne, in the serenity of that luminous day, the rising storm was coming, the tempest born of bodies and hearts. All the variables and variations, the contrasts and nuances, the violence and gentleness, the conflict and the concord, made up the torrential stream tumbling the grains of sand and carrying off the earth that gives life. Drop by drop until the earth is carried away from the roses that are going to die. There were, however, great silences. One had to catch his breath. It was also necessary to have contact again with "the others," to cling to them or to clash with them. It was the journey. Even while listening, I thought of the *Passions* of Johann Sebastian Bach, of those specific moments, either before or after the chorales, when certain phrases were being sung or when "It Is Finished" was being sung. It is necessary for the instruments alone to have their word, so that the word of man can have its full weight. And we were all together in it.

As discreetly as possible, I looked at the different faces, with such varied looks. I listened to the voices, which ran the gamut of ways to speak, to live, to suffer, to hope and to despair, to guess the death that approached step by step. And all this happened in a setting so simple, so peaceful, so perfectly on the human scale. The internal tension was only the greater in its contrast; it was less intense out in the light because together we refused to lose our heads, to lose heart.

I see again the faces of the Ebbeckes, the husband there for his wife. Without her, he would not have been there. She was Jewish; he was not. She was alarmed already by the evil that approached him and would take him. I see again the Peterses. She looked at him admiringly in the face of threatening discovery. He, who was not timid before a crowd, was intimidated by her, who was so small beside him.

I see again the Gaucks. He was a rough-hewn man, an iron-willed Social Democrat, so gently watchful over his "turtle-dove," who tremblingly gave herself to the task at hand, whatever happened.

I see again M. Blumenfeld, and the fineness of his look and

his voice, which conveyed the measure of his courage. He was a man ready to die facing straight ahead.

I see again Mme Marx gazing at her daughter, a young girl, without illusion, without undue emotion, but with such tenderness and with many *why's*. Why had she come into the world only to end up there? And the look of the daughter where flashes of the joy of living were meant for her mother, where the movements of the lips and forehead could not hide the fight against fear.

I see again the look of so many others whose names I have lost. Oh, shame on my memory! Forgive me for no longer being able to name you, but to write your names was to risk surrendering you . . .

We found ourselves in the house. In your midst, friends so little known, I felt a little like some kind of magnifying glass in the sun. I received and concentrated a few rays of hope and suffering. What fire, small though it be, could be born in that instant? After the storms of the camps, you lived a few days of respite, but one should not delude you. Within these four walls, one question passes from one to the other, recharging and discharging its terrifying potential: love, beauty, justice. The Ebbeckes, the Peterses, the Gaucks, the Marxes, threatened by the heel of hate, lassitude, lies, horror. Is it possible? Is it simply the human situation? Think of the masses—to the ends of the earth. It cannot be the ultimate condition . . . But if it were true? And the house becomes a vase where the essence of suffering and hope is distilled and is gone with the wind of springtime.

The meetings, the acquaintances, the plans. What would happen? We waited. Going down very often from Vassieux or Chapelle-en-Vercors by the Grands-Goulets route, I stopped each time to be brought up to date on the menace. Nothing.

July 1942. The Ebbeckes were in bad shape. Regarding him, was it already the omen of the sickness that would take him in 1946? As for her, non-Aryan, recognized because of the fame of her husband, we had reason to think that she had been denounced to the shameful *milice*. We had to get them out of there. We had no means. Our home, in Romans-sur-Isère, was so closely watched by the several informers imported into that loyal country that there could be no question of taking them with us. That would be the same as turning them over. They had to be in a quiet place, not too far away so as not to lose the contact that they so badly needed more than ever. They needed a little "honeymoon" before what was to happen to them, something they foresaw in a confused way. What gratitude we owed to M. Royannet, yesterday unknown to us, today offering us the refuge of a temporarily unused oil press. It was difficult to get to, well hidden under the trees, a house that a stranger would never suspect. The memory of that trip into the valley—their baggage now visible now invisible—how different from the baggage that they carried at the time of their first flight! Their life was threatened by gnawing evil and watchful police. There was the refuge: the heavy door, the millstone, the angled pedestal on which it turned, the hearth where the mash was heated, the press, now the odor—so peculiar and varied depending upon the direction of the wind. Everything here was yellow and brown, perfume and color. A tiny window, just big enough to see the heavy branches that leaned toward the house as if to protect it from despair. Everything was bathed in the humidity of the earth and air and mist rising from the current of the river. It was their Venice for a week, their Koenig-See, their salvation.

One Sunday in July, wanting to think things through for the others and for the family, it was absolutely necessary for me to take a few hours of silence, a retreat out of reach of the interruptions for an indispensable inner sifting of thought.

For such a long time now we had had alerts day and night, the shocking upheaval of special cases, the trips with headlights extinguished from Romans to Die by the Rousset Pass and the famous descent, the game of hide-and-seek with the *milice* in the gorges of the Bourne to the Combe-Laval or the Lente Forest. And the visit one night of the *"grand chef,"* full of questions and threats. All that might cloud one's vision. Fluster is forbidden to him who has the care of souls. It was necessary to leave the children and the others hidden in the city in the care of the woman who watched over the house, and to get to the farm, the most isolated, perhaps, of the Vercors at the Saint-Alexis Pass. M. and Mme Doveau lived there. We had known each other for years. During the summer, the cattle from the low country were brought there to feed on the immense pastures spread out from the plateau to the dizzying cliffs. Beginning with the first nice days, the owner, M. Doveau, would go out to place supplies in the almost virgin forests reaching from Glandasse to the Grand-Veymont and the Grande-Moucherolle. Once the deposits of supplies were in safe places, he began his search for medicinal plants. He left Monday morning and returned Saturday. After gathering and drying them, he would start out again, this time with a donkey. "I need that solitude and the forest animals in order to live," he often told me. He was a unique help in those hard times.

I would sleep in the barn, with which I was familiar. There were several exits, and if necessary, there were the hay chutes over the stalls. Just what I needed. I left my motorcycle behind the piles of wood. "If someone asks you whose it is, you tell them that a person looking for mushrooms left it there. Goodnight and thanks."

The barn. The darkest of nights. The noise of the cows chewing their cuds, scratching, stamping, mooing. A place to curl up must be chosen in view of the always possible "visit." It could not be in this year's hay, nor too far from a door, nor in hay that was too old, full of prickles. But there were a few bunches of straw and a window facing the forest. The old tent cloth was spread out. Everything was possible except silence! To the cows were added the rats and the noise of insects of every kind. That still would have been nothing if there had not been thoughts. They exuded from every crack and flowed from every sheet of tin on the roof. They made an uproar in the middle of the night. I had to struggle for inner silence and for listening and for decisions, for essential options—those on which everything would hinge. The tensest dialogue is one which almost or completely becomes a monologue: "Yes or no? Is it serious? Is it worth it? Can one involve the future of his loved ones, the children who have not asked to enter the arena? Are we led? By whom? By what? Is it possible that we

161

are loved by a sovereign God? Is he weak? Then of what use is he? Is he strong? Then what is he doing? The deported children, the multiplying of horrors, the organized terrors, the senseless wars, these theologies of fools or choirboys, the choice of institution rather than event?" In the barn, everything was ringing with these themes, all was a fugue, everything was counterpoint . . . Why? . . . repetition in every key.

In that night of why's arose all the why's heard or known, recent or ancient, the stammered or shouted why's, in one faith or in another or in the absence of faith. They arose and were such that there was nothing left but to flee in whatever form of unfaith. And that was not thinkable—there and then.

It was then that a voice began to be heard, very deformed at first by traditions and habits, by repetition and convention. Slowly it imposed itself, finding its own precise tone, situation, and condition. For an instant it was audible only in the words of the phrase: "Why . . . Why . . ." A silence under the power of an irresistible gentleness imposed itself. I heard more clearly: "Why, why . . . I said it before you and for you, and with you I say it, even here and with the friends at Pont-de-Manne and elsewhere, be they this or that. I said it, and I say it, and I shall say it again and for all men, particularly for those who do not even suspect that I said it and cried it out before them. Go down with and into the why of men. I am there with you." And it was this certainty that I must not remain in solitude, that I must no longer stay there, that I must take to the road when day came, that I must . . .

Before dawn I watched for the first rays of light, the first glimmerings in the forest, the first dance of trees animated by daylight, from classic to baroque, from the pines to the beech trees. There they were. All was ready. It was still necessary to wait for the kitchen window to open so that I could take leave of my friends. A hinge squeaked. A shadowy movement in the opening. Surprise—entrée—explanations. "You are crazy. So long." Never had the descent from La Chapelle or from Grands-Goulets been made at such speed. A skid on the last hairpin turn. Nothing serious. Romans was there. Our house at the top of avenue Berthelot. The motor without its muffler announced my arrival. There was the gate, and on the other side was she who had heard everything, who waited, who knew and yet did not know.

"Who sent you word?"

"Of what?"

"Last night there was a police raid at Pont-de-Manne. Go quickly. They are waiting for you."

Anything that could be compromising was left in those open, hesitant, yet firm hands there at the edge of the garden. Anything that could accentuate the demeanor of an ecclesiastical functionary was stressed. On the way to Écancière and Saint-Nazaire-en-Royans, the police recognized the local pastor and greeted him lightly. The bridge on the Bourne, our house—no one. At the hotel everything seemed dead, burned out, paralyzed. The Egyptian in his office seemed dismayed. (We were to learn later that he had known the night before that a raid would take place!) Disorder in the bedrooms. Shadows entered and let slip a word to me in their language: "Quickly, go see M. Bitsch. He'll tell you . . . It is frightful. Tell us where we can flee—the forest?"

I had time to whisper a word to one of the calmer men: "The forest. They have never dared stick their nose or their foot in it, but it is not easy to reach."

And again the Egyptian coming and going and trying to guess what was being said. Then, I was on top of a kind of ladder at the home of the proprietor of the hotel. Mme Bitsch had left for a few days' rest with her family and had not seen the raid during the night.

The friend, looking and sounding as if pierced with thorns, said to me: "Yes, last night the *milice* and perhaps camouflaged Germans arrived. I am German-Swiss, so I understood. They gave orders. People shouted. They searched; the people hid. The women begged and cried, but they were seized. The people fought. The *milice* pulled them by the arms and pushed them into the truck like animals going to slaughter. For the moment they have taken only the Jews. Poor Mme Marx and her daughter. If you had seen them . . . They remained straight and calm and proud. You see, there is almost no one left. Some

of them are at the Saint-Jean jail, the 'politicals' perhaps. I
don't know. The gendarmes from Saint-Jean came by this
morning. They said you could go to see them at the jail, at the
gendarmerie, you know, upstairs. Gauck was left here. His
wife and the little Lévy woman are hiding in the bushes at the
entrance of the forest. It won't be easy to get them out of there.
There is only the road, the river, and the mountain cliffs."

Time could not be wasted. First, to the prison at Saint-Jean.
The gendarmes had said to go right away. The two young
women would have to wait. They were not in too great danger.
They would be supplied with food and would have blankets. At
the gendarmerie, I learned that all that the authorities of the
area could do would be done to avoid the worst. The prisoners
felt it and whispered that the gendarmes had helped and encouraged them, bringing them a glass of water, the visit, of
which the Prisoner of Love spoke. Alas! We would lose trace of
almost all of them. Almost all were lost. Peters was pulled out
of there only to be assassinated later on.

Back again to the hotel. Life had begun to pick up. The
shadow of the Egyptian prowled about. Was this house a trap?
Dear M. Bitsch took me into a room so that we could not be
overheard, and told me that M. David, the Kahns, and two
others were hidden in a storeroom closed by a glass door hidden
by some furniture. M. Blumenfeld was going to be lodged in a
landowner's home in the little village of Combovin at the foot
of the Vercors wall, on the west side, toward the Rhone Valley.
The others would follow other paths, at the end of which
liberty would open its arms.

But how could we deliver the two young Jewish women from
the closed and silent world where they were? It was a beautiful
night. Gauck knew how to reach them. The *milice* did not stay
too close to the Vercors forests. They were happy just to watch
the roads coming from it. That was at least something. The
women would have to be passed through the holes of the net.
That night at Romans, the plan was decided. The next morning
a mother, leader of older Girl Scouts, would take several girls
who were authorized by their parents to take part in the adventure. The knapsacks were stuffed with food for the day and

two Girl Scout uniforms. False cards were ready. My daughter was in the group. In the bus, no trouble. Elsewhere the group passed an inspection point without being counted. They found the two young women, who changed clothes. They took the bus again and passed through the control, not without nervousness. Then we had to find a lodging for each of the two escapees.

Mme Gauck reacted rather well. The camps had not left their mark on her. We took her to a family of farmers, very humble folk, discerning and courageous. The children were too young to be an obstacle to the new presence. It was there that she would wait and find her husband at the time of the Liberation. For Mme Lévy, it was another story. She was so strongly marked by the debilitating force of the camps that she was prostrate most of the day. She no longer got up from the divan put at her disposal. She took her meals in bed, like a sick child. When we had to leave the city to flee the increasing German threats, she returned to Pont-de-Manne and from there followed the channel of Abbé Glasberg's protégés toward other refuges.

Mme Peters was at our house at Romans as long as the house was not too dangerous for her. Her husband was placed as a farm worker near Die, thanks to Pastor Pierre Loux.

Dear Peters, you were officially a gardener. We would see you coming and immediately you would lead us in the cantatas and the *Passions* of Bach. Many still remember your evenings of song. Perhaps you were singing in a low voice on the road from Die to Chamaloc or Romeyer—I don't know—when the German police met you. Their sudden appearance made you lose your head. You threw yourself into a ditch. The motorcyclists came back, grabbed you, questioned, tortured, and beat you at the side of the road. Dear Peters, what energy Mme Peters showed after that shock, she who was so fragile! She had to earn her daily bread doing housework in different homes. Habitué of the opera, she lived in stairways and kitchens, doing heavy work. She was able to hang on until her departure for free Germany. She had fought, going forward, as a true witness of the final victory.

Former guests of Pont-de-Manne, the old tollhouse no longer exists. It is better that way. No place, no memorial should be placed there. May a red rosebush be planted there. Before writing these lines, I went back to see M. and Mme H. Bitsch and the ruins, the Bourne, the flowers and poplars. It is not possible that all this had lived and suffered in vain. That which was sown is still in the furrows of the world, for tomorrow.

14.

Order out of Disorder

PASTOR E. C. FABRE

Things were going badly. The flow of the hunted ones increased in the valley. We were submerged. The net was filling; the drag-net was going to be dreadful. I went one night as far as Annecy. Brother Chapal and his house were there. Both were more and more suspect. One must double his caution, look like a beggar or a deliveryman. In spite of everything, inside a smile reigned with peace.

We were going together to ask advice of the highest author-ity in the area, the commander of the gendarmerie. May he be blessed! There was no remedy; there was only the poor pallia-tive of making known afar that everything here was more dan-gerous from day to day. But there was the dialogue, the search-ing together, the exchange in these hard times, the reality of sympathy, which was a considerable force.

Then I was again at Chedde, and Father Berger was wait-ing for me at the top of his stairs. The threshold of that home, that entrance so simple, that large cross on the wall, a few flowers: nothing else. We were together to listen, if possible to hear, to understand, to receive all because we had nothing, nothing. The country was saturated with people. And the bewildered arrivals, their most elementary common sense swallowed up in fear, lent themselves to all the stupidities possible either wanting to be recognized or making themselves undesirable. One could write a book!

What was happening higher up, beyond the steep slope of Chedde, beyond the Servoz? With heart and body heavy enough to collapse, it was necessary to trust yourself to the famous mountain train that shakes you enough to break your bones. In the station at Houches, there could be police spies and we had to seize the opportunity of the stop at the viaduct at Vaudagne. Here in the cold woods, the paths cover you, entwine you, hide you from the cloak and dagger people. The Chavants: all seemed dead. Houses must be avoided. From a little break in the fields, a trail led to G. Lasserre's chalet. Silence. A little boy opened the door: "Yes, Mama is here." She came, looking wan. We went quickly into the living room: a corner, a small table, two chairs. "What news of your husband [a prisoner]?" Silence.

"A message has come. He has been sent to a discipline camp. What is going to happen?" Silence before the little window opening upon those terrific mountains.

"And here, how are things going with you?"

"There are too many of us. We cannot hold on any longer. The children and I have to do everything." Silence again before the cold of the autumn that flowed from the glaciers. "A cup of tea." Not a five o'clock tea of ladies and teacups; but that which is closer to the communion cup, in suffering and hope; the night that comes in the daytime also.

The little boy who opened the door came closer. "Tell me, Mama, when will it no longer be church?" (Imposed silence.) Indeed, in the last few moments a full dozen guests sheltered in the house had recovered confidence, coming and going. We decided that all the "hidden ones" in the house would leave as soon as possible. For them and for the family that received them, it was absolutely necessary. It was the most elementary security.

Among the sheltered ones, there were two or three known friends who would help to convince the others. I went up to the rooms and found the Ebbeckes. He was in bad shape, but he understood. She went to convince the women. Another one to tell and upon whom we could count was Dr. Mayer. Where was he? No one knew. I found him in the little shed built in the meadow, cutting wood for Mme Lasserre. Dear friend Mayer, if only everyone had had your understanding of the times and events . . . Cutting wood with so much care and humility while your companions were being served in bed. I thought of a few psalms which had been lived before being written by those of your people.

One group went up toward Chamonix. The other group would be hidden in the shepherds' huts, which were abandoned at this time of year, up above the Anterne Pass. Rendezvous was to be at the foot of the first pole of the electric line that went up toward the sanatoriums on the plateau and which was at the base of the slopes of Chedde, not far from the factories. The pole could easily be seen from the train. They were to gather there without using flashlights or making noise. It was made very clear that if the little group was visible from the road or the train, no one would go find them to lead them out. The group would play into the hands of the police.

We went up to Chamonix to see how things were going. Very badly. The adjutant of the gendarmerie said to us: "Don't let them gather anymore in the streets, and they had better hide their unusual costumes. And don't let them beg for tobacco, particularly the women; they shouldn't be seen so much. I can't guarantee anything if this continues." How many, without knowing it, and who will never know it, owe their lives to that officer. They never saw in him anything but a functionary like the others!

The train descended. The Vaudagne viaduct! The slopes of Chedde. Were they at the foot of the pole? Were they visible? Were they hidden? Were they there?

But what could we do? What were our efforts in the midst of these tragedies of every sort?

15.

On the Wisdom of the Humble . . .

PASTOR E. C. FABRE

The title of this chapter refers to a simple person's knowledge of plants and their particular qualities. It can also apply to the communication that is established in the human jungle between unpretentious people, without special talents, at the level where existence itself is in the balance. These few lines are written to give the floor, if you will, to a few unknown people who took part in the adventure.

We were on the station platform at La Roche-sur-Foron. I had just dispersed a group of candidates. We were waiting for the train to come up. They were not to gather on the departure platform until the last minute. I would give them the sign by putting on my knapsack. I was sitting alone beside a wagon and reading, or pretending to read, the newspaper. A station employee passed very near me and, while swinging his lantern, said, "You have some more again this morning?" I half-pretended astonishment, waiting to see what would follow. He studied me for an instant and added, "This morning there will be an inspection on all the trains after Bonneville." What could

I do? To leave them on the station platform would be impossible. They would all gather and attract attention. The trainman continued without hesitating: "Have them board the train. Make them get off in small groups at each station, like tourists on an outing. They can take the following train." I overcame all the arguing and got them to agree on the stops, the details. None of them fell into the trap that day.

I had never noticed that employee before. I never met him again.

I was in the station at Saint-Marcellin above the Isère River, between Grenoble and Valence. Regularly each week I stayed in this little town until the express between Saint-Marcellin and Romans came, around midnight. It was the time when, in order to keep awake, one smoked I don't know what mixture of string, straw, and other stuff. The express arrived, and as always I was getting ready to climb into the car at the end when the conductor came up to me, looked me in the eye, and rapidly murmured a few words: "Checklist, searches along the way, arrests." Before I had time to think, he opened a locked freight car and pushed me in, saying, "You do go to Romans, don't you?" I found myself in complete darkness and could distinguish a pile of blankets only with my hands, feet, knees, and head. I could do nothing except wait until someone opened the door.

If only the conductor would not forget! If only he himself was not an agent setting a trap! I carefully listened to every noise. I recognized by the sound the moment we crossed the viaduct of Saint-Lattier and when we reached the part of the track that pressed close to the mountain. I also recognized the peculiar sound of the train on the plain of Saint-Paul, the approach to the station signaled by the clash of the switches, the echoing sound when the train entered the station, and the end of the braking.

The noise of a lock. The door slid open, and a hand was extended; I shook it. A signal; the train left again. I never learned anything about what happened that night. The sky was starry. The noise of the express crossing the big bridge over the Isère came back to me. The town seemed to be asleep. A simple thing could awaken it, like the day when a crowd of women lay down on the tracks in the station to prevent an S.T.O. [forced labor] train from leaving. Or like that early morning when the whole town came to the station to welcome, without advance notice, a trainload of mountain folk from Tarentaise and Maurienne.

16.

The Search for
the Team That Did Not Return

PASTOR E. C. FABRE

They had not yet returned. They had been gone for three days. There were signs of bad weather; clouds were gathering lower and lower. The Buet was over ten thousand feet high and the ridge of the Cheval-Blanc was quickly covered with ice. It was a long way for someone carrying a load and tired. It was necessary to go to the Audemards' at Chedde to get news. It was their thirteen-year-old son who had left with André Morel. One had to go without attracting attention because the house was known as a relay station.

They had not yet come back. With extraordinary self-control, the young mother gave a few details about their departure. The people had been difficult, unknown. André Morel and René had had to take them even though they were not used to doing this, almost under threat. The father was still working at the factory but would soon return. Between rapid replies, the young woman left the kitchen and went into her little daughter's bedroom. They feared that she had polio.

J. G. Wagner, Emile Bernis, and I found ourselves in the alleys of the mill town, crushed by the absence, the noise of the rapids, the confusion caused by the loss of security that we felt, the humming of the factory. We waited at the exit to make our plans with René's father. We heard singing coming from the doors of some houses. How could one still sing?

The decision was made: in bringing up certain boarders of Mme Lasserre to the chalets of Villy, we would take the same route that André Morel and René must have taken. M. Audemard would come with us because he knew better than anyone else what was called the Enfer de Trez-les-Eaux and the passages on the crest of the Cheval-Blanc. J. G. Wagner and Emile Bernis were part of the team. Our sacks were quickly ready. Because we would certainly have to serve as porters also, we took a minimum for ourselves: tubes of concentrated milk, powdered cereals, dried fruit, and sugar in our pockets; ice axes, ropes, and compasses because the fog was heavy and landmarks were rare in places.

In any other season and circumstances and company the route would have been a lovely hike of twenty-four hours at the most. We were to pass below the sanatorium of Guébriand, at the foot of the peak of Pormenaz, Ecuelle, Villy, the abandoned chalets, the Salenton Pass, the Buet, the crest of the Cheval-Blanc, and the Vieux Pass, going around the base of the Corbeaux summit, which was at the border. But we had to lead our *passants* farther on to the Barberine. The return would be by the Montets Pass or by the Loria pinnacle, which was not frequented, and the chalets of Loria. I had previously hiked to that citadel, where one could see without being seen.

Evening fell quickly. Those who were given the word in the morning were at the rendezvous. We had to threaten to throw their flashlights in the rapids if they used them. The climb under the cables, from pole to pole, was steep for beginners and those not so young. The complaints started: "Carry our sacks." "We can't walk if we can't see where we're going." In the beginning we remained unmoved. We had to preserve our strength for farther on. We, too, were carrying heavy loads because we were going to supply a group already settled in the abandoned chalets on this route. For those whom we were going to see again, and for those whom we were bringing, we carried supplies for several days—a side of mutton, flour, sugar, bacon, and butter.

The complaints became more insistent, and threats succeeded the complaints. "It is shameful to treat us this way. We are going to sit here on the ground and wait for daylight." We were obliged to remain deaf. The trip was very slow. If only day would not break while we were still in the zone that could be watched at a great distance with binoculars. What had our *passants* done all day long? They didn't get up until noon. Had they helped anyone, even to chop some wood?

When we judged that we were between the Aiguille Noire and the rocks of the Fiz, we stopped and put their sacks on top of ours. And then we were on our way again. "Another hour," we said, "and the climb will be less difficult. Walk along without grumbling, please. Complaints and gossiping are more tiring than the climb." New protests, new complaints. "You accepted this route. You said that you had climbed mountains—show it."

"We can't see anything."

"Neither can we."

The climb became exhausting for us with double and triple loads. Would we arrive with enough strength left to look for the two missing persons, to bring back one of them if he were wounded? Relieved of their sacks, our "volunteers" dragged behind. We had to pull them, push them—those unfortunates who, to hear them talk, had scaled the Meije or the Cervin! We refused to give in to the wish for frequent halts. Nothing cuts strength more than chilling the muscles. The business world had ill-prepared most of them. Two of them seemed to be totally out of their element in this world where money had no power.

We were at the threshold of the high valley. The going would be easier. The sawtooth of the Diosaz was not very far to our right. The path going up to the chalets became visible. We halted. The sacks were put down and redistributed. "Here is

175

the path for you to follow. Walk in two groups, leaving about a quarter of an hour apart. We'll go on ahead to make necessary preparations. We'll unload and come back to meet you if we can. Think of those we're searching for. We still have a long way to go to find them." There was some muttering, but also some very clear acquiescence. We left at a better pace. Where were the two we were searching for? Had they fallen into an ambush? Had they slipped on some rock? Ice was forming even then, soundlessly and invisibly. Was one of them wounded? A few clouds announced the dawn. The mass of rocks of the Fiz seemed overwhelmingly menacing.

The Ecuelle chalets did not give us any clues to the solution of our problem. Finally, the Villy chalets. A few traces. They had passed by there. We decided to take a brief rest and then go to meet the two groups. At the rate that we had walked, we were a good hour ahead of them. We also had to leave the promised supplies with those who were waiting here and who had heard nothing.

Scarcely had we begun to relax our aching muscles when the sound of voices came to us, and beams of flashlights. It was the police who guarded the borders. We prepared ourselves so that we would seem to be innocent hikers, after having hidden our supplies under a pile of old wood in a corner that might serve for cheese-making in season. Bad situation. If only André Morel and René, along with the couple and their would-be porter whom they were leading, had not fallen into the hands of the police. We heard steps—knocking on the doors—foreign languages. It was not the *milice* of death but our *passants*. Since they had been left to themselves, fear had given them wings and muscles to carry their sacks. We would have gained many hours, therefore, if we had been firmer.

We held counsel all together. "Here you risk nothing. Snow is coming, which hides all tracks. But that's no reason to make others. You will be spotted immediately by reconnaissance planes, and from afar by the customs men who patrol the crests in good weather. For a few days you will not be in any danger. No one will come to look for you here. When it is possible, we will pass you across in turn. We will show you the provisions.

176

Now we are going to look for those who haven't come back. It is much farther on, higher up on the mountain. Time is running out. Don't forget that they were leading three refugees in order to pass them into Switzerland. You are on the way, much closer than many others."

We prepared our sacks, and especially our pockets. We stuffed them so as not to have to stop to eat. Daylight was almost here. We should be at the Salenton Pass. At the moment of leave-taking, a scene broke out. A couple of tea merchants, who had infiltrated among the persons recommended by CIMADE or by the Glasberg Committee, took us aside. "We will never stay here alone. You want to kill us, to rob us. If you don't take us back to Chamonix today, we will do everything we can to be seen, and we'll inform against you!" Wild threats poured out, from the most vulgar to the most subtle. Several of the *passants* stood in the background, unhappy and ashamed before that flood of insane invectives. We called those who were there to witness that neither we nor CIMADE had ever asked for money from those whom we attempted to help. We did not even ask for gratitude. We did only what we had to do—and what we must do again. Nothing helped. A man used to possessing others through money is no longer a man. That monstrous biped is not even a dog that licks the hand of him who feeds him. And that kind reproduces itself in the world of men. Will it take over one day?

We decided, to our great regret, to leave Emile Bernis with the group. He would take the two wild men to Chamonix if nothing else could be done.

We were on the way again. It was long, the climb to the Salenton Pass. It was daylight, and there was great danger of being spotted by the watchers. We were in a hurry to go over to the other side of the crest. From time to time while walking along, we took a swallow of sweetened condensed milk straight from the tube, or a spoonful of powdered cereal, or a prune. The summit of the Buet, at last. A little fresh snow was on the ground. There were tracks. Someone had stretched out in the shelter, several people in fact. There were the remains of a meal and two little bottles of Armagnac. The snow was trampled around the shelter. We could reconstruct what had happened. Three of them had taken cover; the other two had remained outside. André and René had not known how or had not been able to prevent these novices from giving themselves the illusion of warmth by drinking alcohol. Already we thought: they had drunk their judgment. What would we find?

Anxiety grew. We quickly took the little crest toward the peak of Genévrier. At any other time, what a beautiful trip! Rarely do tourists venture into this wilderness. It was seldom visited by chamois hunters, more often by smugglers. It was the type of country the latter needed—complete wilderness! The falls of the glacier of Trez-les-Eaux and the big Nol were on one side; on the other some rather steep precipices toward Sixt. A few tracks were visible. In fact, some cable ends had been shaken. Farther, under a slab was a primitive shelter and a few remains of a meal. People had eaten there and had even stretched out in the snow. It was such a small space that it could not have held the five. How had they done it? Outside the shelter under the slab, there was only the ridge. Had they stayed there long? No. It was not possible.

We continued the route used already for other crossings. The tracks disappeared. We lost time searching on the Cheval-Blanc —nothing. They had not gone toward the Vieux Pass. We went down to the glacier and rather soon found ice-ax marks, footprints, and evidences of sliding. The caravan had not crossed the pass. They had chosen instead the path that goes down to the Enfer de Trez-les-Eaux. Why? There was no exit there, and there was no other route so difficult, so laborious. What had happened? Had they taken the trail which came from the chalets of Loria and ended in the abyss on the "two thousand meter level" below the peak? The torrent coming from the glacier could not be followed to its junction with the waters of the Bérard. The jumble of rocks was impassable, especially at night. At one end of the half-frozen snow, there were a few tracks. Not far from there, among the rocks and a bit of grass, someone had sat or lain down. Someone had again eaten and drunk; a new bottle of Armagnac. Footprints in all directions attracted our attention. Someone had walked around there for a long time. A little farther down there were traces of sliding among the grass and bushes that were beginning to appear.

Day was ending. Loria overwhelmed us with its forbidding cliffs; the two summits towered above us. We hurried along. We had to be out of there before nightfall. The easy passage by the chalets would lengthen our journey too much. We had to find Morel and René and find out what had happened to them. They must have been picked up by the mountain police. Then we were at a small café on the Buet, across from the station. A flood of news hit us—an avalanche. "They passed here. The young boy looked very tired. The monsieur, no one knows how he did it: at night there where you passed, led by the noise of the water, he came to find help. I mean porters. The people were dead, except one who was in very bad shape. Eleven guides and porters went up with poles, ropes, sacks—everything they needed. The man and woman were dead. They were quickly buried in the Vallorcine cemetery. It seems they leave two children, poor things. The *milice* did not see anything. The monsieur paid the guides with the money found on the dead people. They say that they died of fear and alcohol. They were not people for the mountains."

We could not wait for the end of the details. The train, perhaps the last of the day, was entering the station. I was only able to hear again, "And you do that for nothing . . . " To which M. Audemard answered upon leaving, "And it will be done again—it must be done again."

We were even more shaken by our thoughts than by the train. You are responsible, people were going to say. You should not have taken that kind of people on such an adventure. Easy to say when a person is outside the situation, outside the desperate appeals, outside the need to discern the true from the false in what is told him. One must have time. But he does not, cannot have it. It is snatched from him. Easy to say when a person finds himself before beings in whom instinctive reactions—visceral they call them—habits, and preconceived ideas win out over all the rest. Easy to say when one is not in the dilemma: to be informed against and stopped along with those involved with you, or to try to believe the words and the looks that seek to be sincere. Who killed? We or their lie? We or their faith in money?

At Chamonix I left M. Audemard and J. G. Wagner in the train. On the station platform I found—André Morel.

17.

The Witness to the Drama Speaks

PASTOR ANDRÉ MOREL

Sent to Haute-Savoie by CIMADE to organize an escape chain to Switzerland, I had become acquainted at Chedde with Louis Audemard, who was the leader of the Protestant Boy Scouts at Chamonix and head electrician by profession at a factory making chemical products. He had shown me the route, long but sure, that he used to pass agents of the British Intelligence Service into Switzerland.

The bishop of Annecy pointed out the monastery at Tamié as a refuge for the men while waiting for the crossing, and the convent of Chavanod for the women. The Protestant parsonage at Annecy completed the setup for waiting.[1] I stayed in a hotel

1. From all parts the refugees sent by CIMADE converged upon the parsonage at Annecy. They were housed in all the rooms, even the attic. One night the social hall was already full when twenty Jews arrived. The balcony of the church was transformed into a dormitory. The tradition of the right of asylum in the church was never more evident. To feed everyone, the maquis furnished the parsonage with false ration cards. A restaurant owner

at Chedde where telegrams like this would reach me: "Send three ice axes on such a day, at such an hour." Being unable to make all the trips myself, I was helped by Louis Audemard and his family, and by friends like Georges Casalis. I was primarily occupied with young Jews that Mme André Philip had helped to escape from le Chambon-sur-Lignon. Therefore most were formerly from Gurs, guided and helped by CIMADE. All of them crossed over without incident. I am unable to tell the number of trips that we made.

Once again I was the guest of my friends the Audemards. They were very anxious about their little girl; the doctor had just diagnosed a case of polio. Then an Austrian couple arrived, refugees at Chamonix for a year or two with their two children. The boy was a Scout in the troop at Chamonix. The girl was younger. The parents, M. and Mme H.—he was rather tall, she was small—seemed to be in their fifties. Their residence permit had expired. They begged Louis Audemard to "pass" them. There was a long discussion. They were no longer young enough to try that route. In any case, the children could not do it. They would get to Switzerland through Annemasse and join a brother of Monsieur H., refugee at Lausanne, for whom Louis Audemard had served as guide. The couple insisted determinedly. Seeing the family situation of my friends, I proposed to make the trip. It was decided that the young Audemard, René, would accompany me. Rendezvous was set for the next morning.

We prepared the sacks at Chedde. They were not abnormally heavy. It was said afterward that they contained a fortune in gold ingots, but this was not true—the only thing of value was a collection of new stamps. With them arrived a guest, Rudolf W., twenty-five years old, supposedly a *"porteur"* for M. and Mme H. I believe he was Czechoslovakian.

We left early in the afternoon for the cabins at Moëde, where

in the city brought a well-filled basket each night. Neither the pastor's family nor the fugitives ever lacked for anything.

Up at dawn, Pastor Chapal would find his night's guests standing in the kitchen, trying to swallow breakfast with throats choked by anxiety. The guide would come, and the bus would go toward the border.

we spent the night. Leaving early in the morning, I would normally have had time to guide them and to come back to Vallorcine to take the last train for Chedde. We walked very slowly, going up beside the rapids of the Diosaz. I had to take the sack of Monsieur H., who wanted to stop all the time. We arrived at the summit of the Buet around 4:00 P.M. in the fog and rain. We were within sight of the border pass, which we could reach in two or three hours. It was worth attempting, especially since the weather kept us safe from the ever possible guards.

We put on the knapsacks and started out. The chorus of wailing grew. The weather was turning very bad—snow flurries and an approaching storm. I had to give a hand first to M. and then to Mme H. The one named Rudi was sufficiently encumbered with his own sack. René had enough to do in his role as porter. Night fell. We had covered very little ground since the summit. We reached a shelter for chamois hunters, which offered a little protection from the north wind. We crouched against one another to share our body warmth. I took care of René. The husband and wife argued over a little blanket. The weather cleared. The chain of Mont-Blanc appeared grandiose in the moonlight among the clouds.

The next morning, the third day of our adventure, at the first signs of light we were on our way. All of us had our feet more or less frozen. The sun began to shine. We made slow progress on the ridge, although it was rather wide. To the right we were about twenty-eight hundred feet above the crater of Trez-les-Eaux. I not only had to carry Monsieur H.'s sack but to hold him up with his arm around my neck. His courage was gone. I was surprised and annoyed that a man who had to save his skin should give up the struggle like this. He repeated: "We want to go down. We want some tea." I tried, exhorting and pulling him, to make him climb the ridge, which rose again toward the border pass, toward Switzerland. Freedom was there, before us, within shouting distance. It seemed that I would have to carry him on my shoulders. He weighed 175 pounds and I 120! About noon we decided—Rudi and I—to give up the escape and try to reach Vallorcine, over five thousand feet down in the valley. Rudi helped Mme H. and I took Monsieur.

We arrived below the boulders in the hollow of Trez-les-Eaux. There it was necessary to stand up again and walk. That effort was no longer possible for them. Night fell. I hid the now-famous knapsack behind a big rock, easily recognizable. I left my companions in a meadow not far from the rapids that came from the glacier and went to look for help.

I walked part of the night, which was fortunately lighted by the moon. Without knowing it, I followed a smugglers' path and arrived long after midnight at the chalets in the hamlet of Nant. I had to knock long and hard at several doors before someone answered. Finally a guide believed me and gathered a small rescue team of eight or ten mountaineers. Without losing any time, we again took the path for Trez-les-Eaux. They outdistanced me and were the first to meet René and Rudi, who had started out before dawn of the fourth day. We arrived together farther on, where M. and Mme H. were lying at the edge of the rapids, their heads in the water, dead.

I still have the impression that this drowning was not accidental. Their suicide shows what degree of suffering and desperation these unfortunate people had reached.

I paid the rescue group with French money from Monsieur H.'s wallet. Some time later a friend took Swiss money to the brother in Lausanne, two hundred francs I believe. It seems that the knapsack was not to be found, and I scarcely troubled myself to go look for it.

I left again with René, leaving Rudi with the guides who carried the two corpses tied to poles. Numb with fatigue, burned by the storm, feet frozen, and heartsick, we took the train at Vallorcine.

I came out of the nightmare when I saw E. C. Fabre, who had come to comfort us with his friendship, on the platform at the Chamonix station.

Rudi had told the story to Monsieur H.'s brother in such a way that the latter wrote a letter which became cause for my arrest, after it was seized by the police. He said that his brother was not a man to take a trip without a large sum of money and other valuables, that I had killed them in order to steal from them—the sack in particular—and that Louis Audemard was an accomplice—he who had passed the brother himself free of charge.

I was arrested, as was Louis Audemard. We took the road to the prison at Annecy before other CIMADE team members. The suspicions cast upon me were very serious. We had been in prison for six days when the sack was found. Due to this fact in itself, the matter appeared in another light, and we were temporarily freed. I was sentenced to one month in jail, the minimum it seems, thanks to the testimony of Pastors Eberhard and Casalis and Father Berger.

18.

. . . And the Children of the Dead

PASTOR E. C. FABRE

What could we do with the young boy and the little girl whose parents died in the hell at Trez-les-Eaux?

For the moment they were with our friends the Audemards, but that could not last. We had been accused by the uncle in Lausanne of abducting the children. André Morel was in jail. The day that the gendarmes came to take him, Father Berger— very well liked at Chedde—wanted to accompany him. There was a sort of procession in the little town, a gesture of sympathy and protest.

The sack had not been found. It was snowing. We had to wait till the first day of sunshine. Could even the blackbirds visit Trez-les-Eaux?

It was decided that I would try to "pass" the two children, who knew nothing yet about the death of their parents. It would be best to pass them through Annemasse. How? Once there, we would see.

We left on a cold morning, in an old wooden train without a corridor.

Annemasse! The border station with all its charm. The little city. We had to find the Protestant church without asking and without arousing suspicion. Apparently it was one of the most heavily watched places. So be it. We walked back and forth. All attempts to pass the children were in vain. Failure followed failure. At each street corner: what to do with these children? And to think that all came together here, that everything was so small. Life was near, within grasp. There were certainly solutions, and they piled up on one another until they enclosed the children in death like so many of their brothers. How long the hours seemed, and how disappointing the men.

We would have to go all out. Perhaps it would be at my expense; we would see. In navy terms they say, "as God wills." I took the children back to the station and left them in the waiting room, saying, "Just a minute!" On the door I read: *Commissaire spécial.* A dry response: "Entrez." Smoke. Uniforms. Revolvers on the wall. Unmistakable odor of police stations. I asked for the inspector in person. I had vital business with him. Here was my card. Another door. The chief himself. Brief introduction. We sat facing each other. "I have come to ask your advice, man to man. We'll both be frank, you and I, I am sure. This is the story. . . . What shall we do? They are there, in the waiting room."

The inspector got up and shook hands. "You run a great risk. Leave the children. I'll take over. Good-bye." It was understood that once on the other side the children would ask for Suzanne de Dietrich. Everything would be arranged for them to join their uncle.

Annemasse, Chedde again, Chamonix, and Chedde once more; La Roche-sur-Foron and Romans-sur-Isère. That line of metal tying together so many human dramas and those mountains. Between those heights, the mass of Mont-Blanc and the Vercors, how many looks filled with hope tried to recognize them in passing! And all this in the night seemed to me a tiny drop in the hollow of the Master's hand.

19.

The Victims of the Drama Speak

MARTHE BESAG
ANNIE EBBEKE
DR. HEINRICH MAYER

Marthe Besag (who had to leave le Coteau Fleuri in August 1942 with her elderly mother and her twin daughters under the circumstances described by Pastor Donadille, pp. 113-16):

We spent nights in barns and in the grass of the forest. The inhabitants of the region were devoted and courageous.

Sunday. We were a little sad when we heard church bells ringing. But a young man came to us. He was going to lead worship in a peasant's kitchen. The neighbors heard and came to join us. Rarely in a cathedral has a gathered community been so attentive and so moved; rarely has the Lord's Prayer been said with so much feeling.

A workman immediately made us a dormitory in his shop. Early in the morning he brought milk, coffee, bread, and jam from his home. May the Lord protect you all, dear courageous Huguenots!

We had to leave the region. The population had intervened too openly in our favor, and our presence was putting them in danger.

Another departure by night. We walked about twelve miles across fields, up hill and down dale, crossing rivers and swamps. The slopes were steep, and we slipped on the dry pine needles.

We were divided into small groups. The three of us found lodgings in the home of a kind old lady who lived alone with a sick girl. The contrast was disconcerting. Yesterday we slept on ferns, trembling from the cold; today we had a luxurious bedroom. For a week we ate cold potatoes; now we had abundant meals. There in the high places the days were endless. We never went out of our bedroom or to the window. However, we could not remain there either. Nowhere would we be undisturbed in this great and beautiful country. We endangered those who welcomed us. We had to cross into Switzerland.

We were three, my twins and I. Where was my oldest, Frida, placed as a mother's helper in le Chambon? No one could give me exact information. The twins were separated; one was to attempt the border crossing within a short time. Good-bye, dear child! Will we see each other again? Her attempt was a success. We had to wait and wait. And the two of us had to find another place to hide. At night we left the house that sheltered us.

Finally someone came for us. We took leave of our good hosts. "In the past it was we who were the persecuted; today it is you," they said, thinking of the sufferings of their ancestors, the Huguenots. In many a home, behind the alcoves, one could distinguish a hidden stairway that led to a hiding place. We understood their prudence.

We reached the locality near the Swiss border without incident. At last, here was a solution! A pastor gave us God's blessing for the trip. A group gathered at the appointed hour in the shade of a few trees. Fifteen minutes passed, then thirty minutes, forty-five minutes. It was raining. We shivered and waited. More than an hour had passed. Steps. Someone whistled: friend or enemy? Cautiously we left the shade. Friend! "You cannot leave today. The car is broken down."

Again we waited whole days in a big room in an unknown

house. And then we received the sad news. Our child had been deported! We wanted to scream in pain, but the expression of our suffering had to wait along with everything else.[1] We would attempt the crossing the next day.

We approached the border in a group. Then we two—alone, calm, and certain of being under divine protection—walked toward the city on the other side of the border. No customs agent, no gendarme from either side stopped us.

We were in Switzerland, the country of our prayers. But weeks would pass before we would feel really safe. Good friends received and clothed us. But again a camp and the straw! For how long?

Annie Ebbeke:

September 1942. After our long meandering from Gurs to Pont-de-Manne, to Romans and the Fabres' home, we came to Chedde and were received like so many others by the friends of CIMADE, Father Berger and André Morel. All was ready for a crossing in complete safety. We were divided into small groups of five or six persons. Hans and I were with two Dutch Jews and Dr. Mayer and Nagelstein.

First stage, Argentière. The Protestant chapel, including the basement, served as our resting place. The pastor offered us the evening soup. A paid guide came to get us at nightfall. The weather was good; we were extremely hopeful and believed the nightmare finished. But we were not in good shape. With difficulty we climbed the slopes of Charamillon, toward the Balme Pass. Behind us Mont-Blanc sparkled in the moonlight, preceded by the mass of the Aiguille Verte and the Dru. We arrived at the pass at the end of our strength, but happy. The guide gave us a few directions before leaving us: "You have one foot in Switzerland. Go down toward le Chatelard and Trient." Our group hesitated, then took off too much to the left. The rocks became steeper and steeper. We followed a ridge

1. Pastor Donadille told about Frida's arrest, p. 116.

on the abrupt slopes. We wandered for hours. The wind had changed; it was raining. We were exhausted and seized with fear and discouragement. In spite of the rain, we stopped under the tall brush and slept. Early in the morning we took up our journey again. Suddenly, from a hollow in the land appeared customs agents. They were French. We tried to explain. They were understanding and set us on the right path, pointing out a few landmarks. We finally arrived at Tête Noire and found a small Swiss hotel, at which we were welcomed. Such joy—a room and a bed! We telegraphed to our friends in Zurich. They offered to finance a bond. We gave all the information required by the Swiss police. All was in order. Nagelstein's fiancée arrived. We were saved.

A messenger came around noon. We were to go immediately to the police station at Trient. A truck came to get us, with an armed escort. What did that mean?

At the Swiss station a very unsympathetic officer informed us that since midnight, refugees were no longer admitted into Switzerland. He was going to send us back to France. No discussion was possible with that brute. The customs men who witnessed the scene took pity on us and gave us a few provisions. We were put into a truck and unloaded at the foot of the Swiss slopes of the Balme Pass.

We had to climb back up, dragging ourselves from exhaustion and consternation. Hours of struggle and hopelessness. Fog covered the ground; the high mountain was hidden in cotton. It was very cold. We began making our way down.

Hans was trembling from fever. We hid in the hollow of a rock. Dr. Mayer went for news, which turned out to be very bad. Switzerland no longer accepted anyone; the Chamonix Valley was closed by cordons of police. The pastor at Argentière was expecting us, but he was under close surveillance and it was better that we not stay. Supper was served when we arrived. But in the early morning hours we had to take the train to Chedde once more.

Surprised to be still alive, we found ourselves again with Mme Lasserre. When she saw that Hans was so sick, she gave us her room. She settled the other members of the group as best she could. Hans was delirious and needed a doctor, but the doctor was at Chamonix. We gave it up.

Several days passed. Pastor Fabre arrived, worried for us and for the Lasserres. He was going to lead us to the chalets, deserted during that season, where we would be out of reach of the police.

Our friends led us up and warned us that we must carefully measure our daily rations of the food that we took with us. In the joy of being safe, the provisions diminished rapidly. We had to ration ourselves. Four potatoes a day, then three, then two. . . Nagelstein complained. Dr. Mayer chided him and spoke of the extreme limits of hunger endurance.

We were down to one potato and a chunk of bread per day. In the middle of the night someone knocked at the door. Excitement. . . It was Pastor Fabre, who had brought supplies. But we would soon have to go back down. We risked being blocked by the storm that would blow for days and nights.

Below, we waited, divided among several houses. One day Father Revol took us to Saint-Gervais. We learned from two Jesuit priests that our Zurich friends were working for us, and that Pastor Boegner had obtained permission from the Swiss federal authorities for refugees presented by CIMADE and Catholic or Jewish organizations to be admitted into Switzerland.

We started out, led by a guide, from Fayet to Annemasse. He abandoned us at a bridge that we had to cross. We ran into French gendarmes. They reassured us, indicating the road to follow. They were in the habit of doing this sort of thing; they helped French defectors to cross the border. They refused any remuneration and wished us good luck.

Another soldier, a Swiss, led us to the police station. Oh, those police stations! We were transported to one of the harshest camps, near Geneva. The bad treatment overwhelmed us. We had neither mattress nor straw and had to sleep on the bare ground or on icy tiles. We were moved from camp to camp, each one as primitive as the last. It was said that Switzerland was counting on a German victory at that time . . .

In January 1944 we were freed, thanks to our friends in

Zurich. All work was forbidden. We moved from place to place. Finally we found a small boardinghouse where Hans was authorized to work at his piano for several hours per week. Artists from Basel were passing through and heard him play. They hired him as an instructor for soloists at the Basel theater. At last to be able to earn one's livelihood and to have a small apartment! Life became almost normal again.

But not for long, unfortunately. Hans was again taken by the illness that was sapping his strength. He could not fight, and left us in 1946. I remained alone.

Dr. Mayer:

I knew the same wanderings. In Switzerland, from camp to camp, I cleaned toilets and peeled potatoes for the Swiss soldiers, until the day that I could be a doctor again in a camp near Basel. Later I was director of a home for refugees near Lugano. My wife and son joined me there. From there, we left for America in May 1947.

How was my morale during that time? I was often near despair but never at the end of my rope. The Twenty-third Psalm always sustained and inspired me.

In the camps, among my companions in misery as well as among the guards, I met as many very good people as bad ones. Many French people welcomed me as though I were their son or brother, even to the point of risking their lives for me. Others, forgetting that we were human beings, seemed to enjoy seeing us starving and lying in the mud. Among the internees, some helped one another; others, evil to the core, thought only of money above all else.

Pastor Boegner, presiding at a worship service at Gurs, took as the theme of his sermon the words of the women going to the tomb on Easter morning: "Who will roll away the stone for us?" Those words went straight to my heart, and I have thought of them thousands of times since then in the most critical situations.

I never hated the Nazis, even though they made me suffer so much in body and soul.

I would not want to relive those years for anything in the world. But they led me to become more of a believer than I had ever been. They gave me that something that makes a man unshakable, so that nothing can take away his faith. Christ would not be what he is for us without his suffering and his death.

20.

At the Side of the Road

PROF. GEORGES CASALIS

"There were also many women there,
looking on from afar. . . ."
—Matthew 27:55

To Andrew Young, Atlanta, Georgia

I hesitated a long time before writing these lines. If it were necessary, the affair of *Le Vicaire* would remind us how dangerous,
scandalous, and impossible it was to speak out, so that in the
majority of cases we were silent and were accomplices to the
martyrdom of Israel. Yes, we needed Hochhuth, after Schwartz-
Bart and many others, to tell us again that at the time of the
cremation ovens, the only Christian attitude would have been a
solemn declaration of *all* the churches, inviting Christians to
wear the yellow star, sign of the shame and the glory of the Son
of David. I am among those who believe that that witness and
the obedience of Christians would have been enough to make

the Nazis back down. Immediately after the Liberation, I expressed these things[1] very badly and incompletely in the conviction that only the truth before Israel, our only fidelity after the horrible years, consisted of a public confession of our guilt and an unflagging desire for reparation. The friendship of Israel offered to us in spite of everything, the dialogue for many years between Jews and Christians around the Old Testament at Strasbourg, rubbing elbows and getting to know the person and message of André Neher,[2] and the indispensable collaboration at the heart of demonstrations of *l'Amitié judéo-chrétienne*—all these miraculous gifts decidedly testify that grace and pardon are always stronger than betrayal of brothers and complicity, active or shamefully passive, with the hangmen.

There was no question, therefore, that this book of memories would take on the character of a glorification. "We all have a Jew, the alibi of a bad conscience," as C. Zuckmayer has his Devil's General say, "but what does that amount to in the face of all the others?" Perhaps it is necessary that, in the time and generation of "Hitler? Never heard of him," we merely have the humility to witness to that epoch as we knew it.

I affirm here that as of 1933 the existence of concentration camps was known; that before 1940 the fate of the interned German Jews was known; that from 1941 on there was information about the massive exterminations and their horrors. I attest that in 1942 in Lyons I had precise information about the making of soap from the grease of the massacred Jews. Those who timidly dared to say what they scarcely dared to believe only met a shrug of the shoulders and were quickly accused of gullible excitability. We have relived that since, by an implacable logic: the civilized Christian conscience does not like to be confronted with the monstrous mirror of torture. All the denials, no matter how official, cannot represent a shadow of an excuse.

You will find here a few episodes, landmarks along that road to Israel's Calvary, alongside of which we cowardly remained spectators, just as many did years ago in Jerusalem.

1. In *Le Semeur* (F.F.A.C.E.), nos. 3–4, pp. 341 ff.
2. Cf. especially *L'Existence juive* (le Seuil).

At Lyons on the Croix-Rousse, the winding alleys and interminable steps offered, if not good hiding places, at least a few routes permitting one to change his refuge in case of alert. To go between the Montée de la Boucle, where Roland de Pury lived, and the Montée des Lilas takes only a few minutes on foot. That is to say that on the nights of police raids, usually announced by a discreet message from the prefecture of the Rhone, the plan of "communicating vases" was used to the fullest. When we were absent, the key was left with our cleaning lady not far away on the quai Saint-Clair. It was not unusual to return at night and unexpectedly find six people bivouacking in our home under the care of my brother, a medical student, who might be preparing brushes and paste for his next round of subversive postering. There were often surprising moments of human communion, as profound as they were silent. This was especially the case one day in September 1942 when, sent to the south after ten days in prison for secretly crossing the line of demarcation, I arrived home about five o'clock in the morning. I had all the difficulty in the world persuading my wife, who was sleeping in the midst of a real caravan, that my visit was not that of the ever-expected Gestapo.

About that same time, a permanent guest found refuge with us. It was René Courtin, who at the Liberation became a cabinet minister for a while. He had three "authentic" identity cards, two of which were hidden in a flour can that wisdom and chance always kept full, like that of the widow of Sarepta. The comings and goings that our friend was obliged to undertake would not have been of concern if there had not come into our lives at that time a hunted Jew, who acted in a crazily imprudent manner because of the proximity of danger. He came and went ceaselessly night and day, unable to remain still, talking all the time, without any consideration, continuing conversations through the doors of the most secret places where one tried to escape from him. Perfectly at home, he took possession of everything and everybody, putting us sometimes outdoors, especially when we learned that others also received his visit and were faithfully informed about our way of life at the house. He went back and forth endlessly at all hours, day and night, and earned us the following letter from our landlord, a good old man, not very reassuring, who lived just above us and could hear everything through the back staircase:

Madame,

A stranger came to us at two o'clock in the morning and again at three-thirty to get back into your apartment to sleep. We would be much obliged if you would not permit anyone to come at such an hour to ask for you. It would be preferable if you had no one in your apartment when you are absent.

Yours truly,
M.T.

However, nothing happened. A benediction of sorts seemed to attach itself to this Jew's steps; and there was a great feeling of emptiness in the house the day he disappeared forever without our even knowing what became of him. His name was Emmanuel.

Another unforgettable visit was that of M. and Mme W. That admirable German couple came to us only the night after their hiding place at Villeurbanne had become too uncertain. First thing in the morning, they left to walk all day long and to talk endlessly in the narrow streets, closely linked together. They were tactful and naïvely confident, and so eager to be helpful to us. One day during that radiant and terrible autumn of 1942, they found, they thought, the means of helping the lady of the house. "Let us take your little one for a walk." For several days they ambled, beaming, through the Tête-d'Or Park, pushing the carriage of our child, whom they cared for in an exemplary fashion—and who guarded them. After some time news arrived from CIMADE: the passage into Switzerland was organized, the date set. Suddenly their faces darkened. "But it is Yom Kippur. And if you are on a trip, you can't celebrate properly. No, such a departure would not be blessed. We shall leave later on." Some time afterward they did cross the Swiss border, and we learned that these true children of Abraham had found a restful place out of harm's reach.

As André Morel has said, the best way to cross into Switzerland passed by the Buet, and in those last months of the existence of the Unoccupied Zone a rather efficient system had been worked out. From refuges in the Drôme or the Cevennes, the refugees were sent down to Lyons. At their arrival, they were directed to the Chamonix Valley by those who led the convoys. From there they were led into Switzerland by the mountain guides. Did we have a premonition of the events of 6 November 1942? Did we want to shelter as many people as possible before winter? At any rate, autumn of 1942 was a time of intense activity on the Buet line. It was in those conditions that I was called to help. Right away, my first trip consisted of leading a convoy and passing it over.

Perrache station. There were two boys, rawboned from clandestineness and undernourishment. We recognized one another in silence. It was raining. We knew that La Roche-sur-Foron was the most critical point of the trip. The Vichy police, a few *miliciens*, would climb into the train and examine papers. What were the boys' false cards worth? Was it not less dangerous, as we had been advised, to try to avoid the identity check by pretending to leave and then returning to the train at the last minute when the inspection was finished? I tossed around these ideas and conveyed them to the two boys in the corridor. Suddenly I noticed a bit of excitement at the other end of the car. The police were passing through the train today. A decision was quickly made. I opened the door of the moving train. The boys slid onto the step over the tracks . . . and reappeared a bit pale ten minutes later, having passed without incident those unexpected tests of a surprise inspection and a few tunnels.

The little train at Fayet-Saint-Gervais; then Chedde and the incredibly natural hospitality of the Audemard family. It was decided that we should leave very quickly in order to spend the night in the chalets at Moëde. Because I did not know the way, one of the children accompanied me. It was a long afternoon hike. Evening fell, and the weather got better. In spite of yourself, the charm and peace of that long path behind the crest of the Aiguilles Rouges overcame you. The young boy and I quickly became friends and kidded some before going to sleep in the hay.

The next day at dawn, we scaled the Buet in the splendor of sky and sunshine. The entire Mont-Blanc range and the entire Chamonix Valley were bursting with light. The two boys followed badly; their pathetic shoes threatened to fall apart. They had only too many reasons not to be thrilled with admiration. I had to urge them on energetically to reach the summit and to descend the long Cheval-Blanc ridge, holding onto the steel cable with which it was equipped.

Once the Buet and the Cheval-Blanc had been crossed, we found ourselves in a small valley entirely carpeted with big rocks. We had to go from rock to rock and climb back to the Vieux Pass, which was the border, a projecting tip of Switzerland in French territory. From there we could see Barberine. The match was won. Two hours of descent, a few steep banks to cross. The Swiss customs post was in sight. The false identity cards were burned, but I took back the food ration cards for others.

We separated coldly, like the strangers that we were to one another. Probably the two boys realized that, compared to them, we were rich. We did not have to save our skins. Besides, in the glory of that autumn afternoon, I had mixed feelings: the satisfaction of a guide having led his difficult clients to their goal; pleasure at having outsmarted the occupation powers; the good feeling of having enjoyed a deep breath of fresh air. The boys were going on to their uprooted lives. I was returning to my family, my house, my vocation. Had I done more than distract myself for a few hours? Had it just been a time to give charity? How they must have hated me—and with reason. Ah! How sad that help, although effective, is poisoned because it carries none of the traits of compassion, because it gladdens him who gives instead of killing him. Not for an instant during those thirty-six hours—except perhaps when they were on the outside steps of the train—had the boys and I really met; not one time, except perhaps then, did I tremble with them, and then it was probably for myself in the first place.

We left one another. I watched them go down toward their destiny, harassed and without visible joy, children of the people of the Exodus who have never found rest and who despise our civilizations of abundance, our repugnant existences, our satisfied consciences. No, they were not yet at the goal; they would reach it only with the coming of the kingdom, and we with them, if before that they have awakened us . . . But meanwhile they were going to run into the Swiss patrol, and with a little luck they would be sent back to France under pretext of inviolable neutrality and lack of provisions to feed these "foreigners." And everything would have to be started over if they were given to an overzealous French patrol. Otherwise, it would be the Swiss camps for months, years perhaps. Man must hold onto life, all the same!

We climbed back toward France and reached the ridge a little above the pass that led to Vallorcine. The afternoon clouds began to show the colors of sundown. Unconcerned and light-hearted, with one foot in France, the other in Switzerland, the boy and I began to devour our last provisions. Suddenly below us, on the Swiss side, we saw two men emerge whom we recognized as French guards, more from their army carbines than from their makeshift uniforms. Instinctively we crossed the border into France to hide. They arrived at the pass below us. We were sixty feet from them, slightly higher than they. Then they stopped, breathless, spitting, looking toward the valley. "Do you see them?" one of them asked.

"No," said the other as he adjusted the big binoculars and searched among the rocks. "It's impossible that they could have gone so fast."

"They must have hidden. Let's go look."

And then they began to come toward us. The end of the carbine passed two feet from my shoes. We were standing up, exposed, silent, waiting for them to raise their heads, or for a stone to roll, or for the wing of a fly to make a noise. There was a brief moment of intolerable tension. But they quickened their pace, made some noise. We went back into Switzerland, crawling on our stomachs this time. We watched them search the paths, looking behind and under the big rocks. Then I understood, belatedly, that the little French flag seen on the north cliff that morning indicated the presence of a post occupied by those two men. All day long they had followed us with the binoculars and had arrived, by cutting across Switzerland, just in time to catch us as we crossed into France. "Your game would have been up if, as in certain Old Testament accounts, the Lord had not placed his angel between you and those who pursued you," Karl Barth said to me some time later.[3]

There was no longer any question of going back down to Vallorcine. It was twilight; the weather turned bad; the provisions were exhausted. There was only one solution—to go back over the Vieux Pass, climb the ridge of the Cheval-Blanc, and go down by the chalets at Moëde to Chedde. So we started out again across Switzerland toward our morning's route. I wondered how the boy would hold up. We had already been walking for fifteen hours. But friendship, complicity, and that exhilarating feeling of having been miraculously saved gave us legs, even though the moon came up and a violent wind blew across it phantomlike clouds which broke from time to time into big snowflakes. At midnight we were at the summit of Buet in the midst of howling winds that whipped us and snow that stung us. To the south, the spectacle of Mont-Blanc playing hide-and-seek in the dance of the clouds was fantastic. There was no question of bivouacking there; but where was the way down? "This way," the boy said to me with absolute authority. And taking the lead of our Alpinist's cord at the moment I was beginning to turn in circles, he got us down like an old mountaineer, sure of his route in spite of everything.

At two o'clock in the morning we were at the bottom of the slope, clinging to a long stretch of rocks. We had been walking for twenty-one hours. I spotted a big rock where we could camp. At the moment we approached, I heard a voice ring out, "If there is someone who wants to sleep here, you can come on." Convinced that we had fallen upon a patrol, I went forward, resigned, like a robot . . . to find André Morel bivouacking with four Jews. Having sensed the coming of bad weather, he had gone beyond Moëde in order to be nearer the goal the next morning whatever the atmospheric conditions might be. We embraced one another, broke into nervous laughter, tried to swallow

3. Editor's note: The pass referred to was probably the Sassey Pass, more gap than pass and very steep on the French side.

a few crackers that would not go down and—in vain—to warm ourselves.

At dawn we separated, after having explained to André Morel the significance of the French flags on the cliffs and describing the habits of the surveillance patrols on the mountain.

I would not see him again before that day in November when we witnessed for him in Bonneville, without daring too much to look one another in the face. We should have kept the declarations pronounced that day before the tribunal. The judges were astounded, to say the least, by the witnesses coming to take Morel's part, and affirming that the honor of French youth had been to choose solidarity with the oppressed against government and law.[4]

At ten o'clock we were at Chedde, where M. Audemard, who had been very anxious, welcomed us—you can imagine how. Even more so because since the night before, they had been looking in the valley for a man wearing shorts and a Basque beret, hiking on the mountain with a young boy. We went to bed and slept all afternoon. That evening, wearing trousers, very dignified, with the beret in the bottom of a suitcase, I took the night train for Rivesaltes, where Morel had sent me with a message for Dumas after having made me understand that from now on I was an undesirable on the Buet line.

I have never seen the young boy since, but he has a very special place in my friendship.[5]

Some time later, Morel sent word to me: "If someone asks you whether I spent a certain night at your house, be kind enough to say yes." I looked at my datebook and learned that I had not been in Lyons that night; I concluded that he wanted an alibi. Called before the police commissioner, I told a story of pure fabrication, and left somewhat upset at the thought of the false witness I had borne deliberately, if not cold-bloodedly. Meeting Madeleine Barot, I told her of my reaction and she

4. The cases against Bernis and Fabre and the manner in which the judge said to them, "We are giving you temporary liberty," and the disappearance of some documents in a "fire," have shown how the magistrates of Bonneville participated as much as they could in the "action."

5. René Audemard, whom we have already mentioned.

burst out laughing. "But it was one of the rare things that was true in all that André told the police!" I noticed then that in my datebook were noted all the projects for the use of my time, and that on two or three occasions the pressure of events turned it all upside down, without, of course, my noting the resulting changes. With much difficulty and with the help of my wife, I remembered that, after all, André Morel had spent a very short night with us between two convoys. Although I believed I was lying, it seems that I had told the honest truth. Enough to make one lose his mind. . .

It was about that time that my friend Jacques Saussine died. He was a CIMADE teamworker at the Récébédou camp. He had had an attack of appendicitis that the camp doctor treated by applying hot water bottles. When they operated in Toulouse, it was too late. Jacques, even today your laugh, your vitality, and your faithfulness remain one of the joys of my life.

After the war I returned to Lyons. I again saw the Montée des Lilas and so many places where we made plans and hid, in the difficult communion of shame, horror, and hope. But I especially wanted to go to the quai Saint-Clair to see Mme M. again, our former cleaning woman. She welcomed me as in the past, in the single room, where with her husband, a municipal parks employee, she kept a good number of animals, edible or simply domestic, in a most confined atmosphere. We talked about different people, and before leaving I wanted to say thank you to her who—a witness to everything—could have brought catastrophe upon us with a word. She stopped me with a gesture. "Why? Each one is master of his home, and you have the right to welcome whom you wish. Besides . . ." Then she lowered her eyes and her ruddy face became scarlet. "I understood and then . . . I also had a Jew hidden in my house." I said no more, but I meditated a long time upon that lesson—the example of that simple sacrifice of all privacy, in that room where three people, one of whom was a hunted stranger, had lived long months in the company of chickens, rabbits, cats, and a dog whose bark more than once must have led the refugee to disappear into his hiding place.

I should have mentioned moving to Moncoutant, a big town at the boundary of the Vendée and the Poitou. Crossing at Saint-Étienne, we had with us a political refugee, Mme H. Until then, she had been at le Chambon-sur-Lignon, but it was necessary to go elsewhere. Her identity card was obviously false. At the crossing point we put our younger baby in her arms. As upon another occasion, the damaging papers were in the bottom of the basket where our older child lay. In the two instances, the German soldier—poor fellow, away from his own God knows how long—played with the smiling child. Whew! Mme H. knew that her husband, a former journalist from the Saar, had been deported and that she would never see him again. In spite of that, she kept her extraordinary serenity, courage, and vitality. Often in the course of sickness or difficult adjustments, she was like a grandmother in the house. She was also adopted by the parishioners, who pretended to believe in her Lorraine origins. (Because Forbach had been destroyed, all those who did not know how to speak French were said to have been born there.) One day in 1945 she left, never to return. England, Australia . . . still serene, she lives there with her children and sends news.

The epic story of Noirveau must be written, that Vendean village of the Bocage where in 1943 eight families hid eight defectors and seven Jews, not to mention some boarders for "supplementary feeding." When someone arrived unexpectedly, he often found evidence of a place rapidly cleared at the table, a pair of slippers left in the hall, an odor of cigarette smoke floating in the air. One day—denunciation? Or chance? The Gestapo arrived in two black cars and took one of the village leaders, an elderly woman, N. F. She was "grilled" for forty-eight hours during which she conscientiously played the idiot. She was released with a few good words of this nature: "You see whom you risk lodging if we had not warned you." She returned exhausted. "That's what it is to put on an act!"

The night of the arrest it had been necessary to move the "inhabitants" very quickly and to take them by dirt roads a little farther along. Among them were a young Jewish woman and her two children, too obviously typed to be left among the Vendeans. The village was emptied and found itself alone, but not for long, because others were brought there with all the accompanying material and emotional problems. The world of distress and that of resolute protest rubbed elbows here each day in the shelter of the thick hedges and with the support of the exceptionally generous food. At the Liberation this village, which merits a special place among the resistant communities, had the curious experience of lodging for several months an old German-loving colonel, two shaven-headed women, and a child, found one day in the neighboring jail. Probably this extraordinary reversal of things was necessary in order for us to understand the difference between the partisan spirit and the service of Christ by humble people.

We must also speak of our little group of F.F.I.: all those boys who prepared for war without believing too much that they would fight it, and who with all sorts of other refugees—Alsatian, Russian, and other fugitives—formed a strangely sympathetic and unstable company, excited and often unbearable. They were well known by the gendarmerie, which closed its eyes and even arranged to let Big Sam escape the day they could not avoid arresting him when he was riding a bicycle on the national highway and did not have papers. The boys occupied the time as well as they could, performing Molière's *The Hypochondriac* [*Le Malade imaginaire*], singing a whole cantata by J. S. Bach, writing rough drafts of idyllic tales, working in the fields, and inventing crazy ways of listening to the British radio.

One day in July 1944 they left, mobilized by the commanding staff, and immediately Camille was killed, very stupidly. He left simply, as he had lived, proclaiming his faith very clearly to the last moment. Was it being shepherd to the flock to remain alive while those whom one had encouraged to leave died? For Daniel, the son of N. F. of Noirveau, death was long and painful. Made prisoner with Jean at the time of the trouble at Montmorillon, he was deported, experienced long suffering, and died at Dora. It was long afterward that I was able to find his body in the French cemetery in Berlin and send it back to his family. Jean came back.

I could continue thus for many pages and speak of the students, both boys and girls, who tried to continue to study and prepare exams in the camps of the Unoccupied Zone. A telegraphed S O S, told us one day that they were to be deported, which made us realize the extent of our powerlessness. There were also L. G., the painter, and his wife, who, awaiting certain deportation, were concerned only about saving an admirable work of art; T. N., who one day while on a mission suddenly was heard reciting the *Credo* in the midst of the bombs that were falling from everywhere; T. P., who did not hesitate at the height of the occupation to denounce the horrors and lies of Nazism publicly; the *Fédé* camp[6] in Mollans (Drôme), where in July 1942 we had forty-five Jews among sixty campers. That camp, whose occupants were hungry because of supply difficulties, had for its theme the mystery of Israel, heart and key of history, thorn in the flesh of humanity and reminder that the living God never disavows his Word.

If only we were capable of never forgetting that because of this Word, all anti-Semitism and all racial discrimination, all contempt, all violence, all egotistical withdrawal, and every refusal of human solidarity are forever condemned and absolutely impossible! To be the people of God is decidedly not to have a shelter out of reach and a resting place here on earth in green pastures. It is to advance into the midst of pain and injustice, hands and heart dirty, and voluntarily in communion with those who are oppressed, waiting and preparing the roads to liberty . . . until the day when every tear will be wiped from crying eyes. It is then that all Israel, children of the Old Testament and of the New Testament finally reunited in a common happiness, will meet their Lord, the Crucified-Resurrected.

6. French Student Christian Movement.

21.

By Way of Conclusion

PROF. GEORGES CASALIS

I have reread these texts, often surprised that it was something we had actually lived through, at the same time incredulous and more than once amazed upon turning a page to rediscover some word or gesture or face that has disappeared forever. And little by little I measured the enormous gift that was and that remains for us the encounter of all these brothers of secrecy, exile, and deportation. Oh, I well know the price they have paid for what they have given us! And who would not prefer to have never had to write this book?

It would be unpardonable so soon after the concentration camps, the deportations, and the tortures—and in a universe where all this is far from having disappeared—to speculate upon the spiritual benefit that we gained from our timid contacts with those who were to be the victims. Our first and only feeling should be shame for having been weak and unable to stop it. We must never forget that our hands are covered with the blood of our brothers; and yet in the midst of all this which remains our permanent guilt, we know that a grace was given to us which changes nothing of the horror, but which the horror would not know how to destroy either. It seems without doubt that when a man is confronted with death, those who, in such a situation, stand the least bit in solidarity with him, receive from him infinitely more than they can give. Previously the Apostle Paul wrote a powerful sentence: "So death is at work in us, but life in you" (2 Cor. 4:12). Doubtlessly he spoke here explicitly of the mystery in virtue of which he who, in his time and place, participated in the passion of Christ, is the source of life for all who surround him or whom he meets. But is it otherwise with *them*? Is it otherwise with whoever suffers persecution, discrimination, or torture for whatever reason? All wrong or injustice, all oppression or violence suffered— do they not send us back to the scandal of the Cross? All impoverishment, every hunted being, all abandonment—are they not the mirror of the Man of Sorrow?

I remember during this period having spoken of CIMADE and its work before the members of a well-established parish in a large city in Switzerland. The audience passed noticeably through contradictory feelings: incredulity, fright, impotence, pity. At the end there was a long silence; then one person rose and asked me a question that will be engraved forever in my memory: "But these people for whom you go to such trouble and take so many risks, are they 'interesting'?" Stunned by the enormity of the naïveté and self-righteousness that was just expressed, I stammered a response both brutal and off-balance, saying that we had never had the time to ask ourselves the question, caught as we were in the urgency and tragedy of the situations that we faced. A woman's voice spoke up then. "Are you sure that you yourself are so very 'interesting,' and do you think that Christ came to us because we were 'interesting'?" The evening was over; but since then I have lived with that word, which has often been a safeguard and compass for me.

In the beginning, we thought we would help those in distress, but we discovered that it was they who came to our aid, compelling us by their presence and their unavoidable expectation to come out of ourselves, our comforts and our cowardice, our silences and our complicities. Their presence and their suffering brought us back to life, that is, to something like an open and offered existence, to the discovery of the true sense and center of ourselves: "the other," the meeting with whom saves us from that form of death worse than all others—egotistical self-centeredness and unfeeling isolation. We thought we went to them, but in reality it was they who came to us. They visited, helped, and liberated us. Their deaths accompany us always, unforgettable and present, revealing the true face of man in this world, a mirror in which we would recognize forever the hideousness of our complacent self-gratification and guilty security. Is it exaggerated to say that they forced us to understand that "the reasons for living are preferable to life itself," as was repeated often by one of us, and to live unceasingly at the very heart of the gospel? It is they who led us to the center of the great prophecy of the last judgment in Matthew 25; in each of them, whatever he was, it was the Christ who came to us as the rejected, the outlaw, and the crucified. In loving them, it was his love that we received. When they invaded our houses and our lives, greatly disturbing everything, it was his mercy and his joy that took possession. I can say now that it was not a case of calculation or planning, but, on the contrary, each time we forgot it and saw only the surface of things. But each time also, we knew afterward that Christ had blessed us. All our failures brought us to the foot of the Cross; all our successes to the entrance of the empty tomb. The presence of eternity, the expectation of the kingdom inaugurated by Christ's victorious death, also became our daily bread. In brief, these people gave to our lives for always their true dimensions. If only they had taught us to live unceasingly the mystery of encounter with our neighbor.

Straight off, they began in us reflection that is far from being finished and pushes us continually toward a new understanding of solidarity and presence: a partial action, maladroit, powerless. It began to appear to us then that immediate action limited to distressing events was dangerously incomplete, tragically mutilated. In this line of thinking, global analysis necessarily shaped itself—the taking of social and political positions. Charity, reduced to its means only and enclosed within its own limits, is decidedly too restricted; it does not exempt us from a larger and longer perspective. On the contrary, it implies this. As the country priest of Bernanos said one day to the priest of Torcy, "Justice is the expansion of charity and its triumphal entry." An involvement, however total it might be at the level of charity, but not accompanied by a resolute struggle for the establishment of justice, would be blind and finally sterile. How often have we realized the cruel truth of the saying about "Christian charity that has pure hands but no hands"!

And that is why more than one among us was led at this period to take a stand and to take deliberate actions at the level of the Resistance and political struggle. Even if, as I pointed out, we observed more than once that one must not confuse the service of man with a national or partisan commitment, it is clear that little by little we began to recognize and to put resolutely to work the political dimension of Christian existence.

It is clear, also, that as charity pushed us to want liberty, dignity, and life for those who called to us, the political action that this implied could not go in another direction. It was not just a question then of resistance to the Nazis and national independence. Our political involvement went far beyond France and the occupation years. A permanent world perspective opened before us. Who would be surprised, then, that many of us should be found in all the struggles for man fought since 1945? Resistance to the rearmament of Germany, fight for the independence of colonized peoples, refusal of atomic armaments, active participation in the elaboration of a theology and an ethic of revolution. . . Thus it will be as long as the world lasts.

And it is not the cruel character of failures suffered or the provisional and never guaranteed aspects of victories won that can discourage us or release us from our responsibility in this area. On the contrary, in the perspective and hope of the kingdom, all that is temporary and relative becomes suddenly significant and decisive. We know that our actions cannot bring about fulfillment, nor even truly prepare it. We believe, however, that fulfillment is sketched in a certain number of attitudes and movements that it evokes and guides. To refuse them is to make light of the true character of hope, which, like faith and love, is borne by a Word become flesh once for all and continuously flesh again. That is to say, also, to make light of history, society, and structures of a world where man must and can wish continually to live better than he did yesterday. Justice is that desire to permit all to be and to become truly themselves during the course of their brief existence.

They alone who see in the gospel a spiritualism without historical dimensions and a message of religious escapism, will be surprised at the present face of CIMADE, with its will for significant presence among the destitute whoever they may be, but also for action in the great international organizations and sometimes the indispensable clandestineness. But the Holy Spirit always volatilizes the most solid Christian caricatures of Christ's message. It is he who, today as yesterday, keeps us alert in face of all the attacks on the life of man: oppression in all its forms, underdevelopment, hunger, and the ugly litany of all racisms constantly reborn. Service and witness have been able to take and will continue to take new forms; they will remain our permanent raison d'être.

Let us say again that to take this path, CIMADE led us normally to discover that we were not alone along the road. From all directions men, divided Christians or atheists, members of parties or alone, fought for the future of man in this world. From its beginnings, but how much more today, we knew that we were destined to travel together, indispensable companions in spite of our ideological or spiritual differences. That which is specific in what each one brings to the construction of a human order of justice and liberty is not always clear in the beginning. But one thing is certain. There is no authentic specificity that authorizes abstention or noninvolvement. It is in working together, in cooperation and dialogue that one discovers and expresses himself through what he has that is most irreducible and most essential also for a common task. The fact of being in a network of multiple relations with the most diverse men and organizations, far from reducing each one to being only an intersection without color or personality, on the contrary accents the characteristics and perspectives of each and gives to the whole a polyphonic richness and a universal openness outside of which nothing truly human is created.

CIMADE, as it was yesterday, as it is today, as we hope it will be tomorrow—that is, constantly different, in the same movement of faithfulness to Christ and to historical becoming in which it witnesses and wants to be constantly represented— is in the heart of the ecumenical movement, and singularly in the midst of the little French Protestant family, it makes a significant appeal. The gospel will undoubtedly never be understood—and less than ever in this century of great human mobility—as a factor of conservation or immobility. It is in movement, with much flexibility and spirit of invention, it is in listening to others and in the attention to all that they bring to the human community, that the church is faithful to its Lord. There is no doubt that this return to a Christianity lived as an unfinished adventure, in the refusal of sterilizing conformity and organized oppression, presents risks and exposes those who engage in it to many errors. Undoubtedly CIMADE has committed some and will commit others; but who does not see, since the passage among us of Jesus of Nazareth, that the worst error is the refusal of risk and that the Spirit and man cannot live in our too sure words and congealed structures?

That is why many of us give thanks for this breath of air and this challenge to which the Lord has exposed the church by giving it CIMADE—bold, poor, and inventive—some time ago. May this dynamism not slip into dullness, caution, and proved methods. May we always become again brothers of the poor through being ourselves authentic beggars of the Spirit.

22.

CIMADE Today

(*Comité Inter-Mouvements Auprès Des Evacués;* today: *Service Oecuménique d'Entraide*—French Ecumenical Service to the Dispossessed)

CIMADE: today these initials have become a name, the origin of which is unknown for the most part; the committee itself has become service. Instead of an "intermovement" coordination, mention is made of an ecumenical dimension, but its initial vocation has not changed: from yesterday's displaced persons to political refugees, to migrant workers, to foreigners. CIMADE has enlarged its field of encounter; it has remained faithful to its desire to work with uprooted people.

To be uprooted is to have been torn from one's land, his family, from surroundings and activities that constitute a normal sphere of equilibrium. It is to have no longer "a place to lay his head." This uprootedness, which continues to have political causes—for refugees from the East, for the Greeks or Portuguese fleeing a regime that is intolerable to them—also has socioeconomic origins now. If men coming from Africa or Algeria

This chapter did not appear in the original French edition.

accept the hard lot of migrant workers, it is because of political or economic forces in their native countries which make them leave. And it is the relationship of similar forces in the host countries that profits from their displacement: double exploitation, double uprootedness. But, since its origin, the evangelical ferment of the action of CIMADE—its ecumenical dimension and its various interventions in France and in the Third World —has been the quest for justice on earth in a world that we cannot ignore.

Today, although the borders are no longer lined with barbed wire, it is with those who suffer, those who are for a time the victims of history, that CIMADE will affirm its solidarity whatever their nationality, race, political or religious positions. A rapid sketch of the history of CIMADE since 1944–45 gives a better understanding of the evolution of this movement from action with interned Jews to solidarity with the Third World:

In a destroyed France—in Normandy, Alsace, the north— CIMADE established barracks and sent young teamworkers to live there for three or four years, putting into action all the formulas of aid possible in cooperation with other French and foreign organizations.

The same concern to embody reconciliation led to organizing international teams in Germany in 1947. In Mainz and Berlin, CIMADE contributed to the reopening of dialogue between the young people of Germany and France.

In France, the camps emptied of Jewish survivors were full of Germans and collaborators. At the request of a member of the National Committee of the Resistance, CIMADE gave to these new prisoners the same witness that it had shared in the past with their victims. Thus CIMADE affirmed its solidarity with those who are deprived of their liberty.

Following the war, Central Europe experienced the turmoil caused by displaced persons. In 1949 CIMADE created a reception and immigration service. It organized a distribution center which at that time annually provided more than fifty tons of clothing. Aid to political refugees still has a large place in the activities of CIMADE in Paris.

The Protestant parish at Dakar, composed mainly of Europeans, decided to open a dispensary among the poor and in 1955 asked CIMADE's cooperation in this undertaking. Four years later, CIMADE was left the entire responsibility in Senegal at the dawn of independence. Today the dispensary cares for a hundred patients each morning. A literacy course for men, a homemakers' school, and education activities have been added. The committee responsible for the center is composed of Africans and Europeans—Catholics, Protestants, and Muslims. In the dialogue with the Third World that CIMADE has undertaken since 1956 in France as well as overseas, the center at Dakar has had an exemplary value because of the quality of cooperation it has been able to establish between Africans and Europeans.

Throughout the somber hours of the Algerian war, CIMADE discovered some new uprooted persons: "the stokers of Europe," the migrant workers. Present in Algeria, present in the Muslim quarters of Paris, Lyons, and Marseilles, CIMADE, at the same time that it dangerously affirmed its fellowship with enemy communities, discovered the ties between migration and development. Because a country is underdeveloped, unemployed laborers emigrate to zones of economic growth. But the drain of laborers in the countries of origin contributes to keeping those countries in a state of stagnation from which they cannot free themselves. Much later the desire to break this vicious circle guided the action of CIMADE in the Third World.

Decolonization also led to displaced persons. Repatriated persons originating from Indochina, including Cambodia and Laos, were placed in camps. CIMADE is now present in one of these camps at Sainte-Livrade in the department of le Lot. Then came repatriated Frenchmen from Algeria; then ex-Harkis (Algerians who served in the French army) who were settled for better or worse in southeastern France. A CIMADE team at St. Laurent des Arbres in the department of le Gard has, for the last several years, set as a goal the reconciliation of the French rural communities and the Muslims.

Activities with migrant workers, which had begun with Algerians, spread to Africans and then to Portuguese workers.

Beyond serving to welcome, to be the first stage of friendship, the need to work for individual improvement for the workers has become clear. That explains the considerable literacy program put into action by CIMADE.

But the destiny of an individual cannot be separated from that of his people; to aid in the improvement of the worker cannot as a consequence cut him off from his roots, from his country. That is why the accent today is put on the necessity to make the men of the Third World responsible for their collective destiny and to assist that awakening of conscience in those whom we meet. Clearly refusing to be simply a relief organization, CIMADE tries to work in depth with migrant workers in Nanterre, Marseilles, and Lyons.

CIMADE saw most of its preoccupations in France thrust into the foreground in May 1968. "We are all German Jews," was heard in the streets of Paris. A few weeks later the expulsion of foreigners led Catholic, Jewish, and Protestant religious authorities to take a very firm stand. During that month of May, we were preoccupied with the questions of food and medicine. Above all, it was necessary once again to be there "at the meeting of the people of God and history."

For CIMADE today, it is a question of avoiding disagreement between doctrine and practice, between global projects and individual actions. Activity with political refugees is taking a new dimension, enlarging itself to include the victims of police regimes from Portugal, Greece, and Haiti. The time of solidarity in awareness has arrived.

That is why it appears that service can become twisted if it is situated solely at the level of the passing gesture toward an individual. Without excluding the reception of the migrant worker, the *immediate assistance,* service must force itself to pose the problems in *their total dimension* because for one case resolved there are a thousand other similar ones that remain without solution if this additional effort is not made. Neither do charitable intentions exclude a *reflection upon the problems of our times and of our churches.* Charity in the biblical sense is inseparable from the search for justice.

I. The Urgency of Situations Makes Immediate
Aid Imperative

Whether it is a question of earthquakes in Sicily or the riots of May 1968, current events require us to be there. Then a mobilization for immediate action takes place while waiting for other organizations, better equipped for massive action but necessarily slower starting, to take the relay. For example, in 1968, although certain CIMADE teams rapidly established canteens at food distribution centers, they stopped their activity when municipal canteens were able to function.

Another form of immediate aid is receiving political refugees at CIMADE's headquarters at 176, rue de Grenelle, Paris 7. This means first listening to the refugee, who can finally find someone to speak to in his own language. Next he must be helped through administrative red tape, helped to regularize his stay by facilitating contacts with the many public offices that send the immigrant back and forth. Sometimes it is necessary to give emergency aid—in the form of a loan rather than a gift. Finally we help him to find work. In this respect it is evident that the means of the CIMADE teams are very limited even though it is necessary to find an individual solution for jobs within each man's possibilities. Also, CIMADE has tried setting up a network of friends to whom these visitors can be directed: factory owners, foremen, men of goodwill who try to resolve the cases that CIMADE entrusts to them.

II. Immediate Action Calls for Joint Action

Although important for the individual and indispensable for revealing beyond all theoretical superstructure what the problems are, day-to-day action is, in effect, insignificant in face of the problems encountered as often by political refugees as by migrant workers, prisoners, and internees.

Vis-à-vis political refugees, the concern is to not contribute to the "brain drain" which weakens the poor countries for the greater profit of rich nations of the so-called free world. (There is one doctor for 75,000 inhabitants in Haiti, but 2,000 Haitian doctors are practicing in the United States and Canada.) To come to the aid of refugees, to permit them to reestablish a normal existence, perhaps means that they should be sent to other countries of the Third World where they do not risk persecution. That certainly means sustaining them in their struggle against injustice, whether from the East or West, and even if this struggle has taken forms of violence.

Vis-à-vis migrant workers, efforts made to promote their integration in France could go against the worker's interests and that of his country of origin. To favor integration is to accentuate the break with the place of origin, to enhance the uprootedness. There is a double role to play: first, to be present where the migrant workers are established—in Nanterre, St. Denis, Lyons, Marseilles, or Strasbourg—present not only to be of assistance but to witness in diverse circles of public opinion to the migrant workers' situation in France; to be the *porteparole,* the spokesman for these "stokers of Europe."

The other aspect of the role to play is an effort of education, training, and advancement of the migrant workers. It is their own reflection, their own demands that will permit the accomplishment of two projects undertaken by CIMADE. One aims to have the government take into consideration the idea of "migratory training"; supplying the work market with male adults who have cost our country nothing before their arrival gives them a right to professional training that takes into account the interests of their country of origin as well as those of the host country.

We hope that this formula will become generalized because it enables the migratory phenomenon to avoid continuing inevitably to weaken certain countries of the Third World. But in the second place, if the final goal of the presence of the foreign worker in France is his own training, if it is a question of a new form of cooperation with developing countries, this implies that a *migrant worker statute* should be rapidly put into effect. The worker could then enjoy all his social rights without having to take out French citizenship.

Vis-à-vis prisoners and internees, in addition to regular visits and correspondence with those incarcerated, long-term action is undertaken that aims at the cause and effect of delinquency, the problems posed by the application of penal sentences and the liberation of ex-convicts. At the same time an effort must be made to sensitize Christian circles to the reality of the life of the delinquent and the prisoner. For although one sometimes feels sorry for these unfortunates, rare are the doors that open to the freed prisoner to give him a chance to find a job and a normal existence.

III. Action Demands Reflection by CIMADE
on the Problems of Our Time

This reflection brings us first to the *problems of the Third World,* to the division of the world into "developed and underdeveloped," which is not an incidental thing but the reflection of economic law fundamental to our epoch. In an economy of scarcity, the powerful become constantly richer by confiscating to their profit the plus values of production. And the greatest heresy of our time—yes, the greatest heresy—is the coinciding of the world of the powerful and the world called Christian.

The effort to create ecumenical organizations for development education and world economic and social justice is not a gratuitous gesture of charity toward the most deprived; it is first of all restitution of wealth confiscated abusively. One might or might not feel concerned by this effort, but it is irrefutable that it is in accord with the spirit of the gospel. The foremost form of this restitution is the sensitization of the public to this need—not an appeal to feelings, but an explanation of the right of the countries of the Third World to demand that exploitation cease. The recent declarations of Pope Paul VI, like the positions taken by the World Council of Churches, show a real evolution in this direction.

The other form of action for development is the support of projects in the Third World. In agreement with the government of interested countries, these projects must be studied rationally regarding their economic and political impact. Little by little a series of criteria becomes clear, permitting the better selection of projects that will be supported jointly by Catholic and Protestant organizations and always tied to the need for self-reliance of the concerned populations.

Another direction of CIMADE today is reflection upon the significance of a lived ecumenism without rhetoric or publicity through systematic research on all opportunities of working together among Orthodox, Catholics, and Protestants. The forthcoming opening of a center of documentation on the problems of development, created jointly by CIMADE and the Catholic Committee Against Hunger and for Development, is like a symbol of what we want to show here: that ecumenism is less a way of talking together than a desire to act together; that this action is not in itself its own end but must confront the great problems of the world today; and that each one is concerned in this research. And how could we not cite this letter from a CIMADE team member, a Catholic priest engaged in such an experience with the agreement of his church:

The time of discourse and great reflections today does not seem to me to lead anywhere unless men try, with humility and truth, to live all the consequences of the principles posed in these last decades in relation to the problems enumerated above: to live without fear before this new life, which brings an infinitely larger and more open fullness than that which the beginnings would permit us to foresee; to live in crucifying poverty because points of reference are missing for others who do not live in it, and which we live in relation to society even if we are on the margin; to live in exalted poverty also because it seems to me essentially turned toward the future of the world and of the church, in a human and universally Christian communion to which the churches have accustomed us only with words, and often with barriers placed at the outset to mark the route, in an unconscious but true attitude of people who possess rather than serve the Truth made flesh.

At the present time, in order to achieve its objectives, CIMADE works in four sectors of activity: migrant workers, political refugees, Third World development, and emergency aid.

1. CIMADE is in daily contact with *migrant workers*.

In cooperation with other organizations (the Coordinating Committee for Literacy and Training) and with much volunteer help, it organizes literacy classes and basic adult education.

These are only the first stages of training that must end in a true exchange, a process of reflection pursued together.

Such is the goal of teams established in the migrant milieu, be it Marseilles, Lyons, or the Parisian suburbs of St. Denis or Nanterre. It is also the goal of the Reception Center at Sucy-en-Brie, which houses two hundred workers—Portuguese, Algerians, and others.

2. CIMADE works in many ways, by its services and teams, to help *refugees* and the *exiled* become integrated into French life while respecting their personalities and their own traditions; that is to say, in close collaboration with the persons themselves. This aid is at the same time social (regularizing papers, housing, employment), cultural (literacy, various courses, discussions), and involved in promoting handicrafts (boutique on rue de Grenelle, exhibits, periodic sales of the products of these workmen).

The activities are diversified:

—*Elderly refugees.* A foyer-club attracts about fifty people each week. A much larger group benefits two or three times a year from a distribution of food.

—*Student service.* In relation with other organizations, CIMADE tries to help students in their professional orientation and in obtaining scholarships.

—*Indochinese repatriots.* A CIMADE team has been established since 1966 at Sainte-Livrade in the department of le Lot et Garonne. The most urgent problem is that of the adolescents for whom the possibility of professional training and places of employment must be found. It is also necessary to sensitize a population that is often prejudiced and hostile to the camp.

—*Muslims repatriated from Algeria (ex-Harkis of the French army).* A team residing at St. Laurent des Arbres in the Gard is trying to facilitate the integration of these Arab families, particularly the young people, into the rural environment. Progress is slow.

3. One could say, in a way, that the *problems of the Third World* have been imposed upon CIMADE by its very presence at the center of events.

Thus it is from the experience lived by team members at the relocation centers in Algeria that the most significant awakening of conscience began concerning development.

It was because of the inspiration of this experience that the C.C.S.A. (Christian Committee of Service in Algeria, created at the time of independence) was able to pass from simple assistance to the creation of the *Chantiers Populaire de Reboisement* (Public Reforestation Program), which became in its turn the source of complementary activities adding up to a genuine project of regional development.

Thus also the experience of the Dakar team (Ecumenical Center at Bopp) permitted us to see in the field the possibilities and problems of an insertion into the heart of another culture, into a milieu that was always to be animated and stimulated toward the training of indigenous cadres, with the help of and finally under the direction of local people. It consists of sociomedical work, women's work, and discussion programs on the socioeconomic and cultural level.

4. Finally, whether it is a question of Nigeria, the Middle East, Vietnam, or the revolution of May 1968, it is today's events that make necessary *emergency interventions* by CIMADE, usually in conjunction with the Division of Inter-Church Aid and World Refugee Service of the World Council of Churches. And that means permanent availability and the possibility of mobilizing service teams at any moment. It also prevents CIMADE from stagnating in routine or in its own structures.

For all this work CIMADE disposes of about eighty team members working full time, sent out by groups of two or three in France and in the Third World. Fifty-four of these team-workers are French and twenty-five are foreigners of ten different nationalities. Most of them are under thirty-five years of age. They are Protestant, Catholic, and Orthodox. And each group inspires a larger team of occasional co-workers and volunteers that forms, wherever it finds itself, a true community of service and love.

CIMADE's budget is about 4 million French francs [$800,-000], only 8 percent of which is supported by governmental subsidies, 40 percent by French gifts, and 20 percent by gifts from other countries. The rest comes from various resources, especially receipts from the residence centers. It is clear that CIMADE would have to stop its activity without the support of its generous and faithful donors.

Thus today the work undertaken between 1939 and 1945 by God's underground is continued. And if it happens that we ask ourselves today in these troubled times what is the significance of ecumenical service, we remember that there are more and more men and women of all faiths, believers and nonbelievers, who think that it no longer suffices to talk together in order to understand one another, but that we must risk and serve together and that this service is a sign of the presence in the world of the servant Christ.

I. Anti-Semitic Laws of Vichy

A. Law of 3 October 1940

Article 1. Any person descended from three grandparents of Jewish race, or two grandparents if the spouse is Jewish, is considered Jewish.

Article 2. Access to and exercise of public functions and mandates enumerated herein are forbidden to Jews: . . . . (Following is an enumeration of most public offices and the leading professions of the press, industry, teaching, and the army.)

B. Law of 10 October 1940

Article 1. Foreigners belonging to the Jewish race may be interned in special camps by decision of the prefect of the department of their residence. . . .

Article 3. Foreigners belonging to the Jewish race may at any time be assigned to forced residence by the prefect of the department of their residence.

C. Law of 29 March 1941, creating a General Commission on Jewish Affairs

Article 1. A General Commission on Jewish Affairs, placed under the authority of the head of the government, has been created for the national territory.

Article 2. The Commission on Jewish Affairs is charged with:

a) Proposing to the government all legislative provisions and regulations as well as all measures for putting into effect the decisions signed by the government relative to the status of Jews, their civil and political situation, their legal restriction to exercise functions, employment, professions. . . .

c) The power, taking into account the needs of the national economy, to administrate and to liquidate Jewish goods, in cases where these operations are prescribed by law. . . .

e) Instigating, should the occasion arise with regard to the Jews and within the limits of the laws in force, all police measures demanded in the national interest.

D. Law of 2 June 1941, replacing the law of 3 October 1940 as statute of the Jews. All the essential provisions of the law of 3 October are maintained. . . .

Article 8. Exceptions to the restrictions foreseen by the present law:

a) Jews who have rendered exceptional service to the French State;

b) or whose family has been established in France for at least five generations and has rendered exceptional services to the French State.

E. Law of 2 June 1941, prescribing the census of Jews

Article 1. All persons who are Jewish by definition of the law of 2 June 1941 (same provisions as the law of 3 October 1940), serving as the statute for Jews, must, within one month beginning with the present law, remit to the prefect of the department or the assistant prefect of the zone in which they have their home or their residence, a written declaration indicating that they are Jewish by definition of the law and mentioning their marriage status, their family situation, and the extent of their possessions.

F. Law of 11 December 1942

Article 1. Any person of Jewish race in terms of the law of 2 June 1941 must, within one month dating from the promulgation of the present law, present himself at the police station of his precinct to have the notice "Jew" stamped on his identity card and on his food ration card.

II. Provisions concerning the deportation of Jews in the Unoccupied Zone

Vichy, 4 August 1942

Ministère de l'Intérieur
Direction générale de la Police
Direction de la Police du Territoire et des Étrangers
Dépêche 2.765 P
Le Conseiller d'État, Secrétaire général pour la Police,
à MM. les Préfets régionaux:

To inform you that Israelites, Germans, Austrians, Czechoslovakians, Poles, Estonians, Lithuanians, Latvians, Soviets, Russian refugees, and those from Danzig and the Saar, who entered France after 1 January 1939, will be transferred to the Occupied Zone before 15 September, with the following exceptions:

1. Persons over sixty years old.

2. Unaccompanied children under eighteen years old.
3. Individuals who served in the French army or ex-Allied army for at least three months, or who took part in combat regardless of length of service. Their spouse, parents, or descendants benefit from this same measure.
4. Those who have a French spouse or child.
5. Those having a spouse not belonging to one of the aforementioned nationalities.
6. Those who cannot be transported (for reasons of health).
7. Pregnant women.
8. Father or mother having a child less than five years old.
9. Those whose names appear on the list attached to the circular of 20 January 1941, and on lists here attached.
10. Those who, incorporated or not in groups of foreign workmen, seem not to be able to leave their employment without serious effect on the national economy.
11. Those who are notable for their artistic, literary, or scientific works, and finally those who, in some other way, have rendered notable service to our country.

(These instructions are strictly confidential.)

Signed: CADO

III. Report presented by Pastor Freudenberg to the Provisional Committee of the World Council of Churches, Geneva, 21–23 February 1946

(extracts)

The Provisional Committee decided in February 1939 to name a secretary for refugee affairs to the office of the general secretary. Dr. Adolf Freudenberg, pastor of the Confessing Church in Germany, was appointed and began his work in London under the direction of the late Dr. William Paton and in close contact with the bishop of Chichester, Dr. George Bell, and his International Committee for Refugees.

. . . At the beginning of the war the secretariat was transferred to Geneva, and a small provisional action committee was created, composed of Prof. Adolf Keller, Dr. Visser 't Hooft, Pastor Henriod, and other Swiss members.

In 1939 and 1940 our primary task was to save the largest number possible of "non-Aryan" Christians, German and Austrian, by finding them places in other countries. We appealed to churches and charitable agencies in order to facilitate their emigration. But the responses to that appeal were few; the churches did not yet understand their responsibility toward the persecuted. We were ashamed to think that we Christians had been unable to do anything comparable to the generous efforts of the Jews.

In October 1940, seventy-two hundred Jewish and "non-Aryan" persons coming from southwest Germany were deported to the camp of Gurs in southern France. . . . At this time Pastor Marc Boegner, president of the Protestant Federation of France, asked Pastor Pierre Toureille to be chaplain to the Protestant refugees scattered about or grouped in Companies of Foreign Workmen, while CIMADE aided the refugees inside the camps. . . . The Ecumenical Service for Refugees took the responsibility of financing the work of the chaplaincy and of CIMADE. That was made possible in the beginning by the spontaneity and generosity of the Swiss people, who wanted thus to show their solidarity with the victims of oppression. Later, considerable contributions were received from our Swedish friends, and from 1942 on the American Christian Committee sent large, regular subsidies.

The most critical period for the refugees in France began in the summer of 1942, when Laval gave in to German pressure and delivered to the SS persecutors about ten thousand Jews and non-Aryans to whom refuge had been given in France. This blow to the honor of the nation awakened a spirit of resistance, of Christian responsibility and love of neighbor. The teamworkers of CIMADE and the chaplaincy acted continually on behalf of their protégés by hiding them, obtaining false identity papers, and organizing their flight into Switzerland or Spain. Some CIMADE team members (men and women) were arrested. . . . The assistance offered by many French pastors, by some policemen, maquisards, Communists, and railroad men, and the hospitality of Catholic priests and nuns, as well as numerous rural families, was remarkable. Our Ecumenical Committee contributed in insuring the admission of these refugees into Switzerland, working in close cooperation with the Swiss authorities and other organizations. . . . Hundreds of lives—perhaps indirectly thousands—were saved by our combined efforts.

After Pastor Gruber's internment in a concentration camp in December 1940, one could no longer doubt the Gestapo's determination to exterminate. Nevertheless, a certain number of Germans, courageous women and men, church people and others, continued to aid the Jews and non-Aryans in different ways, not without great risks.

In 1942 we had contact, for a certain time, with a Protestant parish in the Warsaw ghetto. . . . Later we tried to answer the sporadic letters coming from the Protestant community of Theresienstadt in Czechoslovakia, which numbered about three hundred members.

In 1944 the Ecumenical Committee for Refugees published a solemn protest against the extermination of Hungarian Jews in Auschwitz. Other organizations took steps with governments of neutral countries. Public opinion in the entire world was alerted and a tempest of indignation broke loose, which certainly contributed to saving the lives of more than a hundred thousand Jews from Budapest. . . .

When the American Quakers had to leave Italy at the time of the entrance into war of their country against Germany and Italy in 1941, our committee took charge of the Quaker services for several hundred Protestant refugees dispersed in Italy.

In 1942 we made contact with the "Association of Protestants of Central Europe" in Shanghai, a community of five hundred refugees, almost all non-Aryans. That parish had fraternal relations with the Chinese Protestant churches, Anglican pastors, and above all with the courageous pastor of the German colony and his assistant. To come to the aid of numerous parishioners refugeed without resources, we were happy to send considerable funds during three years. That community at

Shanghai was an authentic ecumenical parish, like those of the camps in France.

FINANCES

(in Swiss francs)

Receipts

Year	Sweden	Switzerland	United States	Argentina
1941	6,000	77,000	10,000	—
1942	46,000	81,000	44,000	—
1943	44,000	121,000	241,000	4,000
1944	17,000	49,000	368,000	—

Disbursements (in 1942)

France (aid to refugees, chaplaincy, CIMADE)	148,000
Italy	14,000
Switzerland	18,000
Miscellaneous	3,000
Shanghai	1,500

(for Shanghai, 1943–45, average per year about 25,000)

IV. Members of the Ecumenical Committee for Refugees (in 1942)

Prof. D. A. Keller: Central European Office of Interchurch Aid, Geneva

Dr. W. A. Visser 't Hooft: General Secretary of the World Council of Churches

Pastor H. L. Henriod: General Secretary of the World Alliance for International Friendship Through the Churches, Geneva

Alec Cramer, M.D.: Member of the International Committee of the Red Cross, Geneva

Pastor Charles Guillon: World Committee of YMCA, Geneva

Pastor Nils Ehrenström: Director of the Department of Studies of the World Council of Churches, Geneva

Pastor A. Freudenberg: Committee Secretary

CORRESPONDING MEMBERS

Prof. D. F. Siegmond-Schultze, Zurich

Pastor Paul Vogt: President of Fraternal Aid for the Confess-

ing Church in Germany, and Chaplain to Refugees in Switzerland
Mme Gertrud Kurz, from Berne (co-opted in 1943)

V. Mme Marthe Besag confirms the account of Jeanne Merle d'Aubigné

Victim herself of deportation from Baden in October 1940, she describes it as follows:

Elderly men, paralytics, the sick, the mentally infirm, and many children found themselves in the removal of seven thousand to eight thousand Jews. The trip lasted four days. The barrier was raised, then was closed. Fortunately no one knew how long this exile would last. An asphalt road for two kilometers, barbed wire, barracks and more barracks—a desertlike, depressing sight. Behind the barbed wire, ravaged faces turned toward us. Not a tree, not a bush; gendarmes . . .

We entered the barracks assigned to us. It was empty and windowless. Not a bed or a chair. About sixty people were crowded into each barracks—old people, children, the sick. They were stretched out on straw mattresses and trembling from nervousness, from cold, and soon from hunger. The men and women were separated and grouped into different sectors surrounded with barbed wire. They were able to see one another once a week.

After three months I received the first news from my husband. (He was in England.) Then two months of silence. One dark day, the darkest of that hard year in camp, a letter came. My husband had lost his sight. He lived without help and needed his wife, who saw her time wasted behind barbed wire. Swallow your grief. You are never alone; sixty people are watching you.

The earth softened by the rain was transformed into a morass that gave off foul odors. No road. Whether it was a child or a sick or old person (they were numerous), it mattered little; each one had to wade through that mud in the rain, the snow, or the storm in order to reach the latrines. Depending upon the location of the barracks, the trip was from one to ten minutes. There were many who lacked the strength to go that far and fell—to remain prostrate in the mud.

From that mud came dysentery. Rats carried it. It attacked young and old alike, who were unable to shake it off. When at night you saw those poorest of the poor wracked with pain before you, then the bourgeois died in you. You had no remedy? On your knees at the foot of the sickbed, you invoked God, and God helped you. The ill became quiet, often even finding sleep. The ill were glad to know that you watched at night. Did they see the hand that guided, did they know who helped you?

A night did not pass without agonies. Early in the morning a truck came to gather the death harvest. Some men loaded the corpses, rolled in a gray blanket, and tried to forget their distress in joking or singing. They crossed the sector after having placed the bodies in coffins. The truck then carried off its load—five, ten, twenty coffins which it took to the cemetery near the camp. The cemetery soon counted two thousand bodies thrown into the muddy water. Horrible spectacle of a coffin dropped into the water, which splashed! Dysentery ravaged among us all winter. Follow a diet? Impossible! You had only carrots, artichokes, and dried peas. Such was the hell of the camp.

VI. Attitude of the International Committee of the Red Cross

We do not have the necessary information to be able to make an overall judgment on the program of the International Red Cross concerning the civilian victims of the Hitlerian regime and the genocide it undertook. We had been disappointed to meet only with coldness and diplomatic reserve, particularly when we had tried to call upon it for aid to the tortured Jewish population in Poland. However, we can find three precise reasons for that attitude:

1. Until 1943 almost all the war prisoners were held by the Axis powers. Since Hitler had no consideration for the principles of respect for the rights of men as the International Red Cross had formulated them, the situation of war prisoners was made even crueler and more arbitrary. That situation remained the primary preoccupation of the Red Cross; and it was often able to ease the situation, thanks to discreet complicity between its representatives and some sympathetic Germans.

2. According to the rules of the Red Cross, all its members had to be well-known Swiss personalities. They were inde-

pendent of the federal government. But the IRC in time of war had a large political responsibility vis-à-vis Switzerland, and was similarly tied to a strict neutrality which could prevent its letting itself respond by spontaneous reactions.

3. During the last war the Swiss assumed the representation of forty-three countries. The Swiss consulates were charged with the protection of people from these countries. Particularly in the Axis countries and occupied territories, their task was terribly difficult and even dangerous. Their work put them in direct contact with branches of the IRC, and together they accomplished their humanitarian task, thanks to secret negotiations made with tact and caution. Thousands of men threatened with assassination, among them a very large number of Jews, owe their lives to these emissaries of neutral Switzerland. Many of these led rescue operations on a large scale with unparalleled boldness and intelligence. To all of them we extend our thanks.

In order to see more clearly all these problems, we recommend the excellent book by Werner Rings: *Advocaten des Feindes, das Abenteuer der politischen Neutralität* (Vienna and Düsseldorf: Econ, 1966). [*Advocates of the Enemy: The Adventure of Political Neutrality.*]

VII. Joint memorandum from the secretariat of the World Council of Churches and the World Jewish Congress in Geneva, sent 19 March 1943 to the high commissioner of the League of Nations in London

PREFACE

As its introduction indicates, this memorandum was not born solely on the initiative of its authors. It was conceived as a constructive addition to the exchange of ideas begun in February 1943 between the United States and Great Britain on the urgent problem of refugees. This is particularly true for item 2 of this document from Geneva, concerning temporary refuge in neutral countries, while item 3 refers to an earlier exchange between Jews coming under the Palestine Mandate in danger in the Axis countries and German civilian internees in the Allied countries.

TEXT

The secretariats of the World Council of Churches and of the World Jewish Congress have noted with great satisfaction the memorandums exchanged between the governments of the United States of America and Great Britain on the present situation of refugees in Europe, and their decision to meet at Ottawa with a view to preliminary exploration of ways and means for combined action by the representatives of their governments.

Having studied the suggestions and proposals contained in the memorandums of the two governments, the secretariats of the World Council of Churches and of the World Jewish Congress beg to express their views on the above-mentioned topic.

While welcoming most warmly the determination of the Allied governments to bring help to persecuted people of all races, nationalities, and religions, fleeing from Axis terror, they wish to emphasize that the most urgent and acute problem, which requires immediate action, is the situation of the Jewish communities under direct or indirect Nazi control.

The secretariats of the World Council of Churches and of the World Jewish Congress have in their possession most reliable reports indicating that the campaign of deliberate extermination of the Jews organized by Nazi officials in nearly all countries of Europe under their control, is now at its climax. They therefore beg to call the attention of the Allied governments to the absolute necessity of organizing without delay a rescue operation for the persecuted Jewish communities, on the following lines:

1. Measures for immediate rescue should have priority over the study of postwar arrangements.

2. The rescue operation should enable the neutral states to grant temporary asylum to the Jews who reach their borders.

For this purpose a definite guarantee by the governments of the United States of America and Great Britain, and possibly by other Allied governments including the British dominions, should be given to the neutral states—a guarantee that all refugees entering their territories would be enabled to be repatriated or to reemigrate as soon as possible after the end of the war.

In view of the special characteristics of the Jewish problem, in view of the attitude adopted in the past by many European governments, and furthermore, in view of the present attitude of absolute political neutrality adopted during the hostilities by the neutral countries, it may be stated that giving assurance of prompt repatriation of refugees upon the termination of hostilities would not be considered, in the present circumstances, a sufficient guarantee by the neutral states.

Only explicit and comprehensive guarantees of reemigration of the refugees, given by the Anglo-Saxon powers as reinforcement of any assurances of repatriation that may be given by the Allied governments in exile, can lead the neutral countries to adopt a more liberal and understanding attitude toward Jewish refugees.

These guarantees should provide for facilities concerning the supply of food and funds for the maintenance of refugees during their stay in the neutral countries.

3. A plan for exchange of Jews in Germany and the territories under German control for German civilians in North and South America, Palestine, and other countries, should be pressed forward by all possible means.

We should like to stress the fact that the number of nationals of Axis countries living in Allied countries—particularly in North and South America—exceeds by far the number of nationals of Allied countries living in Axis countries.

We feel that in spite of the great difficulties, which we do not underestimate, a workable plan of exchanging Jews for Germans would constitute an important method of rescuing a considerable number of persecuted people from the countries under Nazi control.

In view of the immediate urgency of the situation, the admission of Jews to the exchange plan should be granted *en bloc* to the greatest possible number, as conditions no longer allow time-wasting and in many cases fruitless individual investigations. This plan might include wartime security measures.

Concrete proposals should be submitted without delay to the governments representing Allied interests in Germany by the governments of the United States and Great Britain.

The International Red Cross Committee may also be approached by the Allied governments and asked for support in this matter.

P.S. A copy of this memorandum was forwarded by Pastor Visser 't Hooft to the United States ambassador at the American Legation in Bern, with request to forward it to the American government, to the Federal Council of Churches in America, and to the American branch of the World Jewish Congress.

A copy was sent by the general secretary of the WJC, G. M. Riegner, to the minister of Great Britain in Bern, S. J. Morton, with request to forward it to the government of His Majesty and to ask that the latter communicate it to the archbishop of Canterbury, if possible, and to the British Section of the World Jewish Congress.

A third copy was forwarded by Dr. William Paton, representative of the World Council of Churches in Great Britain, to the high commissioner for refugees of the League of Nations, Sir Herbert Emerson, in London.

VIII. The plight of Jews in Hungary

(Extract from the Ecumenical Press and Information Service, no. 26, June 1944, pp. 125–26)

The Ecumenical Commission for Refugees, whose headquarters is in Geneva, published the following declaration:

The goal of the Ecumenical Commission for Refugees is to aid materially and morally refugees of all beliefs. Its principal task, therefore, is to relieve the sufferings of refugees rather than to protest against the treatment inflicted upon them. But there are cases where the only aid that can be given is that of solemn public protest. Such is the case today. According to reliable reports, about 400,000 Hungarian Jews have been deported so far, under inhuman conditions. Those who did not die en route have been conducted to the camp of Auschwitz in Upper Silesia, where for two years hundreds of thousands of Jews have systematically been put to death. Christians cannot remain silent before such a crime. We appeal to our brother Christians in Hungary to raise their voices with ours and do all that is within their power to stop the continuation of these monstrous acts. We call upon Christians of all countries to unite in prayer and supplication that God have mercy upon the Jewish people.